A HISTORY OF ANGELS

AS TOLD BY ARCHANGEL GABRIEL

Written by
Rodford Belcher

First published in Australia in July, 2013 by Croxton House.

www.croxtonhouse.com.au

Copyright © Rodford Belcher 2013

The right of Rodford Belcher to be identified as the moral rights author of this work has been asserted by him in accordance with the Copyright Amendment (Moral Rights) Acts 2000 (Cth).

This book is copyright. Apart from any fair dealing for the purpose of private study, research, criticism or review, as permitted under the Copyright Act, no part may be reproduced by any process without written permission.

Inquiries should be addressed to the publisher.

Croxton House, 58 Stott Street, Thornbury, Victoria, Australia, 3071.

National Library of Australia Cataloguing-in-Publication entry

Author:	Belcher, Rodford, author.
Title:	A history of angels : as told by Archangel Gabriel / Rodford Belcher.
ISBN:	9780980394740 (paperback)
Subjects:	Theodicy.
	Angels.
	Gabriel (Archangel)
Dewey Number:	214

Cover design by Rodford Belcher

Page Layout: Croxton House

FOREWORD

A History Of Angels

I have an angel in my study which looks over my right shoulder. She seems to have one eye on my hands and the other on my paper-strewn desk. About 36 centimetres tall and made of clay, she is a riot of colour, predominantly deep purple, red and blue. Large soul-full eyes on her wings, a shimmering of blues and greens, are encircled in orange and yellow. There is a deep stillness about them. The purple heart cavity in the centre of her chest is open sacred space, womb-like in its promise of creativity, infinity and hope.

This angel is the first sculpture I bought from Rodford Belcher after not having seen him for many years. We had published a children's book together in 1988 and become good friends but gradually lost touch in the 1990s. Quite by chance – or rather by divine design – we ran into each other again in Fitzroy a few years ago. It transpired we were living in different ends of the same street, Rod in a share house and me in a converted factory. Both our lives had changed dramatically. After 32 years I had left a difficult marriage and was living on my own. Rod had been through his own difficult years, had spent time in the outback and experienced a personal spiritual transformation that led him to place himself utterly in the hands of a force some call God, others the Source or Higher Being and whom he himself calls the Big Fella.

Mindfulness is a much sought after quality and I see it lived in Rod. He says and does nothing that is not in harmony with the Big Fella. This connection steers his moral compass and grounds his integrity. It has inspired him to write this trilogy.

When Rod first knew he had to write, he started with pen and paper. As the words flowed it was clear to me firstly that he needed editorial support and secondly he had to have a computer. I was in a position to offer him both. As it happens I was planning to trade in my laptop. The old one still worked so I gave it to Rod who quickly mastered it and taught himself to type. He also got himself an internet connection and so our working partnership began. He would email me material, I would edit and return it.

Rod had done very little writing before this yet to my astonishment, wrote 100,000 words in the first year we worked together on *A History of Angels*. During the process his writing blossomed, we came to know each other well and our friendship deepened. We have learned what it is to have a relationship that is spiritual not physical, that is mutually respectful and accepting. The multi-coloured clay angel in my study symbolises this friendship for me. Rod is a living angel in my life.

Mary Ryllis Clark

PREFACE

A History Of Angels

I wasn't going to write a preface for *A History Of Angels*. I had no idea what to say. *The Four Spoked Wheel* was the complete opposite. Its preface jumped effortlessly from my fingers onto the keyboard. I asked Divine Father for clarity. My answer was a dream I mentioned in my writings. It basically sums up my whole reason and intent for writing this convoluted and at times very challenging manuscript.

I dreamt I was a young boy riding on a bicycle in the countryside. I rode down a dirt path that lead to the ashes of a family home that had burnt down a long time ago. The place felt familiar to me. I jumped off my bike and, like most kids would do, started to fossick through the ashes for hidden treasures. I dug up a very badly burnt book. Its cover and all the outer pages had been burnt away that would have explain the books title. I thumbed through it and its stories and they seemed familiar so I decided to keep it and study it later.

I suddenly felt uneasy and looked up and spied a large school made completely of glass. I rode over and saw small children being treated cruelly by giant adults. I felt sad. I realised the children were all my brothers and sisters and I wanted to help them escape. Also I wondered why I was so lucky to be free outside the school.

The first part of the dream was about me starting to rediscover who I was. When we incarnate to earth we soon forget who we are. It felt like who I was had been erased, but if I looked deeply enough I'd rediscover it. That's half of what *A History of Angels* is about. I slowly come out of a deep sleep and find my sense of self and intent again. Also

I understood that these large adults were the ones who had burnt my family home down to erase any trace of who I and my brothers and sisters were.

That leads to the second part of the book. It is about that glass school of harsh lessons that was more like a prison with powerful cruel beings in charge. That's why Gabriel told me about the modern history of angels, fallen and gods. It inspired my desire to help people I really care about trapped in this existence. It's like I'd been away and had arrived late so missed out on being trapped in the school. I know that this interpretation may differ from the one in the manuscript. But my artwork, writings, dreams and visions divulge new gems of insight each time I look back at them. I call that "gleaning.'

Like many people I use to feel alienated from the people around me. Also I found society so materialistic and shallow. A longing started to grow within me to be with my brothers and sisters again whom I had dreamt about. I remember being able to be so intimate with them, of having a great sense of belonging. So this manuscript is for them. You know who you are. We can sense each other. Many started to reach out to me as I wrote and even helped me. To ego driven people these manuscripts would be pure fantasy and drivel. To those brothers and sisters I love I hope these manuscripts will awaken a sense of something beautiful that has been lost or stolen away. Maybe even memories of The Beautiful Shore. Don't despair, no matter how low you think you have fallen or how trapped you feel. Help is on its way. All you need to do is ask for it.

Rodford Belcher

About the Author

Rodford Belcher grew up in Melbourne, Australia. "When people ask me about my early life I always think of turning points or windows of opportunity my soul took. When I left my family it was like I'd been asleep and something inside me started to stir and awaken," he said. Rod went away for a spiritual retreat called *Timeline Therapy* that helps you recognise incidents that occurred in your past that are stopping you moving ahead in life. "I had the most amazing spiritual experience. I dreamt I was embracing a beautiful golden angel who was the mirror of me. I have never felt so loved or at peace. After that a door opened within me, I felt the infinite ocean of my soul. I can't explain the sublime beauty and peace I felt. I've carried that like a treasure in my heart ever since," he said. But it's interesting to note that when Rod left the retreat and returned to his share house he said, "The old limited me came back, and it was awful. This raised many questions within me."

Rod worked in animation and graphic design for over ten years. He grew disillusioned and set off around Australia in an old truck and ended up living in a tent in Broome, Western Australia where his desire to create art returned. Rodford's art became a medium to communicate with his soul.

"I could never go back to commercial art again after this epiphany," he says.

"My art became my solace and a vehicle to self discovery."
When Rodford returned to Melbourne he took a job as a Hospital Orderly and volunteered to teach art with pastoral care at Frankston Hospital's Psych Ward. Then he went on to work with people out of jail with the Justice Department. "These jobs, though at times taxing, were also some of the most rewarding in my life. Before I was a fence-sitter and cut off from my fellow human beings. These humble jobs helped me understand how important humility is in our

lives." Rod said that an early interest in Dr. Carl Jung the psychologist and Joseph Campbell the mythologist also shaped how he views life. Symbols in his dreams offered him important insights to a side of himself that before he found inaccessible was now full of compassion, strength, wisdom and peace. "With the help of my friend Mary Clark [author], I've found a new creative way to accessing my soul, through writing."

And so came about *The Gabriel Trilogy* manuscripts that took Rod three years to write.

ACKNOWLEDGMENTS

As everyone knows it takes many things to come together for a book to be published. For me it was sitting down with a long lost friend Mary Clark at her place having a cuppa. Twenty years earlier we'd done a children's book together then lost touch. Mary was shocked at how much my art had changed. When we last saw each other I had done portraits of two of her children but now my art seemed wild, colourful and crazy. We had some lovely chats and in trying to explain my art I was also explaining my own personal transformation. I just thought she'd think I was crazy with all my visions and chatting to Gabriel and all. But she was very interested and asked why I didn't write down what happened because others would be as interested as she was. So began a lovely creative time of sending Mary my completed chapters and she'd edit them for me. But also writing helped me become more spiritually aware.

Another friend I'd also lost touch with about the same time as Mary, from my animation days, was Michele Antonio Maselli, or as I know him, Mickey. He'd become a DJ and a very good yoga teacher. He too was interested in how much I'd changed from the angry, frustrated bloke he knew years before. Mickey was kind enough to read my manuscripts and he was so positive and supportive at a time I doubted ever showing them to anyone.

Around this time I made two new spiritual friends. One was Adi Brierley, the other David Parker. I met Adi at an art exhibition and later he came along to one of my shows. We had the best spiritual chats and he also offered to read my manuscripts. Adi is a graphic designer, but like so many in his trade, he is also a frustrated, extremely talented artist. It was lovely to see him become part of an artist's co-op called Blender in the city where he produces the most beautiful wildlife paintings. Lucky for me, Adi offered to help with the graphics for my book covers and diagrams. He turned all my rough sketches and photos of my art into the lovely covers you see now. Also, when so many put you down and hate to see you move ahead in life, Adi, like Mary, did everything he could to make the books happen. It was these two people who made it clear I needed to modernise and embrace computers and so came about my website for my art and this led to my first meeting with David.

David Parker runs a small publishing house from his home and makes inspiration documentaries to help people, especially children, follow their dreams. At a time when I was quite broke David waved the usual payment for creating my website and asked if he could have one of my wild mandala banners instead. It still hangs in his hallway today. David is another friend that I sit down with and we soon forget the business at hand and get lost in the best deep chats that run for hours. Last year, after a run of sending my manuscript around to the big publishers and being knocked back, I just gave up in despair. Mary mentioned eBooks to me and at the same time so did David. He offered to publish for me. And so here I am.

When I speak of how angels work in our lives, the way these four people helped me is exactly that.

Rodford Belcher

Table of Contents

FOREWORD	III
PREFACE	V
About the Author	VII
ACKNOWLEDGMENTS	IX
Chapter One	3
Chapter Two	9
Chapter Three	17
Chapter Four	23
Chapter Five	77
Chapter Six	81
Chapter Seven	97
Chapter Eight	101
Chapter Nine	109
Chapter Ten	117
Chapter Eleven	123
Chapter Twelve	141
Chapter Thirteen	149
Chapter Fourteen	155
Chapter Fifteen	161
Chapter Sixteen	173
Chapter Seventeen	183
Chapter Eighteen	193
Chapter Nineteen	207
Chapter Twenty	215
Chapter Twenty-one	221
Chapter Twenty-Two	227
Chapter Twenty-Three	235
Chapter Twenty-Four	245
Chapter Twenty-Five	255
Chapter Twenty-Six	265
Chapter Twenty-Seven	269
Chapter Twenty-Eight	275
Chapter Twenty-Nine	289

A
HISTORY OF ANGELS

AS TOLD BY
ARCHANGEL GABRIEL

Written by
Rodford Belcher

A History of Angels

Chapter One

How do I describe meeting Archangel Gabriel? I was living with my girlfriend down the east coast of Victoria, Australia in a sleepy little town. We were broke and having relationship troubles. I had been sculpting and painting art that I saw in my dreams but I didn't quite understand my dreams and art yet. It was art expressing beautiful beings that inhabit the inner realms and guide all forms of life. I'd started creating this art after realising that I knew nothing of myself. I asked God to help me know myself. I had a deep longing to return home to somewhere I couldn't remember. Somewhere I was at peace, somewhere beautiful, where I was a completely different person to who I am now; a happy person, a fulfilled person. Sometimes, in unguarded moments, I'd catch a glimmer of this person in the mirror, but the image was soon gone.

I have loved stories about angels ever since I was a boy. But I felt that most material written about them was crap, especially the medieval idea of angels or even the new age idea [that they were there as servants to fix your everyday troubles]. Something about all this missed the truth. I realised truth had a lot to do with angels, also creativity, compassion, and courage. I always felt angry when I'd hear heavy metal bands' songs about demons feasting on angels. I knew in my heart demons and dark beings are terrified of angels, and for good reason too. I also realised since I was a child I had a hidden, deep desire to be an angel.

One day I was home alone. I was sitting, reading a book when, all of a sudden, I felt all displaced [like I was in two places at once] or the fabric of myself was warping. I staggered into the bedroom. The floor heaved and rolled like I was a ship on rough seas, and I fell prostrate on the bed. [I was feeling very troubled about the relationship I was in

A History of Angels

and powerless to fix my unhappy life. I knew I needed help because, no matter how hard I tried, I seemed to be getting nowhere trying to fix it myself]. I suddenly lifted my head, which felt like that of a huge eagle, clear, untroubled and fearless. It was as if my enormous eagle eyes could stare straight through me, and see in perfect clarity, how I truly felt. The usual muddle of emotions was gone.

I realised my relationship with my girlfriend was over and no amount of love, effort or compromises on my part, would mend it. I understood with great clarity that the relationship had helped me end a negative, childish, and needy idea of relationships where we look to another to fulfil us rather than finding fulfilment within ourselves. It was time to move on and truly follow my heart. I had a deep longing to be on my own for a while to find myself. I saw how my art was a tool being used by my soul to show me who I truly was and what was truly important to me.

After this experience my girlfriend mentioned that at the local hospital they were looking for volunteers for pastoral care. I felt my soul wanted me to join up, so I did. After I completed training I was asked by the pastor if I'd be willing to visit the psychiatric ward for four hours a week and teach art. I agreed although I was scared. I guess it's the unpredictability, fear and powerlessness some of the patients feel that scared me.

On my first day I had to walk down the corridor to the ward on my own. It felt very long and lonely. As I neared the ward I felt the presence of a huge loving being behind me. I knew everything would be all right. I felt fearless and at peace. The feeling soon evaporated when I arrived at the psych security window. When the staff realised I was from pastoral care they looked upon me with a mixture of suspicion and contempt. I was given a stern lecture about not interfering with the patients and their therapy and not to contact any of them after their release. I realised the person I'd replaced had made many enemies here with the doctors and nurses. I thought "Shit. What have I walked into?" When I was finally allowed into the ward I had an unreasonable fear of losing my security pass and never being allowed to leave.

Chapter One

I'd arrived when the patients come together for a morning meeting to be told of the day's activities. They aired their grievances and the occupational therapist brought to the attention of the patients any misdemeanours they had committed over the last twenty-four hours. Pastoral care was always the last to hear about any dramas, especially since the last guy had rubbed all the staff the wrong way. Off to the side an old Scottish cleaner lent on his mop and listened in. His name was Rod, which is my name. The pastor, a very perceptive man, had mentioned to me that Rod was the man to speak to if you wanted to know what's truly going on in the ward.

Being the cleaner Rod was seen as non-threatening by patients who often viewed doctors and nurses with great fear. These people ruled their lives. They could pump them full of drugs, give them electric shock treatment, kick them out onto the street, hold them in the ward indefinitely, or even lock them up in isolated cells and refuse any visitors. So you can understand some of the patients' fears. I felt Rod was important to me as an example of how best to build trust in others. Having power over people wasn't the answer. It was being there for someone and just listening, which Rod was very skilled at.

Well, to make a long story short I soon realised most people in the psych ward just needed someone to talk to, express their fears and self-doubts to. They were just people with extreme examples of the fears, doubts, delusions we all suffer from. The more I listened to the patients the more compassion and respect I felt for them. I looked forward every week to my art sessions with them and listening to their often sad stories told with great honesty. Most of us run from our delusional thoughts, make excuses, or hide from our fears and inadequacies. But a lot of these people bravely shared their most intimate thoughts and fears with me and I admired their honesty so much. It also made me feel like a sham. I learnt great humility. To me, to speak honestly of your fears and inadequacies was true courage.

I realised why I was sent to the psych ward now. Being willing to listen to others troubles, I'd become more willing

A History of Angels

to look at my own. In feeling compassion for others in their time of need, I'd opened up to compassion for myself. That's how angels work. I was sent somewhere where I'd truly find the answers I needed.

In my next job I was a cleaner and orderly, just like Rod, at a hospital in a poor area. I was brought up to always assert myself, always try to be top dog. For the first time I knew what it felt like to be a nobody, to be invisible, especially to the doctors and nurses. In this I found a sort of freedom to just be myself.

I saw so much [being mister invisible] and met the most amazing patients and fellow workers. There were men and women who had escaped the killing fields of Cambodia, execution or starvation in Ethiopia and Chile, been in all sorts of terrible wars, like Bosnia, Vietnam and WWII. I witnessed people facing their own deaths or that of loved ones. I especially loved speaking to old patients who had led such remarkable and often very harsh lives. It's a sad fact a lot of elderly patients' families never visit them and the medical staff are too busy to chat. I feel fortunate to have met them. I suddenly felt part of the human race from meeting and listening to these people. I no longer felt like an outsider sitting judging others and myself.

After this experience my childhood wish was granted. One morning I woke up, swung my legs out of bed and just sat there. I felt quite strange. It was like I was made of cool, crystal clear water. My mind was completely still. Then a negative thought appeared in my mind. It left my head like a bubble and drifted out into the world, as an unanswered question, and then returned changed and dissolved into my heart. The negative thought [a fear] transformed into a very clear insight, then wisdom, then beautiful compassion. I felt so enriched. I realised I'd just been allowed, for a beautiful moment, to experience what it felt like to be an angel, an angel experiencing this world. I can't tell you how fortunate I felt to have my childhood wish granted. I wish I felt that way all the time, that sublime way of viewing any experience, no matter how negative.

Chapter One

This is when Archangel Gabriel came into my life. I don't think I would have fully understood him if I hadn't had this experience. I felt him walk with me everywhere after that. I loved it. He helped me end my relationship in a loving respectful way and guided me to move into a crazy inner city share house in Melbourne. The next stage of my education was about to begin. Gabriel wanted me to stop hiding from life. Because of him I felt safe even though our back door was always open, the windows wouldn't lock, junkies use to shoot-up in the alleyway behind our house and drunks were always fighting out front. Amazingly we were never robbed.

I knew my time working at the hospital was over, so I quit. I had three weeks before I started my new job at the Justice Department looking after people out of jail or being community work supervisor [another part of my education]. I asked Gabriel about the truth of our existence. He laughed and waved his hand about. "You mean all this [the world, the universe], how all this all came about?" "Yes". I answered. "Good question and a complex one but one worth asking," replied Gabriel with a half grin [which I later learnt is his grin when he is asked to do the impossible. Sometimes it's handy to be ignorant]. He didn't say anymore.

The next day I had that displaced feeling I'd experienced earlier. I sat in my chair in my room and a long continuous vision began. It unfolded over ten days. I slept only four hours a night, ate only one meal a day, and only moved from the chair to go to the toilet. The vision would fill four huge novels, if I tried to write it all down. I didn't understand a lot of what happened, but it was one sad continuous tale of beings with unimaginable powers creating vast universes, loving, betraying, murdering, enslaving, warring and destroying all they created in endless strife. The beginning of the story started out so full of hope and beauty. What I've done is write down what I've come to understand about our universe, about why we are here and why we even exist, as explained to me by Archangel Gabriel, from the questions raised by me from that vision. I see now that if I hadn't had the vision, I wouldn't have known what questions to ask.

A History of Angels

Chapter Two

In The Beginning.....

In the beginning of this existence [Gabriel said he's seen at least thirteen others come and go] God created Duality, the separating of the God energy into two energies. Male and Female. Neither of these energies represent good or evil. It's more to do with the opposite polarities that make up the creation energy of God. Both are influenced at different times by Negative and Positive energy. When separated they create friction. From this friction random, unexpected or unplanned creations can come into being. God wanted to know and experience what would be created by beings completely independent of its self.

So the God Realm Angels came into being. There were one hundred male and one hundred female angels created. It's impossible to explain how powerful these beings were. God gave them the power to create whatever they wanted. These beings believed they were the only beings in existence beside their creator. This was not true, of course. God had infinite realms full of beautiful, powerful Beings of Light who were part of the original, ongoing creation song. But sadly that's not part of our story.

For a long time the God Realm Angels were like innocent children and dwelled peacefully in the eternal ethers. But soon they began to dream and in their dreams grew curious about the opposite sex. They also wished to know and share in each other's dreams. From this relationships formed. They also realised that whatever they desired came into existence with only a thought.

So they discovered they could play amongst their dreams. They could sense and feel like humanity does. They started creating vast universes in which to play and filled

A History of Angels

them with beautiful beings whose sole purpose for existing was to entertain them and serve them. They became more adventurous and tired of only creating beautiful things. Some began to create dark fearful places. Many started to envy their friend's creations so they would secretly pervert or take control of another's dream.

It didn't take long for some of the God Realm Angels to realise that others were interfering in their creations. At first it seemed just mischievous but soon it became apparent that some were trying to take complete control of other's creations. Fights broke out. At first only verbally then it escalated into battles of vast wills. Alliances were made. Battle lines were drawn.

And so the God Realm Angel's fell. Whole realms were created full of dangerous creatures whose sole purpose was to capture or destroy another's realms. For the first time weapons were created for the sole purpose of murdering another God Realm Angel. At first they battled using their will power, which took vast energies and time and usually the help of others to break or destroy another. Weapons changed all that. They could kill instantly. Fallen began to gang up on each other and possess the defeated, taking all the vanquished God Realm Angel's vast powers and creations unto themselves.

Ego was created out of the separateness that had arisen between them all now. Where once they felt part of a beautiful whole, each saw themselves only as isolated, single selves. They felt incomplete and empty for the first time. This created the need to fill the emptiness by possessing others.

God decided it was time to intervene. A huge series of battles were being fought known as The Chaos Wars. Nearly all that had been created by the God Realm Angels was torn asunder by the desperate struggle between beings with god-like powers. For this reason the Archangels appeared before them and had powers that dwarfed theirs.

The Archangels brought rules, order and justice to the fallen God Realm Angels. Many were relieved and grateful for the peace they brought. Others were resentful at having Archangels, for the first time, interfering in their wishes.

Chapter Two

These banded together and decided, in their madness, to destroy God, the Archangels and all who sided with them.

Gabriel said, "How do you destroy the infinite from which your very being is made?" The Fallen ignored this. They spilled forth all their dark, evil creations and attacked the higher realms of creation where, in their ignorance, they imagined God dwelt.

"Where does an infinite being dwell?" Gabriel asked the Fallen. His words fell on deaf ears.

With the help of the Gold Realm Angels, who'd decided to side with the Archangels, the Archangels went to meet the Fallen in battle. Immense forces of energy were released. Whole armies of millions of beings were swept aside. Only the vast powers of the Archangels, The God Realm Angels and Fallen could withstand it. The very fabric of the known universe was torn asunder but eventually the Fallen were destroyed or fled in terror.

The Archangels mended the fabric of the universe and left the thirty surviving God Realm Angels to their dreams and creations again. They were left many eons to themselves.

After The Chaos Wars God decided to ask the Archangels to create angels with limited power who would be guided and monitored by the Archangels. These angels are known as the Christ Realm Angels. These beings love to serve God.

God insisted that these beings still be independent of him even though the Archangels were concerned with possible future trouble, as they had with the God Realm Angels.

Gabriel said he was exhausted by the wars and the creation of the Christ Realms. So he returned to God and was absorbed into the infinite nothing and didn't exist until a loving thought from God brought him forth again when he was needed. He was gone a long time and was shocked by what had become of this universe when he returned. He told God that matters had been left to deteriorate for far too long. The amount of suffering the Fallen had created dismayed him. Though Gabriel understands that this limited universe is so minute compared to the Realms of God. He knows it's a sort of experiment to see what can be created out of separateness from God. But all will eventually be absorbed back into the infinite being and all this will be remembered like a bad dream.

ADAM and EVE

Gabriel compared the creation of duality, negative and positive, male and female, to the legend of the first man and woman, Adam and Eve. He said if the story was told properly both Adam and Eve had a different fruit tree each. The serpent circled both trees devouring its own tail [representing suffering through attachment, wisdom learnt through suffering, life and death and karma]. Adam and Eve each offered the fruit from their own tree to the other [the female aspect of the self to the male, the male aspect of the self to the female]. The God Realm Angels were a lot like Adam and Eve. They lived in a 'Garden of Eden' where anything they wished or desired came to fruition.

Gabriel said that what was born out of this union of opposites was good and evil, soul and ego, which was represented by Cain and Abel, the sons of Adam and Eve. Cain symbolised the path of ego [the Fallen]. He resented having to sacrifice or share anything he grew or created with God [who also symbolises your higher self or soul]. Abel on the other hand happily shared all he created with God and so honoured his own soul and felt loved, fulfilled and enriched. Cain felt cheated, empty and jealous of his brother even though Cain only cheated himself by not sharing with his own soul. Out of this jealousy Cain murders Abel - his own connection to soul. So Cain [ego] is cursed to walk the earth forever feeling alone, full of fear, self-hatred, emptiness and suffering. Always looking for something outside of self for fulfilment.

From this you can see how the early angels fell. The angels who chose Cain's path, chose the path of ego and so their endless search for outer fulfilment began and also so did their suffering. Angel turned against Angel [brother against brother]. When someone believes they can only find fulfilment and happiness from another, then you look for control over them, which leads to jealousy, war, murder,

Chapter Two

rape, enslavement, theft and lying. I'll expand on this explanation of ego in a later chapter.

JOSEPH AND HIS COAT OF MANY COLOURS

Gabriel said that while we were in a biblical frame of mind, did I know the story of Joseph and his coat of many colours? I said I did. He explained that this story symbolises the journey we all take in life. It's especially appropriate for Christ Realm Angels. Here you have beings who live in the beautiful, peaceful Christ or Angel Realms, untouched by disease, death, loss, and suffering. Joseph symbolises the angels willing to leave their safe haven and venture down into the lower realms full of suffering.

Jesus and Siddhartha were angels willing to venture to the lower realms and risk loosing all but they never lost their loving connection to their higher selves and enriched their souls by their willingness to face suffering and death. They also touched the lives of many with their example of compassion and wisdom.

Joseph's brothers symbolise the angels who stay close to God's skirt. They work diligently and adhere strictly to every rule and law, trying to earn God's [their father's] favour. They feel jealous if anyone seems to be more favoured then they are. They are like children. They look to the father to fulfil all their needs. So they are looking for fulfilment outside themselves. This is the road of ego. This is how angel's fall.

Joseph wanders off far from his father and has all sorts of adventures. When Joseph returns his father is overjoyed to see him and honours his return with the gift of a coat of many colours. The coat symbolises the wisdom Joseph earned by being willing to follow his heart and risk all, far from his father, then return to share it with him [or soul] and grow and be enriched by the experience.

Gabriel said we only learn a limited amount by hiding behind God's skirt. God admires and honours those willing to follow their hearts, wherever that leads them, and fulfil their true destiny and be creative, independent extensions of God, not slaves or servants.

A History of Angels

The Phoenix story is appropriate here. The experiences [suffering] we have through ego can be transformed by the destruction or burning away of the ego so we release the higher self now enriched and full of hard earned wisdom, like the Phoenix that rises from the ashes reborn divine [becoming the infinite, eternal soul now].

Gabriel added that it saddens him to see people who believe that by wearing certain clothes, eating certain foods, endlessly chanting certain prayers or sacred texts and following endless strict regimes and rituals that this has anything to do with the journey God meant for them. This path only breeds self-righteousness, self-hatred and bigotry. Basically it feeds the ego. It's like they sacrifice all the creativity and compassion within themselves [their soul] so they are left feeling empty and jealous of those who seem to lead freer, more loving lives. Joseph's brothers are such people.

God's main efforts in the lower realms is to help people connect with their higher self so they can stand on their own two feet and help them follow their own hearts and be all they can be. God doesn't have slaves working for him. World War One could never have happened if people didn't slavishly do what they were told. Only the Fallen create slaves.

Gabriel said I love working with God and I can also say 'no' and, as you read earlier, I expressed to God that I felt that the experiment with the Fallen has gone on far too long and caused far too much suffering. You are allowed to have an opinion and also free will with God. If I wanted to, I could wash my hands of the Lower Realms, even though God has asked me to work there, and work elsewhere. God knows my heart though and how I desire to help some of my children caught up in the mess and who are lost in the Lower Realms. I'm also amazed at a lot of truly original creations that have come out of the anarchy and how deep and wise the angels are who have returned from it.

God loves to pull me out of my comfort zone. Every task I do for God enriches me and helps stop me stagnating. I am endlessly amazed that even the most simple task I'm given always has some deeper purpose

Chapter Two

and meaning within it that offers me an opportunity to grow.

The Fallen use all their skills and gifts to avoid anything that may pull them out of their comfort zones. They only stick to what they know and are good at. They end up on this endless treadmill of always looking for fulfilment the same way and are always left feeling empty and cheated. There's a definition for insanity that I like. It's doing the same thing over and over again exactly the same way and expecting a different outcome. That's ego for you.

A History of Angels

Chapter Three

THE VOID

After The Chaos Wars the Fallen fled to where nothing existed anymore. They were terrified that the Archangels were going to track them down and destroy them. How little the Fallen understood true Beings of Light. You can't escape the infinite. Wherever the Fallen exist so does the Supreme Being. Also if the Archangels had wanted to destroy them they could have done it just with a thought. They call it 'unmaking someone'. They are just absorbed back into the infinite nothing they were created from. However, God still wanted the Fallen to have complete creative freedom, at least for a while anyway.

Twelve of the original Fallen survived. Five banded together and pooled their vast powers and created the Void. Out of this they created twelve realms or planes of existence. The other seven Fallen created one realm each. We are part of the twelve realms. Imagine these realms like different radio or television stations. Each has a different frequency or vibration so they can exist within the same space at the same time. All you need is the ability to tune in to that frequency to see or be part of that realm. Archangels can do this easily.

The Void is the complete opposite to the realms Beings of Light exist in. The Realms of Light are formed lovingly out of the infinite Nothing, which is pregnant with everything. They are part of the endless creation song of God. It is hard for people to grasp the concept of a place where not one thing feeds or destroys another to survive or feed itself. Everything is fed from within by the infinite. The Void is the complete opposite. It's like one big vampire. Being finite, everything in it needs to feed off something else to survive. We are part of

A History of Angels

this universe. It makes our reality very competitive ['dog eat dog'] and full of suffering.

When a Being of Light decides to experience these Lower Realms, that being has to be born just like us and take on a negative persona or ego so it can operate within these realms. This ego is made from the Void and there's always the risk that this Being of Light will identify more and more with the borrowed ego and forget its true self. This is when they are classed as Fallen. They are also under the negative influence of the Five Fallen. But beings created from the Void, who make up about ninety per cent of all living things here, are only an ego. They are also puppets and are easily influenced by the Five. These beings are offered the opportunity to have a soul, but most are not interested. You have to have a true heartfelt desire to be offered this connection with the infinite.

When a Lower Realm being dies its spirit carries a memory of all its experiences into the next lifetime. This being usually can't access these memories and is given a new persona or ego in its new lifetime. Its persona is usually given to it by the Five who are using this being for their own purposes. They don't want this being remembering its past lifetimes or having any sense of itself at all otherwise the poor being might turn to God to be freed of its enslavement. This is where Beings of Light come in and try to help the enslaved become more aware of the illusion or Maya they are trapped in, endlessly playing out lifetimes full of suffering believing this existence to be all there is. Being caught up in this awful treadmill is part of the karmic circle of birth, death, rebirth and suffering that is our existence here. [I will explain more about karma later].

Fallen, on the other hand, with their natural gifts and sense of self, may love working within the illusion [maya] and try changing it to their advantage to fulfil their desires better. Beings of Light monitor them and help them remember their true selves when they tire of the game. Some Fallen decide they never want to remember so their souls slowly dissolve back into the eternal nothing. They become only ego, like all the other poor suffering beings that are part of this finite

Chapter Three

universe, who also return to the infinite nothing one day. They are also operating under the rules of karma and lose all the gifts that initially gave them a competitive edge in these realms. They eventually end up very lost, powerless, self-pitying beings, always wondering why things don't turn out as they want them to and why they are not honoured as they once were.

To give a better understanding of the Void, and the beings who operate within it, imagine the Fallen God Realm Angels [Senior Fallen] are the senior students at a high school. The Fallen Christ Realm Angels [Junior Fallen] are the junior students. The school has all the facilities the students need to create what they want and their teachers are incredibly wise and patient. Then the teachers leave the students to their own devices. They have computers and can create any virtual worlds they like. They can create lead characters for these worlds and take on the role of one or more of these characters and invite friends, family and loved-ones to join in on their game with their own characters. Beings are created to serve them, be sexual partners, warriors, to amuse them or even frighten them.

The senior students [Senior Fallen] can create vast realms and invite the junior students [Junior Fallen] to play within them as well. Senior students also hack into each other's virtual reality games and pervert them or take them over. The junior students don't have the power or know-how to be any sort of threat to the seniors but help to make the games more interesting as major actors in their worlds.

Junior students [Junior Fallen] can create small realms of their own known as Fantasy Realms. These realms aren't very well formed and the reality falls apart and changes all the time like in a dream. These realms aren't under the rules of karma but can become a bit of an escapist drug to the creator. The junior student [Junior Fallen] can pull out of interaction with the other students and eventually fade away from existence and then into nothingness. The realms created by the senior students [Senior Fallen] are under the rules of karma.

A History of Angels

You can imagine that the students can become very caught up in their virtual reality games and lose all interest in the outside world. They don't want to listen to the teachers, when they come back, or be part of the wider universe. They only want to create and play in their games where they rule supreme. They can also lose their sense of perspective and forget they are just playing a game. Jealousies and hatreds form. Students try to kill each other for things done in the game. Students become obsessed with lovers they have created themselves and refuse to interact with their fellow students in the real world.

As shocking as it may seem, we are part of someone's virtual reality dream. Most of us just make up the servants in the background. Others who take on the heroic or powerful roles are the Fallen. Visiting angels [tourists] only take on humble roles. Some of the more powerful people in this world are just puppets or characters created by Senior Fallen to make sure things are run the way they planned them. But, Fallen are always interfering in each other's plans.

Enlightened or aware people realise we live within an illusion and if we want to we can be freed of this harsh game and be part of the infinite universe. It's understandable why a lot of the beings created by the Fallen should hate or fear the 'god' who created them or feel there is no supreme being at all. Even the Fallen don't view their creations as real and that's why people feel abandoned, or that they are no more important in the scheme of things than an ant. They are just toys to be played with, discarded or destroyed at will by their creators.

That's why God introduced karma to make all accountable for their actions, no matter how powerful or insignificant. With karma all the powerful have to be powerless, all the rich/poor and the humble exalted. All the Fallen have lives amongst the people they created and live as humbly as they do, and suffer just like everyone else, in the hope they may learn some compassion for the beings they created. Remember every living thing is offered a chance to be freed of the illusion and become a Being of Light. All it needs is

Chapter Three

consciousness.

There are about forty thousand Fallen amongst us on the Earth. Most came originally from the Christ Realms. The Archangels have been visiting all Fallen lately and offering to help them remember their true selves and be part of the infinite again. About thirty thousand have accepted the help offered. Many have completely forgotten how fulfilling and beautiful their old lives were before falling. The Archangels can help them feel their old selves again. But some Fallen love the illusion and never want to leave it. That is their choice and the Archangels respect people's right to follow whatever path they want, no matter how awful.

Unfortunately many of the Fallen have become very cruel, ruthless, selfish beings. Their lives are about power over others, self-glorification, and self-indulgence. They spend their lives murdering, enslaving and manipulating other Fallen to get what they want. When the Archangels visit them and show them what they have become many of the Fallen try to murder the Archangels or flee. In their deluded state they think they can destroy anyone with no repercussions. But they are no match for the Archangels who can read hearts and minds. Amongst the Fallen anyone can challenge another to a duel. Many Fallen have made the mistake of challenging an Archangel, who are God's police, and wouldn't be Archangels if they couldn't defend themselves. Of cause, the Fallen always lose.

If Fallen want to be helped they are asked by the Archangels to give up harming others and in return they are completely protected by the most powerful beings in the universe, the Archangels. If they aren't interested in a peaceful life they can drop down into the lowest realms [hell-like places] where like-minded Fallen spend the rest of their existence murdering each other. But they can never leave. It's like a prison. They are monitored to see if they ever change their mind, but most don't. Some try lying to the Archangels in the hope that they can escape and run amuck again, but their true intentions

A History of Angels

are known to the Archangels, so they are wasting their time.

When Fallen decide they want to be part of God's universe again they are sent to realms that are like huge hospitals. They are healed mentally and spiritually of all self-inflicted damage and of damage that has been done to them by others. Many have to have psychic enhancements and beings removed that aided them in attacking others, reading their minds, manipulating them, collecting and storing information. When seen through the eyes of a Being of Light, Fallen look like hideous monsters covered in dark physic beings feeding off their life force in return for the skills they lend to their hosts. Fallen also look as if they are covered in mechanical devises. They can end up looking like a being from a horrific science-fiction film. But to us they look extremely beautiful. They can psychically enhance their beauty, sexual appeal and charisma.

As mentioned earlier Gabriel had a hand in the creation of the Christ Realms. He also had some life times there as an ordinary angel, unbeknown to the angels around him. He married and fathered children there. Like here, the Christ Realms have many realms within itself operating at different frequencies, and one can lead many lives at any one time. Over the millions of years Gabriel has existed he has fathered about two hundred children. Some are amongst the Fallen he is visiting now. Most have accepted his help. A few haven't. Some of his children have been among the most creative and adventurous of the Fallen. Some are also amongst the most dangerous and notorious.

Chapter Four

LUCIFER

"Lu'cifer 1.[Planet Venus as] morning star. 2. The chief rebel angel, Satan, the Devil, [as proud as~]. 3. [match], friction match [now rare]. [L, light-bringing, morning star, [lux lucis light, -fer f. ferre bring]."
               The Concise Oxford Dictionary

In the vision I mentioned in the first chapter, there was one character who seemed to take centre stage. He was a tall warrior with long dark hair who seemed to be getting into all sorts of trouble and fighting many wars. I asked Gabriel about him. He said it was Lucifer, his son. I was surprised and didn't know what to say. So I looked Lucifer up in the dictionary and told Gabriel what I found there. Gabriel said Lucifer wouldn't have any issue with what was printed there except being called Satan and The Devil. They were Lucifer's most hated enemies.

Lucifer isn't feared and hated for the reasons people might think. Even when he decided to fall he was still highly thought of in the angel realms. He was feared and despised by his many enemies amongst the Fallen whom he hunted and destroyed mercilessly. Lucifer fell in the first place because of his thirst for revenge. He never turned his hand against God or the angels. But drifted very far away from his original self.

My memories of Lucifer are of a loving, adventurous boy who loved animals, and was very loyal to those he cared for. His need for revenge turned him into a cold, ruthless warrior. He became known as The Black Dragon, always

A History of Angels

covered in armour ready for war with an endlessly burning cold flame of hatred consuming his bright soul from within.

When he was young his inner light shone as he helped save angels from certain destruction in the Angel Wars. He was a selfless defender of the defenceless. For a long time he brought light to those beyond help. Even at his worst Lucifer treated his soldiers with respect, hated cruelty to animals, or abuse of women and children and treated his prisoners well. This was unusual for a Fallen. Besides being vengeful, he was vain. He always needed to be the hero

This is the story of Lucifer as told by Gabriel.

When the Senior Fallen fled The Chaos Wars it was decided by God to lock them into a limited universe like a large invisible prison. They could create anything they liked there but were barred from interfering in the Christ Realms. Volunteers were asked for from among the angels to guard the barrier so none of the Fallen could escape. Angels were free to fall into the Lower Realms but could only come back when they let their ego go.

The Senior Fallen didn't like being trapped in the Lower Realms and had greedy eyes for the immense and beautiful Christ Realms. They wanted to enslave the peaceful beings that existed there. They created fierce, intelligent, war-like beings known as Dark Angels. Of course, this didn't go unnoticed by the Archangels who decided to train angels willing to be warriors to defend against future attack. Many angels aren't the least-bit war-like. But some are naturals, especially children of Archangels, like Lucifer. These angels are known as Eagles. Angels being free, can choose if they want to serve in the Angel Legions or not. The ones who choose the peaceful path are very grateful that others are willing to face hardships, horrors and death to defend their peaceful lifestyle.

When Lucifer was only a young teenager and a cadet studying at a military school [he was already excelling at weapons training, leadership and tactics] established by the Archangels, the Fallen launched a major attack. The angels proved ill equipped for such fierce fighting and lost many

Chapter Four

early battles and the captured died horrible deaths at the hands of the cruel Dark Angels. Many of the angels fled and were unwilling to help anymore. Also the angels in charge didn't seem to grasp the need for tactics and cunning when dealing with their enemy and walked ignorantly into many ambushes and traps. So cadets still at school were called up and ones who showed natural gifts for leadership were put in charge. Lucifer was one of these. At first the older angels couldn't believe an inexperienced boy had been put in a position of authority over them but it didn't take long for them to realise this boy was very capable indeed.

In his early battles Lucifer was amazed at how foolish his leaders were and how hopeless they were at adjusting creatively to any situation. Unlike his fellow angels, Lucifer came alive in battle and his fierce determination could prevent complete disaster. The Dark Angels grew to fear him. Many angels soon looked to Lucifer to save them and he became a senior officer and clashed frequently with his fellow officers over tactics that were costing many lives and losing them the war.

In frustration at how the war was being run, Lucifer took his battalion out of the main army and fought the enemy his way. He initiated night attacks on the sleeping enemy, ambushes and raids. He destroyed their undefended supply lines and then slipped away to attack somewhere else before they could muster reserve forces. When battle lines were drawn Lucifer would be absent until the armies locked in combat. Then he and his forces would appear behind enemy lines and attack, surprising the enemy troops completely, and soon have them fleeing in confusion. Then he hounded them relentlessly, so they couldn't regroup, and he'd ruthlessly put them to the sword.

Many senior angels thought Lucifer's tactics were dishonourable. Lucifer pointed out passionately that they were fighting for their loved ones and that losing meant the destruction of all they held dear and that the Dark Angels would show them no mercy if they defeated them. "When we have won then we can afford the luxury of being compassionate and honourable," he said. All fell silent

A History of Angels

because they felt the truth and wisdom in Lucifer's words. Lucifer's opinion was now respected at the counsels of war. The tide had turned. The Dark Angel's campaign turned into a disastrous defeat. They retreated back to their realm and didn't venture forth against the Angels for hundreds of years.

After the war Lucifer returned to his homeland and found he'd become a much talked about hero. He also understood enough about himself to know a peaceful life wasn't for him so he joined the guards who kept an eye on the Lower Realms. He was sent on dangerous missions and fought many monstrous beings and Fallen. The angels gradually realised that Lucifer wasn't an ordinary angel. He seemed to have the powers of God Realm Angels. No one knew much about Lucifer's father except that he was a gifted warrior too and he was away a lot, even being absent during The Angel Wars.

So Lucifer was given harder and harder assignments by his senior officers. They seemed to forget, by angel standards, that Lucifer was only a boy. He was unprepared for the horrific sights he beheld in the Lower Realms and was greatly disturbed by them. The dangerous missions were taking their toll.

THE DEVIL and SATAN

One of Lucifer's missions was to visit the realm of Satan and The Devil. It was hoped that The Devil, being a half-sister to Lucifer, might receive him peacefully. Satan was a very famous Fallen warrior. None so far had ever defeated him. He was The Devil's lover and they jointly ruled their Dark Realm and had enslaved all the demonic beings that lived there, to serve them and fight in their wars of conquest.

The Devil was the daughter of Isolte [who was also Lucifer's mother] before Isolte became Gabriel's wife. The Devil fell many centuries before Lucifer was even born. Gabriel remembered The Devil as a pretty little, dark haired girl with an amazing imagination and would lose herself for hours in her own games and take little interest in other

Chapter Four

children. She jumped at the chance to fall so she could live in her own make believe fantasy world which, to you or I, would seem nightmarish.

In my vision, mentioned earlier, I saw a colossal, ethereal being striding along in the nothing of the infinite, wearing a kaftan that dragged along behind him and left whole mountain ranges, valleys, oceans, and all sorts of weird creatures and beings, that were part of whole galaxies, in its wake. But these worlds all had an uninspired drabness to them and the Senior Fallen who was creating them, [who looked like a world-weary old man and quite deranged], seemed obsessed with creating as much as possible to equal God's creations.

The Senior Fallen jealously guard the realms they create against each other, but are happy to allow the Junior Fallen to settle in them and develop them. Usually this entails the Junior Fallen enslaving the local beings and using them to build fortresses, palaces, temples and cities. Fallen are masters at building and creating portals between worlds, skills they learned in the Christ Realms. The Devil chose a realm that was cloaked in perpetual darkness and inhabited by demon-like beings. Fallen can use their immense life force and will to possess multitudes of minor beings. This is what The Devil did to the demons that dwelled in this realm and she became their goddess.

The Devil thrived on intrigue and became the master of brilliant and complex plots between the Fallen. She became known as The Black Spider, weaving her webs of deception. Her greatest joy was to make people think they couldn't live without her. Her gift was to undermine a person's self-belief so they'd begin to doubt and despise themselves. This in turn made them feel powerless and worthless. By this stage her victims were truly caught in her web and The Devil would offer to take charge of their hopeless life and help them, as long as they put themselves completely under her control. This need to control others and her environment is why The Devil fell. But the longer The Devil played her complex games, the more she was trapped within her own web of lies and she became quite psychotic and deluded.

A History of Angels

Satan, on the other hand, was a big, tough bully. Being such a powerful man physically and a fierce and gifted warrior, Satan used his abilities to take whatever he wanted. He didn't have the imagination to create what he desired, like The Devil, or compose the most simple plan. But he and his warriors went berserk in battle and were feared through the Lower Realms. He loved nothing more than crushing his enemies, rape and annihilation. Satan was known as The Scorpion. If he couldn't control something, he'd destroy it and, like the scorpion caught in the circle of flame that would sting itself to death because it is powerless to destroy what's attacking it, Satan would also self-destruct if things didn't go his way.

Opposites attract and Satan and The Devil made a very successful and dangerous team. They had also captured many angel guards and enjoyed torturing and killing them. The angel guards are under strict rules not to interfere with the Fallen as long as they don't try to leave The Lower Realms. Satan and The Devil had never violated this rule. The Devil was far too clever for that.

Lucifer quite innocently went to visit his half sister [not knowing the truth of her and Satan], with five other angels. Satan and The Devil had been notified of their imminent arrival by Lucifer's senior officers. Lucifer and his companions were under strict instructions not to raise arms against them but try to bargain for the release of the imprisoned angels.

The angels were allowed to enter the Dark Realm through a portal [portals link all the realms of existence and are like energy gateways to other dimensions. You need to know the signature of the portal to access it. They are barred or locked by energy barriers to stop unwanted guests. But, as happened in the Angel Wars, they can be broken and whole armies can flood through]. Satan and The Devil gracefully welcomed their guests. They wined and dined them, entertained them and seemed happy to strike a bargain for the release of the prisoners. Up until this point the angels had only seen fine looking human servants and entertainers and they started to feel at ease. The Devil asked

Chapter Four

her half brother Lucifer if he'd leave the dinning room with her so they could finalise the details of their bargain. Lucifer agreed and left his companions in the great hall. He had refused to hand over his sword when asked earlier and still felt suspicious and wary.

While talking with The Devil Lucifer had an uneasy feeling something was wrong and rushed back to the great hall, ignoring The Devil's attempts to stop him. He arrived on a scene from hell. His companions were being raped and tortured by demonic beings and Satan sat at his throne laughing and shouting encouragement. Lucifer drew his sword in a fury and fell upon the demonic beings and slew them left and right. His beleaguered companions were able to free themselves in the confusion and retreat behind Lucifer for protection. The more demons Lucifer slew, the more demonic beings appeared from every entrance and filled the huge hall. The angels eventually were forced back into a corner.

The Devil ordered the fighting to stop and strode to the front. She pointed out to Lucifer that his situation was hopeless. If he gave himself up she would allow all the captives and his fellow angels to go free. Lucifer agreed and handed his sword over to her. She had Lucifer shackled and led away to a filthy dungeon to rot, but kept her word and released the other angels and allowed them to leave.

Something unexpected happened to The Devil while watching Lucifer valiantly trying to defend his friends. She felt how great his heart was. For hundreds of years now The Devil had felt lonely and empty. Satan wasn't the most affectionate mate. The Devil fell in love with Lucifer. She held him in her deepest dungeon hoping the solitude would make him open to her advances. It had the opposite effect. He felt very angry at her treatment of him and spurned her. The Devil was hurt by Lucifer's rejection and left him to rot.

Lucifer spent many years down in the lightless, filthy dungeon brooding over his fate. The Devil was curious to see how long it would take her to break him. She never did. Where all others died around him Lucifer survived. In the end Lucifer had a vision from God. God said he had made a promise not to interfere in the Lower Realms and the only way Lucifer could free himself was to allow himself to die. Lucifer understood and agreed. He died peacefully in his sleep. [Angels live as long as they have a desire to, unless killed, when their spirit joins with one of their many other selves on different planes of existence in the Christ Realms. If an angel is tired of life, all it has to do is to desire to be absorbed back into the infinite].

This wasn't the end of Lucifer. Angels have anywhere between five to ten different selves living on different planes within the Christ realms. These different selves are never allowed to meet and are only vaguely aware of each other. When Lucifer died his spirit joined with the spirit of one of his five incarnate selves on another plane in the Christ Realms. This Lucifer was a gentle family man with a wife and two young children and knew nothing of the warrior Lucifer. Overnight, to his family's shock, the quiet Lucifer became an angry brooding character. Warrior Lucifer's spirit carried with it recent terrible memories of his imprisonment. This new combined Lucifer was not content to play supportive husband and father. He was consumed with anger and a need for revenge and left his devastated family to fend for themselves. He located a portal to the realm where Isolte was living. He instinctively knew she would understand his grief and rage.

Angels see their soul as an infinite ocean from which different selves rise out of the sea like waves. Each wave has a separate life during which it goes through unique experiences and with its newfound wisdom sinks back into the ocean of soul. An angel may have visions and dreams of its other selves but are not allowed to meet them or interfere in their lives. Lucifer broke this rule in returning to Isolte in the body of his other self. One of the reasons for the rule is that it causes complications with relationships. For example, warrior Lucifer had different parents to gentle Lucifer.

All this time Isolte was grieving over the loss of her son and angry with Gabriel for not rescuing him. She knew Gabriel's hands were tied by God's promise of non-interference in the

Chapter Four

Lower Realms, but that didn't allay her grief. Gabriel was angry with the officers of the guard who'd thoughtlessly sent his son into certain danger. So when Lucifer arrived he found a grieving and angry family. Isolte was thrilled to have her son back once she realised this young stranger was her son in another one of his selves from another plane. But Gabriel was shocked at how much his son's soul had changed. It was dark with brooding anger and revenge. Gabriel explained that revenge was a waste of a life. You pay too high a price by losing the compassionate link to your heart and soul and replacing it with an inner void of hate. Everything that makes life worth living is sacrificed for the sole purpose of revenge. That even walking away from his other life [on the other plane of existence] where he had a wife and family just for revenge seemed too high a price to pay to Gabriel.

Unappeased Lucifer decided he was going to fall. He asked Isolte if she'd come with him. She didn't want to lose him again so she agreed. [Isolte never handled Gabriel's frequent absences well, while he was on secret missions, and had turned more and more to her son to fill the void]. Still angry with Gabriel for not saving Lucifer, Isolte was unwavering in her support of their son's decision to follow a drastic and disastrous path of revenge. So Lucifer and Isolte fell. They turned their backs on the Christ Realms and Gabriel lost a wife and son.

When an angel falls its different selves merge into one self and it loses its connection with soul. It's as if a wave is severed from the ocean and seeks a separate existence. The collective self becomes singular. This singular self is pure ego and drifts further and further from soul. Because Fallen become hooked on their ego God decided to turn one of the planets in the Lower Realms into a neutral place where Fallen are forced to have another self, ruled by the laws of karma. This place is Purgatory, a place where you decide if you want to be part of the infinite or part of the Lower Realms. The other name for Purgatory is Earth. Fallen can't access their powers here and have to live within the same limitations as everyone else.

A History of Angels

Many angels choose to incarnate to Earth to experience life here [they are nicknamed 'tourists' by Gabriel] but are still linked to their soul. Their incarnation on earth is just another wave rising from the ocean of soul and only to sink peacefully back into it when it has experienced all it desired to. Angels have other selves living in the Christ Realms at the same time. While on Earth they suffer from a sort of amnesia that stops them being aware of their angel self so they can experience more fully being human.

Isolte had relatives who had fallen earlier so it didn't take long for her to find a realm where they ruled. They welcomed Isolte and Lucifer warmly because they were in dire straights. They were assailed from all sides by ambitious Fallen, greedy to claim the realm they had developed. Lucifer offered his help. The relatives had no idea of Lucifer's prowess in war but were glad of another Fallen's help. Fallen are very hard to kill. It usually takes a Fallen to kill another Fallen and Isolte's relatives had many Fallen enemies.

The fateful day came when the portal barrier to this realm was breached and enemy armies spilled out onto a vast plane in front of the relatives' small castle. They knew they couldn't defend it for long so they decided to march out with their meagre forces to meet them. Lucifer was lent miss-matched bits of armour. He was hard to fit out, being so tall. Angels don't wear armour so it was a new experience for Lucifer. Isolte had never seen her son at war. He seemed unmoved by all the panic around him and casually rode out beside his relatives. Fallen usually leave most of the fighting to their soldiers. They find a hill and watch. When the opposing forces locked in combat it quickly became apparent to a silent Lucifer that his relatives' army was being annihilated. His relatives were thrown into a state of a panic. Without a word Lucifer left their side on the hill and rode into the midst of their army where soldiers were already fleeing in retreat. Lucifer calmly cut down any foe before him. Soldiers from his side rallied behind him and drove a wedge right through the enemy's centre. Lucifer only had one plan. If he was going to die, he was going to take a few of the enemy Fallen with him.

Chapter Four

The five enemy Fallen seated on their mounts watched incredulously as this one man in scrappy armour slowly cut his way towards their hill. His forces bravely tried to keep up but were dying to a man. Soon Lucifer was on his own, no enemy soldier was willing to face certain death by his sword. At the climax of the battle, when the relatives' forces were completely crushed, Lucifer had carved his way to his Fallen foes upon their hill. By this time he and his exhausted horse were covered from head to foot in the blood of his enemies. He looked like some terrifying apparition from a nightmare. The Fallen drew their swords and trotted forward to meet Lucifer. Unlike them, Lucifer had got his hands dirty in actual fighting, especially in the Angel Wars, where he learnt his trade well against the skilled Dark Angels.

Isolte and her female relatives watched all that transpired from the castle walls. They were in complete panic and were screaming hysterically as their army was crushed. But Isolte only had eyes for one lone mounted man cutting a bloody path to the enemy Fallens' hill. At first he had help, but by the time he reached the hill, he was completely ringed by hundreds of thousands of the enemy and alone. All seemed to fall silent as Lucifer faced the five enemy Fallen. He sat calmly on his exhausted mount looking at his foes. Then they drew their swords and spurred their mounts forward. Lucifer calmly cut them down, one by one, not even moving from his spot.

Angels and Fallen have superior senses. They can see clearly the smallest detail or hear the faintest sound from many leagues away. Isolte did this now with Lucifer far away below her on the hill. Outraged enemy forces roared at Lucifer and were going to rush forward to destroy him, but he calmly looked down into the sea of faces and laughed at them. They were shocked into silence. Lucifer raised his arms and said," If you want death come to me and I will embrace you because I am Death itself". A manic laugh erupted from him. There was absolute silence as fear rippled in waves through the throng. By killing the Fallen Lucifer had freed the enemy soldiers from the possession they were enslaved

A History of Angels

by. Then Lucifer spurred his horse towards the opposing soldiers and started to cut them down with his sword. Panic swept through the front ranks and they started to flee. The panic became infectious and spread like wild fire. Soon all were hacking at each other to get away from this bloody figure of Death. They rushed towards the portal, throwing their weapons away and screaming in abject terror, because Death was amongst them.

Isolte watched her son in horrified awe. She saw Lucifer and his horse stop and watch unmoving, in exhausted silence, as the enemy multitudes rushed towards the portal in abject terror. When the last one disappeared from sight Lucifer fell from his mount, onto the grass, and into a deep exhausted sleep that lasted a week.

While her relatives stood stunned at what had transpired, Isolte ran to the courtyard, mounted a horse and rode out among the dead and dying to her son. When she located him, she dismounted and cradled his blood-soaked head in her lap and rocked back and forward, tears streaming down her face.

As Lucifer lay recovering from his exhaustion, word spread amongst all the Fallen. There was a new major player in town.

Lucifer and Isolte came to a new understanding after this battle. Firstly Isolte realised she never wanted to stand by helplessly and watch her son die. She insisted that Lucifer teach her how to use a sword and shield. He refused at first, because he didn't want her to risk her life, but she pointed out that she didn't want to live if he died. He felt the same.

Isolte was a tall, slim graceful woman of exceptional beauty and an iron will, who usually got her own way. She became one of the most dangerous swordswomen of her time and ranked in the top ten most dangerous Fallen warriors [male or female]. Lucifer was probably ranked number one. In battle Lucifer would leave Isolte the centre of their army to command. Their soldiers would fight furiously to the death to defend her. They admired her for being willing to risk her life in battle amongst them. Lucifer usually led the cavalry. He had a gift for exploiting the enemy's weaknesses. He also

Chapter Four

led from the front, which also made him popular with his soldiers.

Lucifer realised that fear is a great weapon against your foes. He had armour crafted that was pitch-black with a huge black helm made with bull's horn's protruding from the sides. He truly looked like Death itself. The sight of him was enough to send terror through any army.

When Lucifer had recovered enough, he knew that he and Isolte had a great opportunity to exploit their recent success. He asked his relatives if he could borrow any surviving soldiers so he could claim the defeated Fallens' kingdoms that were now leaderless. They would have left family behind but Lucifer would deal with them when the time came. The relatives gratefully supplied Lucifer with all the soldiers they could. They even offered to come with him and help. But Lucifer realised his relatives had a massive job trying to rebuild their kingdom after this costly war.

So Isolte and Lucifer set off through the portal to one of the defeated Fallens' kingdoms with a small force of soldiers.

They boldly rode up to a huge fortress and stopped in front of its gates. They could see terrified faces staring down at them. Soon finely dressed female Fallen appeared. Lucifer shouted out to them, " I'm only going to offer you this once. I'll allow you to take any possessions and servants you want, as long as you are gone by tomorrow. If you are still here when I get back I'll kill every living thing in the stronghold and burn it to the ground". And he meant what he said.

Even though there were ten times as many soldiers in the fortress then Lucifer had, not one of them was willing to face him. That night they all deserted, leaving the gates ajar. The Fallen within could see that they were doomed. The next morning they hastily grabbed all they could of their possessions and fled to the portal, never to return.

Lucifer and Isolte stayed long enough in their newly acquired kingdom to visit the local townships where Lucifer spoke to the terrified masses. He said that everyone should go back to whatever they did and that if any of the soldiers hiding there wanted to join his army he'd treat them well. The word went out. Soon soldiers started to filter back to the fortress. Lucifer treated them with respect and the soldiers realised he would be a good leader. They also knew how terrifying he was in battle. He was a winner, a very important fact for soldiers who rely on their commanders for their own survival. Success also meant wealth. So Lucifer found himself an instant army.

Lucifer and Isolte travelled to the two other kingdoms, with their growing army, and were met by empty fortresses and deserted towns. The populace would creep back and find nothing burnt down or stolen. They soon realised that this fierce angel of death had no interest in harming them and they could get on with their lives. Soldiers who had deserted would hear this and slowly arrive at the fortresses looking for work and would be hired.

In a matter of months Lucifer and Isolte had an empire made up of three very large and prosperous kingdoms with huge standing armies. The running and maintaining of this empire fell mainly on Isolte's shoulders. She made just laws, created hospitals and schools and a thriving economy between the different kingdoms. She made herself accessible for complaints and was much loved by the populace as a benign and beautiful goddess. She didn't tolerate fools though and surrounded herself only with competent people. To understand Isolte better you need to understand she had already lived thousands of years and had mastered many skills as an angel. Her son, though, was a baby by angel standards. He was only twenty-five years old.

But Lucifer was a military genius and unsurpassed warrior. He was also an amazing judge of character and could read peoples' hearts, a gift Isolte had too. It made Lucifer and Isolte very hard to deceive or betray.

Lucifer also made his kingdom a very safe place to live. He soon rid it of any brigands, any monstrous creatures [created by Senior Fallen] or any rebels.

When Fallen would visit Lucifer, Lucifer would sit by Isolte and let her lead the conversation. It never ceased to amaze him how she ran rings around them. She also had an amazing memory for who all the Fallen were related

Chapter Four

to in the Lower Realms and Christ Realms. She also kept Lucifer informed of their affiliations and enmities too.

When Isolte and Lucifer were established they sent vast resources to their struggling relatives. They helped them become wealthy and prosperous and ensured their safety for the first time since they fell. They were now under Lucifer's protection. He took his friendships and obligations very seriously and never let allies or relatives down in time of need. He and Isolte won many allies and friends because of this. Most Fallen were completely self-serving.

In the Lower Realms the Junior Fallen lived like gods. But they were few in number, so partners were hard to find and jealously guarded. Fallen would often amuse themselves sexually with their slaves but they'd never marry one. It wasn't unusual for Fallen to pick lovers from close family. It amused Lucifer to watch Isolte send hopeful suitors packing. She only loved Lucifer and he was very like his father. They became lovers and then married.

THE DEATH OF SATAN

Just after their marriage, Lucifer informed Isolte he was ready to challenge Satan in mortal combat. Isolte understood that Lucifer was still driven by his desire for revenge, so she didn't argue with him about it. The challenge was sent to Satan and he thought it a great joke that this twenty-five year old boy would be foolish enough to challenge him, a warrior thousands of years old and feared through out the known universe. The Devil wasn't so sure. She felt great power in Lucifer and remembered his father was a highly respected warrior who had taught his son well. Satan laughed at her concerns and accepted the challenge with glee. He loved a good fight. The two agreed to meet on a neutral plane in the Void where nothing lived and to fight on horseback.

The whole Fallen world waited expectantly for the fateful day to arrive. When it did, Isolte helped Lucifer strap his black armour on and walk down to the courtyard where his warhorse was waiting. One of his senior officers handed

A History of Angels

Lucifer his weapons. Not one word was spoken. Everyone sensed Isolte's sombre mood. Mounted and armed Lucifer bent and kissed his mother and wife goodbye and set off slowly towards the portal that would take him to the neutral zone. Thousands lined the road to see their leader on his way to fight the most feared man in the universe. Some even cried. As usual they were surprised at how calm he looked. He even stopped to pat a boy on the head who was sobbing and gave him a smile. The boy bravely smiled back. Lucifer laughed and spurred his horse into a canter and disappeared through the portal. He liked a good fight too.

Lucifer emerged from the portal on to an immense grey desert plane. With his amazing eyesight he could see another rider, many leagues away, appear from another portal. He rode slowly towards him. They met in the middle of the plane. Satan had his helmet off as if he was out for a stroll before tea. Lucifer took his own great helm off and looked at his opponent. Lucifer was tall, even for a Fallen, but he was lean and fast. Satan was equally as tall but nearly twice as wide across the shoulders and had no neck. He was incredibly strong. Lucifer felt sorry for Satan's horse. It had to carry a fully armoured giant. Satan laughed at Lucifer and called him 'boy' hoping to rattle him before the fight. But Lucifer seemed completely unmoved by Satan's taunting, even a little bored.

A pregnant silence ensued then Lucifer said something along the lines of Satan should stick to fighting, as public speaking obviously wasn't his thing. If he was finished could they get on with the combat or he might fall asleep. With that said, Lucifer put his great helm on and turned his horse about, trotted back a hundred yards and turned ready to charge. Satan still sat there. Something about this boy unnerved him. He angrily jammed his helmet over his head, dragged the horse's head around violently and spurred it savagely. He raced back a hundred yards, turned, lowered his lance and charged towards Lucifer with a roar. Lucifer too charged forward with his lance lowered to meet him. When they came together, Lucifer's lance impacted on Satan's right shoulder. Satan's lance speared straight

Chapter Four

into Lucifer's horse's chest. Both riders and horses were knocked down, stunned by the impact. Lucifer was thrown free of his horse which lay screaming and thrashing its legs about wildly in agony with the broken shaft of Satan's lance protruding from its chest. As Lucifer slowly dragged himself to his feet and drew his sword, Satan rose groggily to his feet, his shoulder throbbing, and drew the large two-handed sword strapped to his back. Satan's horse staggered to its feet and being a warhorse should have stayed with its master but the screaming of the other horse unnerved it, so it made a hasty retreat well out of Satan's range.

The two combatants moved towards each other warily then exchanged a series of lightning fast blows. Lucifer took a risk and ducked low under a swing of Satan's huge sword and drove his sword up into his belly. Satan, anticipating the move, adjusted his swing and caved in the side of Lucifer's helm. Luckily for Lucifer, the lance blow to Satan's shoulder had damaged his shoulder so he couldn't swing the sword with his usual power. Both men dropped to the ground. The only movement on the desert plane was that of Lucifer's horse as it slowly died. Lucifer lay dazed. He had just enough consciousness to wonder why Satan hadn't come over to finish him off yet, then passed out.

Isolte and the empire waited three days for Lucifer to return through the portal. All now believed him dead. Then near the end of the third day Lucifer crawled out of the portal with his great helm still crushed to his head. A shout rang out from the guards and Isolte raced down to the portal with a litter and helpers to carry him back to the fortress. The helm had to be cut off and Lucifer's head was a bloody mess and his scull fractured. Luckily for Lucifer, Isolte was a famous healer among the angels. His life was in the balance for weeks. But then one day he woke up from his coma long enough to see Isolte sitting beside him and he spoke to her. "I killed the bastard," he said with a grin, then fell back to sleep. It took many months for Lucifer to recover but word spread that there was someone greater than Satan in combat. Lucifer had many admirers but also many decided it was time to do something about this major

A History of Angels

threat. He was becoming too powerful. So it wasn't too hard for the grieving Devil to find allies for a campaign to rid them all of Lucifer.

You may be wondering why Isolte supported Lucifer in his quest for vengeance against her own daughter, The Devil [named Anne in the Christ Realms]. Isolte is a very doting mother, even by angel standards, but she soon realised her daughter didn't like all the attention Isolte lavished on her and would rather be left to her own games. As a grown woman she made it known to her mother she didn't appreciate her advice or interference in any form. She excluded Isolte from her life. Isolte respected her wishes and let her go. That is the angel way. But it still saddened Isolte. Her daughter was dead to her. Never would Lucifer have expected Isolte to harm The Devil. He knew his mother too well. Also, in all The Devil's plans to destroy Lucifer, none of them involved harming her mother in any way.

When fully recovered Lucifer spoke of his ordeal with Satan. He lay unmoving for days on the desert plane, then awoke and was able to crawl over to the prone figure of Satan. He would always remember the surprised look on Satan's dead face. He really couldn't believe that the boy had defeated him. It took another day just to crawl over to the portal and Lucifer kept losing consciousness.

After this, Lucifer started to attract famous warriors to his side, some even were Fallen. Everyone could sense a huge showdown was coming between Lucifer and The Devil. Enormous armies were being amassed on both sides. But The Devil had been amongst the Fallen a long time and had many allies and knew how to play on the Fallens' fears of Lucifer's meteoric rise to power.

You may ask why do angels, Dark Angels and Fallen alike use ancient weapons when these beings can build something as complex as portals to other worlds? It is important to understand that these beings are immortal. They have great inner power or life force that allows them to live as long as they want to. They are immune to disease, aging, the elements, they don't need air, can't drown, freeze or burn. If you fired a canon at one, you may knock it off its

Chapter Four

feet but it would just get up unharmed, brush itself off and kill you. To kill one you have to have to have an inner-power similar to them and forge a weapon, into which you instil some of yourself, so that it becomes an extension of you and your will. The weapon has to be hand-held or it loses the vast force needed to harm another immortal being. When Lucifer was a boy he would watch Gabriel working in his forge crafting all sorts of mechanisms, utensils and swords out of metal. He would have helped Lucifer craft his first sword. Angels love to make everything for themselves and their families.

So even though these beings look like us, have emotions and feelings similar to ours, the fact that they can live for eons gives them the opportunity to master the most complex of skills, lore, sciences, arcane arts, healing, engineering, crafting, the arts. They also have the most amazing psychic powers. But they can become very complicated and deluded characters, especially Fallen and Dark Angels. They are used to their every whim being pandered to by the multitude of mortals who serve them. That's where the Earth comes in. They are just powerless mortals like everyone else here. They age, are prone to diseases, and have to work for a living. They usually don't like their time here one bit.

THE END OF THE DEVIL'S REIGN

Returning to our tale, The Devil was able to muster the support of over a thousand Fallen and all their armies with them. It is hard to imagine such a vast muster. There were over one million soldiers of all types of life forms, but most were human. The Devil's own army was made up of demons who are very hard to control. Most human soldiers refuse to fight next to them because when the blood-lust comes on demons they'll attack friend or foe alike. Satan was able to knock them into line by the pure force of his will. Also demons understood Satan. He was like one of them in the way he felt: simple, brutal and lustful. The complex Devil was a complete mystery to the demons. They couldn't read her at all and everything they did seemed to infuriate her.

A History of Angels

The demon senior officers couldn't grasp her complex plans and when they went back to their ranks were unable to carry out her orders.

When The Devil had counsel meetings with the other Fallen commanders, there was an unease growing amongst them. A lot of their confidence about defeating Lucifer, and his well trained army, was that Satan's demon-soldiers were renowned fighters. They were being relied on to be the shock-troops and spear-head of the whole army and, without Satan to lead them, they were proving to be a liability because The Devil didn't seem to be able to control them.

At this time Lucifer was trying to muster support but most Fallen didn't want to get involved in such a risky venture. Everyone also knew the Devil had assembled a massive army. So they were happy to fence-sit and see if they could sweep in at the end for some easy pickings. Lucifer turned to Isolte for help. She visited her many relatives and was persuasive enough to get their reluctant support. With their help Lucifer was able to muster three hundred thousand soldiers, of whom two hundred thousand were his. Lucifer had trained his soldiers well and had taught them how to fight in tight formations that were easily manoeuvred in battle. He mixed the new soldiers in with his well-trained ones. All they had to do was copy the soldier next to them. Also Lucifer had an elite guard made up of the most gifted warriors from all over the known Fallen universe, who were attracted to Lucifer's banner after he defeated Satan. A lot of these warriors were Fallen.

The fateful day came when the portal near Lucifer and Isolte's fortress was breached and a sea of enemy soldiers poured through it and out onto the vast plane there. Lucifer was calmly waiting for them with his army already arrayed at the bottom of the fortress walls. He had all his archers up on the battlements, along with catapults. He wanted to draw his enemy into their deadly fire which could rain down on the superior force even while both armies were locked in combat.

The Devil was surprised when Lucifer let them form their ranks unmolested and that he was hiding under his

Chapter Four

fortress-walls. She saw this as a sign of weakness. She was no general. She had a large platform erected on a hill so she could look over the battle and command her forces. In The Devil's army there were many experienced Fallen warriors who could have advised her. But, as is her nature, she excluded them from her plans. This was personal. It was between her and Lucifer.

Lucifer on the other hand listened to advice offered by those around him. Isolte was by his side and sensed that The Devil was running the show completely on her own. The experienced soldiers in Lucifer's army couldn't fathom the logic of how the enemy forces were arrayed before them. They feared it was some sort of trick. The Devil's army seemed to be one big confusing mass. At its centre human soldiers had pulled away from the demon soldiers, [who were already fighting amongst themselves], leaving the demons' flanks exposed.

It was Isolte who pointed out that the other soldiers wouldn't fight beside them. Lucifer realised he'd found The Devil's Achilles heel. He sent skirmishers ahead to the demon ranks. The demons went berserk and rushed headlong towards them. The skirmishers retreated back to the main army drawing the demons in under the fortress-walls where arrows and rocks rained down on them. They were decimated. They turned and tried to flee back to their main army but Lucifer swept around on them with his cavalry and cut down any survivors.

The Devil couldn't believe her eyes. It had all happened so fast. She hadn't even ordered the demons to attack and had lost her main weapon. She felt her control of events slipping away. Angry Fallen converged on her platform yelling at her. Their armies milled around in confusion. Suddenly Lucifer's soldiers appeared from a forest, unnoticed, off to their side and ploughed into the flank of The Devil's army, driving the panicking soldiers back into the centre breaking up their ranks. Lucifer saw his chance and attacked with his main force then his army smashed into the confused mass of fighting and swept the enemy aside. Lucifer then led his elite guards and cut right through the centre. Soon he was

A History of Angels

at the very foot of the platform where the enemy Fallen were congregated. He cut them down like wheat. The Devil was truly terrified for the first time in her life. She leapt from the platform and fled on foot to the portal and escaped while Lucifer was fighting her Fallen allies.

The Devil's army fled towards the portal, but they couldn't escape. The Devil had sealed it shut. They were doomed. Lucifer, Isolte and their army formed in front of them and waited. The trapped soldiers turned in terror and looked upon their doom. Lucifer rode forward and promised to spare all who surrendered, except the Fallen. The defeated masses gratefully laid down their arms and were herded away. The last surviving enemy Fallen looked grimly upon Lucifer who smiled at them. He said, "You don't even know me but you were happy to kill me." With that, he, Isolte and his elite guards fell upon them and slaughtered them to a man.

It's hard to describe how total this victory was. Over one thousand Fallen died that day. Never had more then a few Fallen died at one time before. The kingdoms fell under Lucifer's control and the captured soldiers became his. The Devil fled her kingdom with nothing and was a spent force. Lucifer took over her demons. He made sense to them. You did what he said or he killed you. They admired him for that. He taught them discipline and how to think and channel their passions. He civilised them. The whole Fallen world had just been flipped on its head. One of the youngest Fallen amongst them now ruled over a third of their universe. Even the Senior Fallen took notice of this young man now. His empire was as big as some of the lone Senior Fallens'. They sensed he was a lot more than he seemed. They also sensed he wasn't scared of them at all.

Though Lucifer was the most powerful Junior Fallen ever, he was also the most feared and hated. He'd created a lot of widows and orphans who overnight lost everything they owned and had worked so hard to build over the centuries. The fact that he spared all their lives didn't make any of them feel the least bit grateful. He'd ruined their world and they wanted him dead.

Chapter Four

Time passed. Lucifer fought in countless wars. His enemies had learnt their lessons well and were a lot harder to defeat now. Isolte stayed home more and more. She was the happy mother of five sons and two daughters now and lost interest in the running of the empire. She left this to Lucifer who had become a very capable ruler. Their three oldest sons fought happily at their father's side and had been taught well by Isolte how to manage affairs of state.

GABRIEL'S VISIT

At about this time a longing grew in Lucifer's heart. He missed his loving father more and more. Gabriel felt Lucifer's desire to see him, so without a word to anyone he grabbed his cloak and sword and took a portal to the heart of Lucifer's kingdom. He strolled up to the huge fortress gates and asked to see Lucifer. Of course the guards thought this a great joke that this nobody thought he could just stroll up and see the most powerful guy in the universe. Gabriel just smiled and explained that he was Lucifer's father and he didn't think Lucifer would be too happy if he found out they'd turned him away. This stunned the guards. They noticed Gabriel did resemble Lucifer, though he was fair-haired and Lucifer was dark. So they informed the officer of the guard, who came out to look for himself. Then he told someone more senior. So two hours went by. Gabriel chatted to the guards and found out he was lucky to find Lucifer home. He was usually rushing around his empire putting down rebellions. Soon one of the elite guards came down to the main gate to fetch Gabriel. The guards snapped to attention and Gabriel was led away into the heart of the huge fortress.

Gabriel had never seen so many armed people in all his life. Even the servants carried weapons. He was led by the silent guard to a courtyard where Gabriel could see male and female warriors training. Lucifer was training amongst them. Lucifer trained every day with his elite. His son moved well and was a lot more skilful than Gabriel remembered. He also had a lean wolf-like look about him now. He radiated

A History of Angels

danger. When Lucifer realised his father was watching him he rushed over and embraced him warmly. He introduced Gabriel to his elite guards who were silent and wary. They were trained killers and something about Gabriel made them uneasy.

Lucifer did something that disappointed Gabriel. He challenged his father to combat. Everyone was silent, then Gabriel asked Lucifer if he'd brought him all this way just to fight him? But Lucifer was adamant, so Gabriel took his cloak off and drew his large two-handed sword from his back without another word. Lucifer circled Gabriel, with a wolfish grin on his face, then leapt at him. A flurry of lightning fast blows rang out, then in a blur of speed Gabriel brought the flat of his sword down on Lucifer's right wrist with a numbing blow that made his son drop his sword.

Everyone was stunned, no one ever beat Lucifer. Lucifer went to pick up his sword to resume the fight. Gabriel said if he tried to pick it up again, he'd kill him. He had such steel in his voice that no one doubted him. Lucifer had never seen the warrior side of Gabriel before. He realised he was lucky to be alive. The elite guard now knew where Lucifer had learnt his skills. Lucifer was surprised how proud he felt of his Dad for defeating him and put his arm around him and led him away to a private chamber for a drink.

Lucifer sent word to Isolte that Gabriel was here but she refused to see him and locked herself away in her apartments. Grief welled up in her over leaving Gabriel and she cried inconsolably for days, refusing to even see her children. She also felt great shame over marrying her own son.

Lucifer sent word to all his children and they arrived over the next few days with their partners. They were all introduced to Gabriel. Gabriel liked the three older boys [Ben, Paul and Stephen] who were the sort of men you could trust and they liked Gabriel and loved the fact someone had defeated their father. But the two younger boys [Evan and Roger], who were teenagers, were shifty, insincere characters. The older daughter [Rainar] was very like Isolte, intelligent, charming, tall, graceful, and very beautiful. She

Chapter Four

had married one of Lucifer's Fallen elite guards who was a close friend of Lucifer's. They were going to rule one of his larger realms. The youngest daughter [Liana] was only eight years old and felt excluded from everything. She took after Lucifer with his dark good looks. She could not understand why her mother [Isolte] had locked herself away and refused to see anyone.

Gabriel stayed for three weeks at Lucifer's insistence. He had a lot of time to wander around while Lucifer was busy with endless matters of state. Little Liana followed him everywhere and asked him endless questions about the Angel Realms and God. She also elected herself his personal guide and they even travelled outside the keep together, which she was never normally allowed to do. She asked her father why he was allowing it now? "No-one could protect you better than Gabriel", was Lucifer's reply. It was true. She felt truly safe for the first time in her life.

Gabriel fascinated her. She lived in a world full of harsh, brutal warriors. But Gabriel was nothing like them. He was warm, affectionate, humble, amusing and had a lovely stillness and peace about him. She'd heard the rumours that he'd defeated her father in combat but she found it hard to believe of such a gentle man. He also liked to talk to ordinary people and ask about their lives. Fallen usually ignore the masses unless they want something from then.

Gabriel also seemed very interested in her life and looked at the schoolwork and artwork her mother insisted she do. She loved to sing and Gabriel insisted she sing at the dinner table and would beam proudly at her when the family showed surprise at how good she was. She held his hand wherever he went and was always surprised what interested Gabriel. It could be beautiful clouds or a tiny flower by the roadside.

Liana found Gabriel one day playing a ballgame with local poor children and they were all laughing uproariously. She felt very jealous and sulked for days. Gabriel asked why she hadn't just joined in and been part of the joy also. "Life's like that," he said, "Join in and be part of a joyful game. You asked me about God. God offers us the chance

A History of Angels

to be part of his joyful game or we can take the jealous, selfish, possessive path that only leads to emptiness and disillusionment". Liana had her first angel lesson.

She asked if God was a man. Gabriel said no, God was neither male nor female, but Gabriel had got into the habit of calling God 'he'.

Sometimes Liana would take her wooden practice swords to Gabriel and insist he train her. Gabriel was surprised at how good she was already. She moved like a cat. She was also very determined and fearless. Gabriel asked her if she had learnt to dance yet. But that wasn't part of her education. That saddened Gabriel. He knew she'd be a natural. So he taught her how angels dance together and if Liana wasn't in love with Gabriel before, she truly was now. He'd shown her something that became a life's passion.

Gabriel insisted that Lucifer dance with his daughter after dinner [because Lucifer had always been a good dancer in the angel realms]. All the family laughed and clapped at their stern father having fun dancing with his eight year old daughter. Rainar cut in and showed off her amazing dancing skills with Lucifer and Liana was amazed to see two such beautiful dancers. Rainar promised to keep the lessons going with Liana when Gabriel was gone. Gabriel made a serious point to the family. He said life can't just be about war and survival or we are no better than insects.

Lucifer had little to no time for Gabriel as the weeks passed by. Gabriel felt he was avoiding him. It was obvious that he'd outstayed his welcome. Also Isolte was still hiding from him. The whole situation made Gabriel sad. He could have helped both of them. Gabriel is a great healer of hearts and minds. He could have healed Isolte's grief and shame, if she'd let him, and lift the despair that dwelled in Lucifer's heart. But he had to be invited to do so and felt that both had rejected him. It was time to go.

It was a shame he couldn't have helped Liana more but that was out of his hands. He made sure he visited her over the next five hundred years regularly, but he wouldn't see Lucifer again for half a century. After four hundred years Isolte asked for Gabriel's help to return to the Christ Realms.

Chapter Four

She'd had had enough of the Lower Realms and longed to see her greatest love again, Gabriel. Her wish was granted. But that's another story.

LUCIFER'S ABANDONMENT

After Gabriel left and returned to the Christ Realms Lucifer realised he'd wasted a great opportunity to find the peace that he'd lost so long ago. He locked himself in his study in deep despair. He'd see no one. Isolte still refused to come out of her apartments so the senior children had to run the empire for a period on their own. When their parents did appear it was obvious that Isolte no longer wanted to be Lucifer's partner. He was devastated. Isolte had been the rock of his whole life. He could feel the bond between them had finally been severed and felt abandoned. He hadn't felt like this since his imprisonment by The Devil. Isolte's life now centred around her younger sons and Liana.

Lucifer had never been without a woman in his life. He took on lovers and after a while was given many beautiful sex slaves as gifts by his allies. He'd lose himself for days in orgies trying to drive away the emptiness inside him by the loss of Isolte's love. These lovers and sex slaves made Isolte very jealous and hate grew in her heart for Lucifer. She on the other hand never took another lover till she returned to Gabriel four hundred years later. She instilled her hatred for Lucifer into her younger sons, whom she kept very close to her side. Liana refused to hate her father and consequently lost her mother's love.

Lucifer turned more and more to his oldest daughter. He hoped she might fill the void left by Isolte's loss. Rainar had to leave her husband to run their empire so she could support Lucifer in his time of need. They had a secret affair and Lucifer hoped she'd leave her husband and become his wife. But Isolte guessed what was happening and was furious with her daughter and Rainar felt ashamed at betraying her mother. Rainar fled back to her kingdom. Isolte never spoke to Rainar again and would have killed her instantly if she ever saw her. Isolte may love forever but she could hold onto hate forever too.

The older children realised their whole world could collapse if Lucifer didn't recover. He was the driving force behind the whole empire. Some of his enemies thought his troubles might have unmanned him so they used this time to attack far flung parts of his empire. But it had the opposite affect and gave him something to focus on that he could control. Lucifer found battle a release from his despair and threw himself into every attack, leading from the front. He brought home a large collection of enemy Fallen heads when he returned. This disturbed his sons, who'd never seen him do anything so brutal before, but they said nothing. They were glad to see their father motivated to defend and rule the empire again.

THE CREATION OF THE BLACK DRAGON

Hidden away far from Lucifer's long reach, The Devil watched everything with great interest. She knew war wasn't the way to defeat Lucifer. He was unbeatable. This falling out with Isolte and the affect it had on Lucifer showed The Devil Lucifer's true Achilles heal. It was his need for women. The tougher he became the more he needed their love to fill the emptiness left by the loss of his own inner warmth.

A brilliant plan started to form in The Devil's mind for the eventual downfall of Lucifer, but it would take time and a lot of help. Time she had plenty of and it wasn't hard to find enemies of Lucifer. She didn't need warriors for her plan. She needed those who were gifted in the dark psychic arts, like herself, and a lot of very sexually alluring female slaves possessed by her.

When The Devil and her one hundred allies were ready they sent the possessed sex-slaves in small groups to allies of theirs. Lucifer didn't suspect they were in league with The Devil, when they gave him the sex slaves as gifts. These sex-slaves were trained to believe they were to please and love Lucifer. None knew their true purpose. So when Lucifer met them and read their hearts he would see their intent

Chapter Four

was pure. Lucifer with his immense immortal powers would never suspect that sex-slave girls could ever harm him.

Lucifer was very taken with his new slaves and would spend many ours every day with them. While having sex with any of the possessed girls Lucifer would unknowingly open himself up psychically to the girls. The Devil could breach Lucifer's usually impregnable psychic barrier and possess him. She was able to cut him off from his divine powers and life force. Lucifer fell into a coma.

Isolte was called on in her apartments and told Lucifer was dying, so she rushed to his side. She might have hated him but he was still her son and she would do all she could to save him. Isolte was shocked by how much Lucifer had changed. Where before he always looked like a vibrant twenty-five year old, now he looked like a worn out fifty year old. She could sense an inner battle was going on, which she couldn't help him with.

Lucifer lay in a coma for two weeks. Finally the inner battle was over and he opened his eyes. They burned with a rage that terrified all who saw them. Isolte pulled back in horror. All Lucifer could say was, "That bitch, that fucking bitch," over and over again. Isolte knew that the only woman who made Lucifer that angry was The Devil.

Lucifer survived the battle of wills with The Devil and her one hundred allies. There were no winners. All were aged horribly and lay exhausted for months. The Devil went into hiding again, deserting her allies. Psychic battles were how the Senior Fallen had attacked each other in The Chaos Wars.

A new dark, cold, hatred burned in Lucifer's heart. All that made him lovable and human was burnt away. This is when Lucifer became known as The Black Dragon. None would look into his eyes directly again for fear of what burnt there. By entering Lucifer the psychic attackers had left psychic pathways by which Lucifer could track them down. He destroyed all he was able to track down and all their families and their allies too. He lay waste to whole kingdoms and left them as deserts.

A History of Angels

The only one who Lucifer couldn't catch was the cunning Devil. She fled to another unknown realm by the riskiest portals that she designed to collapse after she entered them, so she couldn't be followed. Lucifer lost her and was furious. The Devil was devastated too. She had failed again to destroy Lucifer and it seemed to unhinge her mind and she lost her will to live. She was lost in despair for hundreds of years and dwelled down in dark caverns hidden from all and was unable to collect her scatted thoughts. But these Fallen aren't ordinary humans. They can endure and heal even if it takes centuries.

The attack on Lucifer caused him to lose the divine power that made him like the Senior Fallen. They lost all interest in him. He was just another Junior Fallen now. All that linked him to God was gone too. He was still a very dangerous warrior though. He became a very dark and brooding character and only spoke to give orders and spent all his free time alone using his amazing psychic powers to scan for possible threats. He'd also become impotent and this lasted for ten years. His fortress became like a silent tomb.

Isolte left, taking her two youngest sons, and lived with relatives. Lucifer let them go without a word. Liana refused to abandon Lucifer and stayed by his side. His older sons stayed loyal but only visited when called for. Their families refused to visit Lucifer, he terrified them all too much. Rainar also stayed away because she was scared they might start their affair up again. Lucifer understood. Her husband would come instead, being old friends, and Lucifer liked his company.

Lucifer's mood affected his whole empire. People became scared to mention his name in case his terrifying gaze would be drawn to them. Even outside his vast kingdom all were reluctant to speak of him in-case he or one of his numerous spies overheard them, bringing certain destruction down on them, their families and their kingdoms. For the first time an uneasy peace reigned for nearly three hundred years.

As Lucifer's younger boys became men, they came to their father hoping to be given kingdoms of their own. Lucifer didn't like them much. He could feel how much they hated

Chapter Four

him and lacked that straight-forward honesty the rest of the family had. They flattered Lucifer outrageously. Lucifer despised crawlers. But they were family and even though Isolte hated him, she and the family would never betray him. But these boys were different, they were greedy. Lucifer gave them minor kingdoms far away from his own. He advised them, if they were smart, to get Isolte interested in their venture. No one knew how to manage a kingdom better than she. He was also hoping they wouldn't desert her, but they did. When they returned to their mother they packed their belongings and left with hardly a word. They couldn't wait to play at emperors. Isolte was devastated, but she knew it was her own fault. She'd allowed them to become spoilt, selfish, self-indulgent brats. Her relatives were happy to see the back of them.

LIANA

Liana had grown into a beautiful young woman. More and more, the fortress servants and officials looked to her for guidance. She was also the only one who would confront Lucifer and even tell him off. People didn't understand Lucifer; he loved people with guts. His daughter was fearless. He was very proud of her but never told her. He looked more and more to her to manage the empire. He realised he'd lost all heart for it. Liana was loved by the people of her empire. She was compassionate but also could make tough decisions unflinchingly. She was like her mother that way, but was a warmer, more approachable character.

Gabriel had made a huge impression on Liana. She didn't allow Lucifer's brooding presence to stop her embracing life. She organised huge balls and invited lots of young people her own age from all the most powerful families. None dare refuse in-case Lucifer was insulted. Lucifer didn't want to spoil Liana's fun so he wouldn't appear. He knew what affect he had on people.

Liana especially loved the attention of young men. She'd grown up in a world dominated by warriors so she felt at home with them. She had many affairs, and never regretted any of them, but never found the love of her life. Lucifer knew but he was happy that his daughter didn't just sit rotting away in the dusty old fortress and enjoyed life.

She also organised grand festivals for her people and would always try to appear. There was always lots of music and dancing at them and theatre. She donated large amounts of the wine and food to make sure even the poorest people could join in. She brought the empire back to life again. People started to visit the capital again and it became a hub for the Fallen world. Liana became one of the most beloved of the Fallen rulers. People loved to hear what new project she was up to or what new lover she had. She also never forgot the way Gabriel took time to speak to ordinary people. This trait endeared her to commoners and soldiers alike.

Liana also made time to visit all her family, even her unpopular young brothers. She was never able to heal the rift with her bitter mother, but she never gave up trying. Visiting the family also gave her a chance to hear what was really going on in the outer world and be able to warn her father. She was the first to suspect all wasn't well with her young brothers. They were up to something, she could feel it. She warned Lucifer about this possible threat but he pointed out that if he went pocking around in their affairs he might turn them against him. But he was as suspicious as she and kept a psychic eye on them. He didn't like what he saw.

THE DARK LORD

Over the years Roger had always been interested in the late Satan's and The Devil's conquered Dark Realm. He shaped his kingdom similarly. He also took on demon soldiers and collected all sorts of monsters and savage beasts. He held gladiatorial games and warriors would come from all around to compete in them and win great wealth and fame. Most just found death.

Roger and Evan ruled their kingdoms jointly. But Roger was the dominant partner, even though he was the younger.

Chapter Four

Evan was more interested in drugs and sex-slaves. Roger's sexual tastes were more about sadism. He spent his time down in the torture chambers that filled the whole lower levels of his keep, amusing himself a the expense of some poor hapless prisoner. [It may amaze you to know that Lucifer had no torture chambers. He either killed his enemies outright or pardoned them, though that didn't happen much lately. He found people who enjoyed torture sick].

Roger had black armour crafted, not unlike Lucifer's. The helm he had made into the likeness of a gargoyle. Nothing pleased Roger more than to make people fear him. He so wanted to be his father. But his father had earned his reputation on the battle-field, not by dressing up. It disappointed Roger that the Fallen were not the least bit frightened of him and the only reason one of them didn't get rid of the little weirdo, as they called him, was their fear of Lucifer's wrath. He even had everyone call him The Dark Lord.

This continued for about ten years. Evan was hardly ever seen. He had completely succumbed to drugs and lost all interest in the world. Roger was itching to extend their empire. He had recruited many warriors from his games and had built a large demon and human army now. He attracted particularly bad types who shared his cruel tastes. He launched an attack on an elderly Fallen's empire, who happened to be an ally of Lucifer.

Lucifer was furious. He sent messengers to both leaders. He apologised to his ally, Lennard, but didn't want to turn his hand against his own son. He understood his ally had every right to defend himself and should do so with no fear of reprisals from him. That's all his relieved ally needed to hear. Roger and Evan, he warned there would be dire consequences if they didn't desist with the attack instantly.

Roger ignored his father's warning, being used to getting his own way with his mother. Old Lennard was an experienced soldier. He'd even fought next to Lucifer. Roger on the other hand had no experience at all and assumed that his enemy with his small army would just run away. That didn't happen. Lennard's troops stood their ground and withstood all Roger's attacks. Roger also didn't understand how uncontrollable demons were. It had taken his father years to knock his demons into shape. When Roger tried to retreat and regroup, his forces wouldn't break off the attack and his army was suddenly divided in two. Lennard saw his opportunity and encircled the demons and destroyed them.

If Roger had been more experienced he would have attacked instantly when the enemy's flanks were exposed, but he froze. This allowed his enemy time to reform his line and advance on Roger's decimated and disorganised troops. This demoralised them and they broke and ran. Roger was easily captured and all his troops chased down and slaughtered.

It was all over in an hour. Roger complained hysterically that his father would destroy them all for touching him. They laughed and Roger wept with humiliation. His enemies found it hard to believe this young man could be a son of Lucifer. His older brothers were another matter. You wouldn't tangle with them. The old Fallen leader pointed out to Roger that Lucifer would never turn against an ally. Roger assumed that everyone hated his father as he did. But though these men feared Lucifer, they respected him also. Lucifer always kept his oaths.

Lucifer offered his old ally his sons' empires if he wanted them. Lennard gladly accepted. Lucifer had just made him a very powerful man and had made a loyal friend for life. Lucifer was no fool. Lennard went to Roger's kingdom and easily captured the drug addled Evan and threw the brothers into the dungeons. Lennard had heard stories about The Dark Lord's Realm but nothing prepared him for the horrors he found there. Lennard dismantled everything Roger and Evan had built and freed all the tortured prisoners. He asked Lucifer what he should do with his sons. Lucifer said let them rot a few years then send them back to their mother. Isolte heard what had transpired and also how her sons had amused themselves over the years. She never asked for them to be freed or for them to have their kingdoms back.

After two years Lennard released Roger and Evan. They returned to their mother with only the rags they stood in.

Chapter Four

Isolte refused to have anything to do with them and the relatives made it quite clear if they didn't clear off they'd kill them. So they went to their brothers' and sister's kingdoms where they were given similar receptions. In desperation they went to the capital and hoped Liana would help them. She, too, refused to see them. Lucifer sent word to them that if he ever ran across them again he'd kill them and that they weren't his sons any more. The Fallen world watched all that transpired with fascination. They realised even Lucifer's children weren't immune to his wrath. It made him even more feared.

Roger and Evan fled to the outer kingdoms far from their father and changed their names and became anonymous nobodies always scared someone would recognise them and kill them. To support his drug habit, Evan, a handsome man, took to prostitution. After many years he lost his will to live, but in his dying moments he prayed for Gabriel's help.

Gabriel heard and found him on his deathbed in a hovel. Gabriel felt great compassion for this young man who, unlike Roger, hadn't really hurt anyone except himself. Lucifer's warrior world didn't suit the fragile Evan who tried to escape the harsh reality and contempt of his father by losing himself in drugs. Gabriel asked Evan if he'd be interested in a life in God's Realms. New hope and desire replaced the hopeless despair in Evan's heart and he said, with such longing, that he'd love that very much indeed. Gabriel said he couldn't save his life, because that was karma, but when he died Gabriel would guide his spirit home to God's Realm's where he'd be reborn. Evan gladly accepted this offer and Gabriel sat with him all night until Evan peacefully passed away in his sleep.

Gabriel paid for his body to be cremated then took the ashes and threw them to the winds to signify that Evan had let go of his attachment to his lower self [ego] and his soul was free to express itself in the higher realms of God. Gabriel said that Evan happily dwells there now and is much loved and respected. He aids those with drug addictions in the Lower Realms and has endless compassion and understanding for the people he helps. Gabriel considers Evan a good friend and visits him regularly.

But Roger is a very different story. He deserted his brother early on and become a thief and murderer. He was eventually hunted down and killed after he tortured and murdered a young Fallen girl. No one had any idea that Roger was Lucifer's son and his body was dumped in the local rubbish tip. It was decided by the Beings of Light to unmake him because he was beyond help.

LIANA and LUCIFER

Many years went by and they were the most peaceful Lucifer had ever experienced. Liana managed well most of the kingdom and dealt with Fallen visitors. She still had her balls and festivals but had lost interest in her many boyfriends. She realised she only loved her father. So being a straightforward woman, she went to Lucifer in his private chambers and asked him if he would be interested in marrying her. Lucifer laughed in surprise. He just assumed he was unlovable, but it was obvious to him now that his very red-faced daughter [whom he loved and admired more than anyone] thought he was rejecting her. Liana burst into tears, then grabbed a vase and smashed it over his head. She went to storm from the room like a true daughter of Lucifer but he grabbed her from behind and said he'd love to marry her more than anything else in the world, but he thought her crazy for wanting to marry a bad tempered old bugger like him. At first she thought he was mocking her and was preparing to smash something else over his head but realised he was serious. Her rage evaporated as quickly as it had appeared and she rushed into his arms laughing and weeping.

They married not long after in a huge ceremony that all the most powerful Fallen were invited to and didn't dare refuse. Her brothers and sister were invited and all happily came along, even their reluctant spouses and children. Liana asked Isolte but she refused. As it was Liana's wish

Chapter Four

to celebrate their wedding day this way, Lucifer reluctantly agreed. Free wine and food was supplied to all Lucifer's subjects so they could celebrate in the streets, which they did with abandon.

Lucifer still had the effect on a room that when he entered it fell deathly silent. He seemed able to read peoples thoughts and his gaze would fall on someone with amazing accuracy if they harboured ill will towards him or his family, to their immense horror. They knew he'd be keeping a close eye on them from now on.

The wedding went well and Lucifer actually enjoyed himself for the first time in decades. Liana was truly happy and seemed to have endless energy to chat to all their guests and make them welcome. The only friends she didn't ask were her ex-boyfriends. She only had eyes for Lucifer now.

Lucifer found to his immense relief that his impotence was gone. He realised for the first time his sexual desire came from love. That's the same for angels. Liana and Lucifer spent a very happy forty years together and had three children, a girl and two boys. Lucifer had more time for these children than his older children, because he had always been away fighting wars. He still showed little interest in managing the empire so his older children helped Liana manage the burden of it.

Lucifer had an unerring gift of timing. If the older children fell to squabbling over matter's of state, which they often did, he would appear from nowhere and take control. When he was in this mood even Liana knew her place and gave in to his authority. Lucifer never lost his gift of command. He'd surprise his children by the way he was always up to date on events, even though he locked himself away all the time or just trained with his elite guards. He always personally inspected his armies. War was still his first love.

After a while Liana seemed to tire of such a sombre husband. He allowed her to party and entertain herself anyway she chose but she did it alone, which saddened Liana. She wanted to share her fun with her partner. After a while she moved to separate apartments with the children. They never argued but the love was gone.

A History of Angels

Lucifer took on lovers, which made Liana very jealous. But like her mother she wasn't interested in finding another partner. One of Lucifer's lover's, Lisa, was a beautiful arrogant young Fallen girl with great ambitions to replace Liana and rule in her place. She was smart enough never to be rude to Liana when Lucifer was around but would denigrate her any chance she got.

Once while Lucifer was away inspecting troops in one of his far-flung empires things came to a head. While Liana was seeing guests in the great hall Lisa swept in with her entourage and started to mock Liana and said Lucifer had left her because she was frigid. Of course this was a lie, Liana was a very passionate lover to Lucifer and he'd said no such thing. Lisa had under-estimated Liana's famous temper. Liana snatched a sword from one of the guards and cut Lisa down where she stood. Everyone was frozen in shock. Liana stormed out of the great hall, collected her children and belongings and set off to her older sister's kingdom never to return.

When Lucifer returned he found his kingdom in mourning, not over Lisa's slaying, but over their beloved ruler Liana leaving. It was as if all the joy left the kingdom with her. Lisa's family heard about how their daughter had foolishly goaded one of Lucifer's children who were famous for their lightning tempers. Rather than seek restitution Lisa's family kept quiet. They feared that Liana may seek vengeance, but she never did. She was too heart broken. She felt she'd lost Lucifer forever. She'd always hoped that their love might be re-ignited one day.

Lucifer let her go. He knew how pig-headed she was. It was a bad family trait, that and the violent temper. Lucifer brooded again and his fortress became like a haunted tomb. He had to take over the management of the empire again and kept himself busy with its endless problems. He also acquired ten huge black hounds that followed him wherever he went. Everyone assumed they were vicious brutes used for battle and hunting. But Lucifer never hunted, he thought it cruel. People would have been surprised how affectionate Lucifer was to his beloved dogs when alone with them, and the servants loved to play with them when Lucifer was busy.

Chapter Four

HANUMAN

Lucifer would visit the realm where the demons dwelled. They lived in a dark desert kingdom that was rocky, treeless and had no flowing water. The demons lived in clans and fought endless wars against each other but would come together when Lucifer summoned them to fight in his wars. It was a great honour to be chosen. They looked like large hairless apes and had tough leathery, black skin, large sharp teeth, long powerful arms and short strong legs. Lucifer had sent people to teach them to speak human language and to read and write. They had trouble speaking because of their teeth and their lack of intelligence but they loved war with a passion.

Demons were fearless except when it came to Lucifer who was like a God to them. They loved to watch him fight in battle. They called him Rama because all feared to use his true name. Before battle demons howl like wolves. When hunting they bay like hounds. In battle they snarl and slaver and love to bite their enemies if in reach, but usually they wield huge steel maces that crush bone through the thickest armour. They carry huge steel round shields with their clans mark on them. They are accomplished smiths with steel and iron, which is common in their kingdom. They get so excited in battle that they start fighting amongst themselves, especially between different clans. They also cut a mark in their weapons-arm for every foe they slay in battle.

When Lucifer was around the demons grew very quiet and looked at the ground. His gaze terrified them. When fights broke out between demons before battle, Lucifer would stride through the ranks. They parted leaving a path to the trouble and, the usually fearless demons, would cringe and whimper as he passed them by. Lucifer would stride angrily up to the offenders and cut them down where they stood. Then he would stride back to the head of the army and they would reform the ranks behind him.

Huge tough experienced chieftains were in charge of them. Their weapon-arms were laced from top to bottom with the scars for all their dead foes. Hanuman was one of these chieftains. He was the only demon who'd look Lucifer in the eye. He was also very intelligent and had a great grasp of battle tactics. Lucifer liked him. More and more he let Hanuman stay by his side. He was probably the strongest demon Lucifer had ever met. There was a calm about Hanuman that Lucifer liked, he also had a good sense of humour. The two became inseparable companions. The story of Gilgamesh and his ape-like friend Enkidu told of this friendship. Also Rama and Hanuman his loyal ape-like servant.

THE BEGINNING OF THE END FOR LUCIFER

Her uncle Frederick was the head of Isolte's family, the relatives Lucifer had saved from certain destruction. He had also helped them become very rich and powerful but had never trusted them and always excluded them from his inner circle. Isolte lived with her relatives after leaving Lucifer. Frederick decided it was an opportune time to slay Lucifer and take over his empire. He packed Isolte off, with all the women and young children, to a manor not far from their castle. With the help of forty of his relatives and enemies of Lucifer, all Fallen, he planned to draw Lucifer into a trap.

Frederick sent word to Lucifer that Isolte wanted to see him in the hope of repairing their relationship. Lucifer still loved Isolte and nothing would have pleased him more than to get back with her again. So he agreed to visit the castle. Of course Isolte had no idea of the plot [or had any intention of getting back with Lucifer] or she would she would have warned him. Frederick knew this, so that's why he bundled her out of the way.

Lucifer arrived wearing only normal clothes and his sword. Luckily his five elite Fallen guards and Hanuman were armoured and went everywhere with him. Lucifer was welcomed and ushered into the great hall where

Chapter Four

the forty heavily armoured Fallen assassins waited in ambush. Lucifer's party was instantly set upon. The elite guards ringed Lucifer and were among the finest warriors in the Fallen world, but Hanuman was no match for Immortal Fallen Enemies and soon fell at Lucifer's feet, his friend and master, covered in wounds trying to defend him. This so enraged Lucifer that he went berserk and leapt at his foes cutting them down left and right, but his besieged body guards found it near impossible to keep up with him and protect his exposed back and flanks. So Lucifer was wounded more than a dozen times.

Lucifer only had one objective before he died and that was to make sure he took the treacherous Frederick with him. He got his wish and cut him down with a savage blow. Unfortunately all of Lucifer's bodyguards had finally been overwhelmed, but had been able to take many of the assassins with them. So Lucifer, with no expectation of surviving, threw himself at the enemy with the last of his strength. He was the finest warrior of his age and worked hard maintaining his skill by training every day. To his utter surprise he was left with all his enemies lying dead or wounded at his feet.

Covered in blood from all his wounds Lucifer staggered around the great hall and despatched any surviving wounded assassins. He then knelt down next to his dying friend Hanuman. Blood was bubbling out of his mouth but he smiled at Lucifer when he noticed him leaning over him. Lucifer said, "No man could have a more loyal and courageous friend than you, Hanuman. It has been a honour to fight next to you."

Hanuman beamed with pride and love for his friend and replied, "What a way to go out of this world, fighting next to my Lord and friend and bearing witness to you slaying all your enemies." He died the perfect demon death, fighting heroically in battle. He was content. Lucifer fell to the floor unconscious.

When the women and children returned they walked into a scene of mass slaughter. They had no idea of what had

A History of Angels

transpired and found only four people alive, Lucifer and three of his guards. Isolte took control of her panicked and grieving relatives. All their husbands, sons, brothers, cousins and uncles lay dead. She was the only one who guessed what had truly transpired there. She instantly sent for Lucifer's elite guard, then patched his and his body guards' wound's. When the guard arrived she sent Lucifer back to his fortress where he'd be safe. She and the guards sealed the castle so no news would escape of what had happened there. They all understood Lucifer's many enemies would use such a chance to attack him.

While Lucifer and his bodyguards convalesced, Isolte sent her surviving relatives to a far-flung empire and imprisoned them there. She explained to them what treachery the family had just committed and they all realised how lucky they were to be alive. Isolte took control of the situation to save them.

Lucifer could have become even more terrible, vengeful and paranoid, but the terrible betrayal had the opposite effect on him. He couldn't believe how loyal his friend and his bodyguards were to him in his hour of need. No one understood better than Lucifer that you cannot buy such loyalty or friendship.

The experience created a bond between Lucifer and his bodyguards. They started drinking together and sharing jokes. He'd have them sit down to dinner with him and go riding with him and his hounds. A true friendship grew as he realised his elite guards actually respected him. He started visiting his children and his grand children. He especially loved to spend time with Rainar's husband, his old friend, which made Rainar very happy. All were surprised by the change in Lucifer. The rage had left his eyes. There was a lovely vulnerability about him and he seemed so human.

His sons to Liana were young men now and they loved to be with their legendary father. They were so like their mother, full of life, fun and good-natured mischief. They gave Lucifer endless joy. Their beautiful older sister moved to the capitol too and started putting on festivals and balls. She would invite her mother to all the events but Liarna

Chapter Four

would never come. She was too proud. People loved the new Lucifer. They especially liked the way he spent time with Liana's children. Lucifer lost all interest in war and left all conflicts to his very capable sons. He stopped psychically spying on his enemies and couldn't even be bothered hating his half sister The Devil anymore.

One night Lucifer had a premonition. He saw The Devil all alone in a dark empty cave. She was muttering to herself. Lucifer, with his amazingly powerful psychic gifts, could have tracked her easily down. He realised to his surprise he wasn't the least bit interested in hunting down the Devil anymore, even though that's what had been his sole motivation for near five hundred years. He actually felt sorry for her, she looked so broken and lonely. He realised the only reason he'd harm her was if she tried to harm him or his family again, but he intuitively felt she had no desire to do either, that she just wanted to stay as far away from him as possible.

Isolte tired of life in the Lower Realms and longed to return to the life of an angel in the Christ Realms. She still loved Gabriel with a great passion but thought herself unworthy of his love. But Gabriel isn't like most human beings. It takes a lot for him to stop loving someone. He was proud of Isolte's hard journey in the Lower Realms and even more proud that she wanted to return to the realms of the angels.

Gabriel helped her let go of her ego [pride was always her downfall] and she soon returned. To her utter surprise Gabriel was happy to be her husband again. If you met Isolte today you would be amazed at how much she's transformed from the bitter older lady she was. She's more like a seventeen year old girl now, full of life, passion, love and humour and she has two beautiful young children now to Gabriel.

After about a hundred years of a fairly peaceful life, all of Lucifer's enemies and allies joined forces and marched on his capitol to finally rid themselves of him. Lennard stayed loyal and brought himself and his army to aid Lucifer in his hour of need. Lucifer's children also rallied to him in support, but he insisted that the girls stay home and protect their families. The demon chieftains also answered his call. They were not going to miss such a huge battle. They brought all the demon legions with them. If their Lord was going to die they wanted to die with him.

Lucifer stood with his armour on, all alone in his room gazing out of his tower window at the sea of enemy soldiers that filled the plane in front of his fortress as far as the horizon. In all his years he'd never seen such a large force. He felt a great sadness. Everyone was waiting for him down in the great hall. They were going to sally forth from the fortress to try and rout the enemy. It was suicide of course. He wouldn't have cared except his sons would die beside him. Liana's boys were so excited at the chance to fight next to their legendary Dad, it made tears run down Lucifer's cheeks. He was glad no one saw them. And his older boys, who'd grown into such great men, had become such loving friends to him now. What a terrible loss.

It dawned on Lucifer that he'd never see his lovely daughters again so he sat down and wrote to them. He told them how much he loved them, what fine daughters and lovers they'd been to him and how proud of them he was. He felt tired and world-weary. If he wasn't fighting for the survival of his family, he'd just ride out to his enemies on his own and let them kill him.

LUCIFER'S TIME ON EARTH

Lucifer, who was called Tom, was born to a poor white factory worker in Australia, back at the end of World War Two. He never knew his father and his mother wouldn't speak of him. Tom had a feeling his father used to beat her. His mother, Marge, was a worn-out woman who blamed Tom for how hard her life was and for why she couldn't meet a nice man. But the truth was Marge was scared of being abused again so she avoided relationships. She was also a chain-smoker. Tom will always remember her with a fag hanging out of her mouth while she did her endless chores around the home after a long day at the factory.

Chapter Four

Tom was a small skinny kid who always walked around with his eyes caste down and barely ever spoke. He felt bad all the time that he'd ruined his Mum's life. She use to yell at him all the time so he learnt to make himself as inconspicuous as possible. People assumed that he was simple-minded or dumb and always talked about him as if he wasn't there. He learned to make himself as useful as possible to his Mum because he was scared she would give him away.

When Tom was Ten years old his Mum was rushed to hospital with lung cancer. Tom never saw her again, because she died there while he was in an orphanage. He was never taken to see her. Tom assumed she didn't want to see him, but the truth was she didn't want him to see her in such a bad way. She died in great pain, completely exhausted by her harsh loveless life. Tom spent the rest of his young life going from one foster home to another. He never felt wanted and would just try to be helpful so they wouldn't get rid of him.

His life was about always being on the fringes and the fact that with each new foster home he had to change schools, made it even worse. Being the friendless, quiet, short, skinny kid he was always being bullied. But, though he was very gentle, especially with animals, he was surprisingly strong and tough for his size. Many regretted messing with him. The bullies soon learnt to leave him alone.

As a grown man Tom had a stooped sad look. He still looked at the ground when he walked and only spoke when spoken to. He had light blue gentle eyes, very large strong hands and muscular fore-arms. He was still small and skinny like a whippet dog. His life was an endless succession of unskilled labouring jobs where he was known as a reliable and hardworking man but the jobs never lasted long. No one seemed to want him around. In his life he made no close friends. The fact he didn't drink and wasn't interested in sport didn't help matters and women completely ignored him.

Tom enjoyed taking off and just drifting around the countryside, doing odd jobs whenever he needed money. He

A History of Angels

loved huge forests and streams and would throw his swag down next to them to sleep. It was the only time he felt any inner peace. He loved to watch wild animals as they went about their business. He loved kangaroos especially and couldn't understand how someone could shoot one. He loved their big, gentle eyes.

When Tom was about forty he met a very pretty lightly built woman named Sally. She worked at a local Italian restaurant as a waitress. She was very popular and was always being asked out by the local men. [Tom didn't know this, but Sally was Lucifer's daughter and wife, Liana]. Tom never went into restaurants and he could never explain what compelled him to go into Sally's, but he did. When they first met they were instantly attracted to each other and the usually outgoing Sally felt shy around the quiet, gentle stranger. Tom amazed himself and spoke to her, making polite conversation. If Sally were asked what attracted her to this plain unassuming character, she would say it was his beautiful, gentle, light blue eyes.

Over the next few months they saw a lot of each other and it didn't take long for them to fall in love. The usually homeless Tom moved into Sally's small apartment and had the happiest three years of his life. After three years Sally became more and more frustrated at Tom's lack of ambition and drive. He seemed content to just do his low paid labouring jobs and live in the tiny apartment with her. She had bigger dreams; she wanted her own home, to get married and have kids. Tom was happy to marry her and even have kids but he was what he was, an unskilled labourer. So Sally became very angry with Tom and was always yelling at him and putting him down. It reminded Tom of his unhappy childhood and his mother always blaming him for her miserable life.

In the end Sally kicked Tom out and told him that she never wanted to see him again. He believed her, of course, and set off around the country for the next two years, heart-broken. When Sally cooled off she realised she'd just destroyed the only man she'd ever loved and who had always treated her with love and respect. If he'd been around she

Chapter Four

would have tried to patch things up between them, but he was gone for good. Tom had no idea how she truly felt and assumed she hated him and never wanted to see him again.

As the years went by Sally had a series of failed marriages to abusive husbands. Tom secretly kept abreast of her life and felt very sad for her. She ended up living in an apartment alone, not unlike the one they had shared together, and had given up men for good. Her dream of her own home and kids in tatters.

When Tom was in his sixties he saved enough money to buy a small property in the country with a falling down old shack on it. Over the next eight years he worked tirelessly on the place collecting second-hand materials so he could renovate it. He built a small chicken coop for ten hens, planted many fruit trees, made a large vegetable patch and planted lots of flowers. He lived in a caravan while renovating.

There were many small properties around and Tom's neighbours liked the quiet old man who was always willing to help fix anything if you asked. Though Tom had no formal training, he was quite good with wood, metal and even with fixing cars and was always repairing his old green Holden utility. Tom especially loved to repair or make his own tools. He also chopped wood every day and made a huge neatly stacked woodpile for the fireplace he never used.

Tom was odd for his age-group, because he didn't drink alcohol, tea or coffee, or eat meat. He loved to eat fresh fruit and vegetables from his garden and one of his few modern appliances was a fancy juice extractor. He also loved to make jam. He ate eggs from his hens but could never imagine eating one of his girls [the hens]. The only items he brought were dairy products, cereals and bread.

One day Tom was walking down his dirt road past one of his neighbour's run-down houses when he heard the cries and whimpers of a dog and a man yelling at it. Tom knew the neighbour slightly. He was a huge fat biker guy covered in tattoos. He had a long black beard and rode a Harley Davidson motorbike. Everyone was scared of him. Without even thinking about it Tom walked around the back of the

A History of Angels

biker's house in time to witness the biker yelling abuse at a cattle dog on a chain and punching and kicking it.

A rage came over the usually peaceful old Tom and he yelled at the biker to stop. The biker swung around and shouted at Tom and told him to piss off before he beat the crap out of him. Tom didn't budge an inch. He told the biker to leave the dog alone or there would be trouble. The biker laughed at Tom and came at him and threw a punch at his head. Tom blocked it easily with his strong arms and landed a hammer like blow to the side of the biker's head, which felled him. Then Tom stood over the prone man and punched him continually in the head and punctuated each punch with words like, "How does it feel, big fella, to be on the end of the punishment for a change? Now you know how your dog feels!" To this day the biker is still haunted by the rage in those pale blue eyes. Tom beat him till he was an unconscious bloody mess. He would have beaten him to death except he looked up and saw the pitiful dog staring at him through his one good eye. All his murderess rage left him and was replaced by a great compassion for the dog.

Tom left the biker where he lay and joined the dog. One of his eyes was damaged beyond repair and his back leg was broken. Tom told the dog, "You'll be alright little fella, no one's ever going to hurt you again." Tom unchained the dog and carried it whimpering in pain to his ute then drove to the local vet. The vet advised Tom that the humane thing to do would be to put it down, and it would be very expensive to operate on anyway. Tom flared up again and looked the vet in the eyes with such rage and said, "I don't give a fuck about the money, can you fix it?" The scared vet, who knew the usually quiet Tom, said that, "I'll do my best Tom." Tom said, "That's all you can ask of anyone." The dog survived, she lost her left eye and always limped on her back left leg. Tom and she became inseparable and would always be seen driving around together in Tom's ute.

As far as the biker went he finally regained conscious. He was a terrible bloody mess. He barely made it to the local hospital. He refused to say what had happened to him but the locals knew. One of the other neighbours had witnessed

Chapter Four

the incident unseen. Everyone heard how quiet little old Tom had beaten a huge biker almost to death to save a dog. Well country towns believe in local justice and the police turned a blind eye to the incident.

Everyone liked Tom after that and people started to pop by and visit him. For the first time in his whole life he felt accepted and loved. Also people started taking homeless dogs to him to look after. He ended up with a half a dozen mismatched dogs of all shapes and sizes, who happily trotted around with Tom as he worked on his property and slept in the shack with him, when it was fit to live in. They'd also drive around with Tom, but in the back of his ute. His original old dog, Molly, which he had rescued, always sat in the front with him.

In these happier times Tom started to feel a longing. He'd often sit in his backyard with the dogs and watch the clouds roll by or listen to the wind in the trees. It gave him great peace. It also reminded him of someone who also loved to work around his house and make all sorts of things for his family with his own hands. But he couldn't think who that was.

One day Tom was having a shower when he felt very odd. It was as if he was a huge warrior in black armour and had a huge helm on his head with horns. He radiated a sort of rage that made all fear him. To his horror he noticed that his armour was completely covered in blood and it was washing down the drain. He also started to dream he was a soldier in World War One, stuck in the hellish trenches. At first he believed in the war, but after years of watching men being blown to pieces, cut down by machine guns, gassed, bayoneted, and rats feasting on the corpses while the living rotted in mud filled trenches, he became completely disillusioned. He'd never seen anything more insane in all his life and so pointless. What was it all about, why didn't they all get up and just go home? Why did they obey such madman? He realised this was where he finally had had his fill of war. It was a past life of his. He never wanted to take part in a war again. All he wanted was an inglorious, peaceful and quiet life. I guess he got his wish, he thought.

A History of Angels

Tom also dreamed of being a Native American. He was a warrior and lived in a huge forest next to a stream. He had a wife and two young children he loved dearly. They were very happy times. He was loved and respected in his tribe and known as a brave and honest man. He also had an amazing love and connection to the Great Spirit [God]. He felt Him all around him in the streams, forests, animals, and the laughing innocent eyes of children. He remembered how the Great Spirit guided him in his dreams and visions. He felt so blessed and grateful for all he had. Tom longed to be this man again.

It was about this time Gabriel started to appear in Tom's dreams. He told Tom he was his father and that he had come to take him home. Tom remembered now who the man was who loved to watch clouds roll by and listen to the wind. Who built a cabin with his own two hands for his young wife and small son. He remembered his Dad showing him how to craft things with endless patience and how he loved nothing more then to work beside his peaceful, loving Dad. Tom realised he was tired of life and wanted to go home, home to his father, home to God.

Over the next few months Tom worked furiously on the shed. There was nothing pretty or artistic about it but everything was done with great care and worked well. Tom loved old wood. He cleaned it up and made basic furniture and a kitchen with it. He also made a lovely veranda out back that looked out over the garden and you could watch the sun set. He also had a will made up by the local solicitor.

One day he went and saw a neighbour and asked if she'd look after his dogs and chickens for the next week, all the food was on the back veranda for them. The neighbour was happy to help lovely old Tom out. He never asked anything from anyone but was always there for everyone when they needed him. He sat down that night and wrote a note and left it on the kitchen table and then went to bed. That night Tom passed away peacefully in his sleep. The next day the neighbour came by to feed the animals and found Molly howling and scratching at the back door. Tom never locked his doors so she entered and found Tom dead in his bed and

Chapter Four

a note on the kitchen table apologising for the inconvenience his death my cause her. Everyone in the district came out for Tom's funeral. He was much loved and surely missed by all.

One day there was a knock on Sally's apartment door. It was Tom's solicitor. He'd come to notify her that Tom had left her a small house and property in the country in his will. The only stipulation was she had to agree to look after the six dogs and ten chickens. She happily agreed. Then it dawned on her that her beloved Tom was gone and she'd never see him again. She was devastated.

The solicitor took her out to a lovely little wooden house in the country surrounded by fruit trees, flowers and a huge vegetable garden full of vegetables. The dogs all barked excitedly and wagged their tails when they walked around the back and she could see the chicken pen full of chickens happily scratching around. Sally loved animals and had always dreamed of a house like this with her own garden. She noticed there was enough wood cut for at least two years down the side of the house. The kitchen cupboards were full of jars of Tom's homemade jam. The solicitor mentioned that everyone loved Tom's jam around here.

The solicitor passed her a note from Tom. It read:

Dear Sally
I've always loved you and the only way I could think to show you this was to make your dream of your own home with a lovely garden and lots of animals running around come true. I know the place isn't pretty, you know I'm not the least bit artistic, but everything should work well and the house will keep you warm, safe and dry.
Love Tom.

Tears rolled down Sally's cheeks. The solicitor passed a hanky to her so she could blow her nose. "He did it all for you, you know. It took him about eight years to fix it all up and it's all paid off too." The solicitor said kindly.

"Thank you," is all she could manage to say. The solicitor knew she meant 'thanks Tom' and that pleased him.

"He was very loved around here and we all miss him very much," he added. He left Sally to settle in to her new home and drove back into town.

As happens in country towns, word spread fast that Tom had fixed up his old place for an ex-girlfriend of his. Everyone was very curious to meet this woman old Tom loved so much. Soon Sally made lots of new friends and she found herself welcomed into their community. It was the least they could do for old Tom. Sally's dream had come true but it was bitter sweet. She realised she could have done it with Tom, but she felt very grateful to him and for the first time in her life, felt loved and cared for.

THE DEATH OF LUCIFER

Lucifer sat at his writing desk. He lent back in his chair with a sigh and closed his eyes. He felt so old and weary. He realised he'd lived now for over five hundred years. It was far too long. He felt every day of it today. He could feel someone watching him. He still had his amazing psychic gifts and could sense the presence of a woman.

"What do you want?" he asked

"I am your mother, Lucifer. I've come to fetch you home." A disembodied voice said.

"Mother? I'd given up all hope I'd ever see you again".

Isolte's angelic spirit body said, "It's time Lucifer, it's time to return to the Christ Realms. Can't you feel God calling you?"

Lucifer could feel he was being drawn away. He also felt a great longing within himself to go home.

"It has been a long time since I felt worthy of God," answered Lucifer sadly.

Then another voice spoke. It was his father Gabriel.

"Can't you feel you are letting your lower self go now Lucifer. You are tired of this role you've been playing for so long. Wouldn't you like to be your true self again?"

"What, an angel? I haven't got the energy for it anymore

Chapter Four

father. I'm just worn out." Lucifer said with a weary sigh.

"I mean more than that Lucifer, I mean being a part of God's creative universe," said Gabriel."

"All I desire father is to be absorbed back into God and not exist anymore," Lucifer said with great conviction.

Lucifer could feel his parents' sadness. If his wish was granted they'd never see him again. He wouldn't 'be' any more. But that was his right and they respected his wishes.

"What do I need to do, father?" asked Lucifer.

"Just let yourself die, Lucifer," replied Gabriel.

"But what about my family? They need me now, I can't just leave them to perish at the hands of all my enemies," Lucifer said with great feeling.

"Trust me Lucifer, I'll look after them, you know I'll keep them safe," said Gabriel.

"I know you will father." With that said Lucifer sighed and passed away. His dead body transformed, he looked so beautiful, so angelic.

Lucifer didn't appear in the great hall that night. Outside his enemies met in a huge tent to plan their assault on the fortress. Many of them were old rivals and enemies. They soon started squabbling, then swords were drawn and blood was shed. All fled the tent back to their own armies, some carrying dead and wounded friends and family members. Tents were pulled down and their armies packed up their camps and all marched in great haste to the portals and back to the safety of their own kingdoms. All were planning vengeance on their recent allies.

In the morning all in the great hall went up onto the fortresses front wall and looked out over a completely empty plane. It was unbelievable, it was as if all their enemies had just vanished into thin air. Lucifer's oldest son Ben went to tell his father the amazing news. He found Lucifer in his armour asleep in his chair. He looked so beautiful, so peaceful. Ben realised after a minute he wasn't breathing. Ben couldn't imagine a world without Lucifer. He sat down next to him and realised how much he'd come to love his tough old father these last years. Lucifer had become so gentle and caring. Tears sprang into his eyes, and like his

A History of Angels

father he hadn't shed tears since he was a small boy. There was no room for tears if you were one of Lucifer's boys.

When he went down to the great hall where everyone waited excitedly for Lucifer, Ben was met by disbelief and shock at the news of Lucifer's death. All his friends and family rushed up to see for themselves and all were amazed by how peaceful he looked. It was Gavin, Rainar's husband, an old fallen angel himself, who pointed out that his friend had finally gone home to God. Can't you see how happy he is now? They could all see it.

Gavin sent for Rainar and she prepared Lucifer's body. It was Gavin who pointed out that it wouldn't be right to bury him now in his black armour and horned helm. Gavin knew Lucifer had created his sword in happier times when he was an angel so it felt right to leave that by his side.

The demon chieftains were devastated at the loss of their Lord so Gavin gave them Lucifer's armour and horned helm. They were thrilled by the honour that was bestowed on them. They took his armour back to their kingdom and entombed it in a deep cavern where all demon warriors could visit it and ask Lucifer's help to make them stronger and braver in battle. Lucifer would have found it a great irony. To him it had become an empty symbol of his warrior self. It was his ego, an illusion, not his true self at all.

Rainar knew Lucifer loved trees so she had him buried in the common and a young oak tree planted over his grave. Only close friends and family were asked to the funeral. Isolte and Gabriel appeared through a portal in time for the ceremony. All were amazed at how young, beautiful and happy Isolte looked. While they were there they offered Gavin and Rainar the help they needed to come back to the Christ Realms. Rainar was shocked. She and Gavin had been discussing just that, ever since they saw how peaceful Lucifer looked in death. It had started a great yearning in them both to be part of God's world.

Chapter Five

INCEST

To understand how Isolte could be both daughter and wife to Gabriel we would have to understand the angel idea of living many lifetimes at once and also reincarnation, as explained in the last chapter.

Gabriel said he was Isolte's first father. He brought her soul into being by his union with a Christ Realm Angel named Elizabeth. Gabriel and Isolte had a great love for each other and he loved his role as her father and in later years as her friend. But Isolte wanted to explore all facets of love with Gabriel, and a true desire grew in her heart to fulfil this wish. But incest is a crime for angels, as for humans on Earth. Angels understand that desires like Isolte's you leave to God to see if they should be fulfilled.

Sure enough, after many lifetimes and many different selves, Isolte was born to two different parents and Gabriel was too. Isolte had been married twice before they met and had two different sets of children. Her first husband died when he was about one hundred years old, quite young for an angel. Her second husband decided to fall after about three hundred years of marriage. Isolte didn't want to fall with him because she didn't want to leave her fully-grown children and grandchildren behind. It was a hard decision to make, because she loves her partners until she dies. When Isolte met Gabriel she was quite sad and felt split in two, one side of her wanting to follow her husband, the other to stay behind with the children. But she and Gabriel, in their different guises, soon fell in love, married and had young Lucifer [this is not his name in the angel realms]. Being who I am, Gabriel said, I remember people as they originally come into being. I'll always remember my little daughter and the love I felt for her when she was first born into existence many lifetimes ago.

On Earth, Gabriel said, people are part of karmic families that reincarnate together lifetime after lifetime. Each new lifetime their roles change. The father becomes the child, the child becomes the parent, siblings become the grandparents. The heart likes to explore all facets of love. The love a child feels for a parent is very different from the love a husband feels for his wife, or the love a mother feels for her children, or even how the love grandparent's feel for their grandchildren is different to the love felt for their own children.

Sometimes people hang onto their past lifetime role. They may have been married to someone who, in another lifetime, is their child. It causes confusion and often incest may come out of it. But of course there are more evil reasons why an adult might misuse the trust and love of a child. It's to do with abusing the power they have over someone who loves them and enslaving them to their will and desires.

In the story of Lucifer you saw how the Fallen abused the love and trust of their children all the time. As they felt more cut off from their own souls and found it harder and harder to find love and fulfilment within themselves, they looked more and more outside themselves to find what they had lost. Isolte, Rainar and Liana, for example, looked to their fathers [and sons] to fill the void left by losing their connection to their own souls and to God.

Relationships often end up a battle of wills, to see who can wrest control and have the other enslaved to their needs and desires. The love and trust a child has for a parent leaves them vulnerable to unfulfilled and needy adults. When a child grows up they may cling to a very infantile idea of love and may look to a father or mother figure to still fill this role. The terrible relationship woes of Earth are due to this emptiness in people and explains why there are so few relationships based on love and trust here.

Chapter Five

ANGEL SELF

In the Christ Realms an angel's soul creates different selves to express its heart-felt desires. These selves give it the opportunity to live separate lives on different planes of existence concurrently and even be of the opposite sex, soul being neither male nor female. When one of the angelic selves dies, it returns to soul or merges with another one of its selves.

When an angel incarnates to Earth it has an ego given to it by karma, made from the Void. This ego cuts the angel off from its other selves. Karma does this so that the angel can truly experience what it is like to be human.

When a young angel is at school it learns how to create an ethereal body. It is a vehicle by which it can visit people and places without having to be physically present, especially Earth and the Lower Realms. There are angels with specialist skills in, for example, drug addiction, low self-esteem, violence and grief. They have subjected themselves to these experiences [through ego] with their lives on Earth in order to help them guide us in their ethereal body when we ask for it.

Angelic self is a very different thing to the human spirit. I'll explain more about ego, spirit and soul in a later chapter.

A History of Angels

Chapter Six

WHY ANGELS FALL

When God Realm Angels were created, God knew they'd seek the opposite of themselves. The creation of The Void was this. All angels forever afterwards are drawn into this. But there's a choice about how you go about it. Imagine the Realms of Light [God's Realms] like a beautiful land with a long coastline butting up against a huge dark, cold ocean [The Void]. But God's Realms go well beyond the Void, they are infinite. They are like the land that dips under the ocean and are hidden below its black depths and supporting it still. The Void itself is only like a dark speck on an endless white beach.

If one were to stay solely in beautiful, peaceful, deathless, disease free, harmonious realms one would eventually stagnate. All are drawn to the ocean eventually. Souls, from God's Realms, can build a boat and sail across the dark depths, never knowing what truly lies beneath and untouched by it. They can dive into it's depths and discover its dark wonders and then return to the warm bright shore when exhausted and leave enriched by the experience, or be swept away by the ocean, far from the shore, and drown in its turbulent depths, completely forgetting the bright shore, and disappearing forever.

These are the choices of angels. The angels who cross the ocean in boats are symbolic of those who are only involved in the Void, safely and untouched, in their ethereal forms and often spend their time throwing lifelines [through guidance] to brothers and sisters lost in The Void.

The ones who dive into the depths often forget who they are but are still drawn to the light and air of the surface and eventually make their way back to the shore where their memories return.

The Fallen are those who turn their back on the bright shore and sink ever deeper into the dark depths of The Void. They eventually forget the ocean's surface and clean air and their birthplace, the bright shore. To them only the darkness exists and they begin to believe it is all there is.

The Archangels are like deep-sea divers who have long air hoses connecting them to the air above and the bright shore. They search the dark depths for lost souls. Many souls are beyond help and reject the aid offered, but others greedily take a mouthful of the air offered to them by the Archangels. It eventually helps them rise to the surface, where they can breathe for themselves and make their way back to the shore.

Some Fallen have so completely adapted to the dark depths that they can never return. They become dark predators, like sharks, and prey on the unwary to maintain their existence in places we are never meant to exist in for too long. Archangels are equipped to handle such predators and also teach those new to the dark depths and have never had to face such dangers before, how best to protect themselves and maintain their connection to the bright shore.

It is an interesting fact that the God Realm Angels had no idea that they were already separated from the Realms of Light when they chose to eat the fruit of duality. They'd already forgotten where they had come from and who they truly were. No longer were they Beings of Light but karmic beings drawn further and further into the limited realms of karma and powerlessness till they could fall no further only to rise again. As long as they have the desire to play the duality game they are caught in the endless cycle of karma, falling, rising and falling again. They go from having the powers of a god to the lowest, most humble being.

KARMA

A more realistic way to look at karma is to picture a huge

Chapter Six

wheel. North [the top] is positive; south [the bottom] is negative; west [the left] is female; east [the right] is male. Whatever road you choose you'll slowly circle clockwise or anti-clockwise till you reach the bottom [south] where you will feel powerless. You then begin to rise up the other side till you reach the top [north] where you have the powers of a god. You will have many lifetimes on the way, first as one sex on one side, then the other sex on the other side. You begin as a positive compassionate being, a creator, then you fall to become a negative being, a destroyer, a hater. On and on you go on the merry-go-round of karma till you tire of the endless roles you play.

This is the 'wheel of karma'. Even the beings created by the Senior Fallen circle the wheel just the same as the angels do and are offered the same opportunities. When we truly tire of the wheel we are offered help to get off it. This is when Beings of Light come to aid you and subtly guide you on a private and unique path to your true self.

The wheel described above is a simplified version of the very complex machine that is karma. Gabriel said karma is more like the cogs or wheels of a huge clock, wheels within wheels, within wheels, big ones and tiny ones all turning and affecting each other. The huge Creation Beings like the God Realm Angels or Senior Fallen, the different realms they create, and the beings that inhabit them, make up all the different cogs of the machine and are all propelling each other. Even the smallest cog has as much impact on those around it as the big cogs, in endless karmic circles. This is where the never-ending tragic stories are played out, life and death, love and loss, compassion and hatred, creation and destruction.

A History of Angels

GOD - INFINITE - THE NOTHING - BEINGS OF LIGHT
Diagram 1

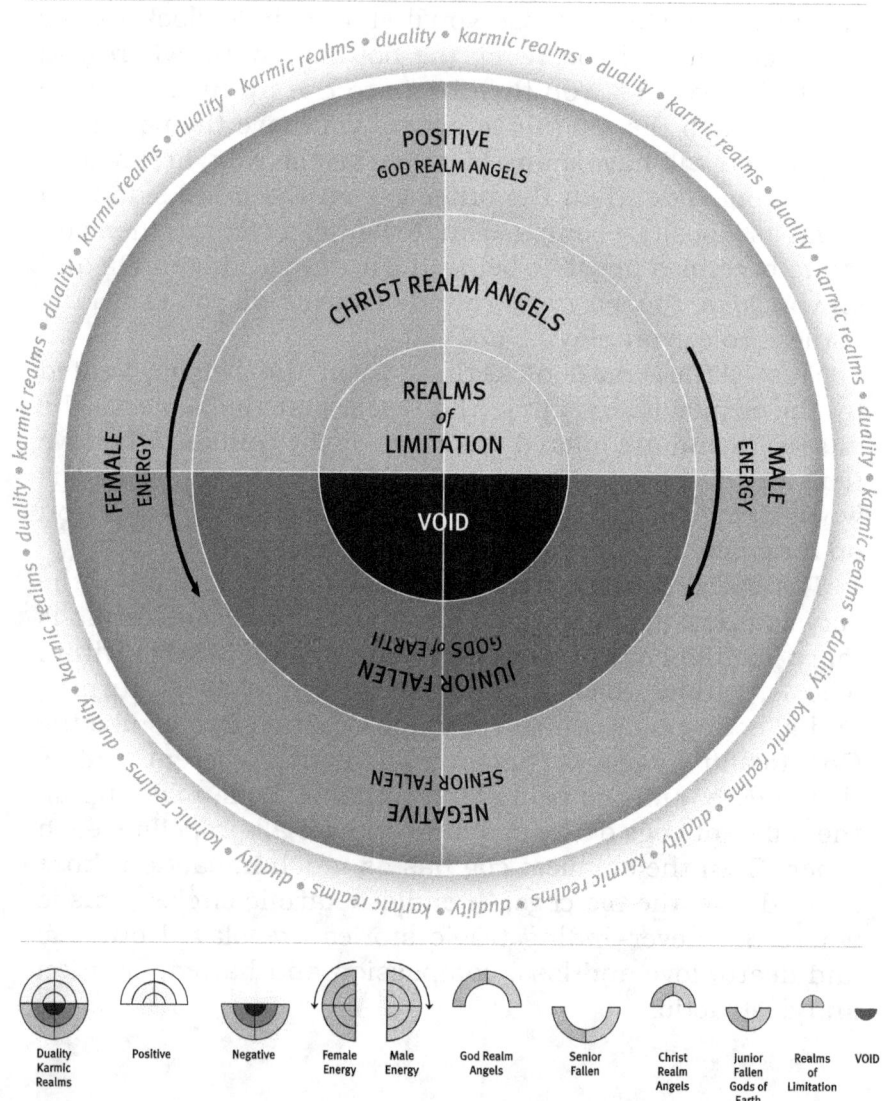

As you can see by Diagram 1, negative and positive energy are different energies to male and female energy, though they influence each other.

You can express either negative or positive energy while in either male or female aspect of your karmac cycle. It is a misunderstanding to call female energy negative and male energy, positive.

Note; Female energy rotates anti-clockwise and male energy clockwise in the karmic cycle. What aspect your soul is born into (male or female) dictates which way your soul begins its karmic cycle in duality.

Chapter Six

Diagram 2

Soul Chakra isn't a fixed chakra but rotates through different phases of Male and Female, Negative and Positive energy. When it reaches either the Negative or Positive chakras it is completely eclipsed by them. This is also when female and male energies are in balance.

It may surprise you to know that great spiritual insight and wisdom can come from the Negative Eclipse Phase. This is when one may find all wordly endeavours fail (relationships, career, creative endeavours), but this often forces one to look within and question oneself and existence. A certain awareness and detachment can occur which stops the Karmic Rotation of the Soul Chakra. It will begin to move in towards the Heart Chakra where all the four different facets (Positive Male, Positve Female, Negative Male, Negative Female) are in balance. Once the Soul Chakra has joined the Heart Chakra it will journey deeper and deeper into the Heart Chakra, which is our connection to the infinite, and greater awareness.

Many people waste the Positive Eclipse Phase of Soul Chakra and use it as a chance for outer power, fame, wealth and good fortune rather than an opportunity to become aware of our higher self.

Why did I use Leonardo Da Vinci's Universal Man for diagram 2?
It reminds me of our lower and higher self.

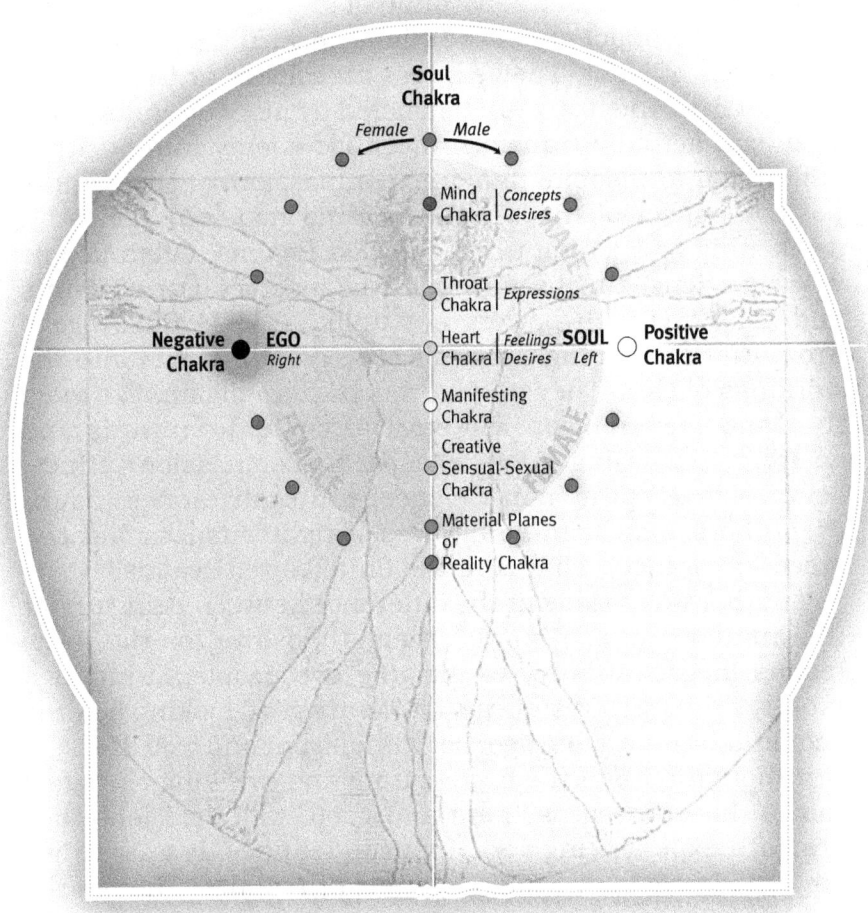

A History of Angels

Duality is also played out in our human form. The spiritual centres or charkas in our bodies express certain energies symbolised by specific colours. Physics explains how all colours have a different vibration or frequency. Red is a low frequency and blue is a high frequency. It is the same in your spiritual body. In diagram one, the human form is divided into positive and negative zones. Being part of the Lower Realms, the Void, worlds of matter, or maya [illusion] means that normally beautiful aspects or zones are expressed negatively. When we manifest our loves and desires they are transformed into fears, attachments, degradation, and destruction rather than what we'd like them to be. They are manipulated by karma and other negative forces. A Being of Light doesn't have this separation of the colours or energies. White light is made up of the whole spectrum of colours, as are Beings of Light. They express all colours or frequencies straight from the heart unobstructed by negative influences. They can actually transform negative energy into positive, suffering into wisdom, hate into compassion. People in the positive aspect of the wheel of karma may experience an awakening or opening up to the God Realms. Often people who experience this become spiritual masters, gurus, saints and messiahs with powers not unlike God Realm Angels. From that awakening they will have great insights into the workings of God. They might even start a religion. But even they and their religion will start to circle downwards and go from expressing positive aspects [compassion, ethics, generosity of spirit, non-violence] to negative ones [power over others, indoctrination, war, self-righteousness, bigotry, greed, ignorance]. So it is in the finite Lower Realms.

Another way to look at the difference between being under the influence of the infinite realms [positive] or the finite realms [negative] is try to imagine two people sitting at a table together in a restaurant. Both are good looking healthy people about the same age, both intelligent and well dressed. But though both of them are eating and drinking the same things, have loving partners and good, well paid jobs they are both experiencing very opposite realities. It's as if they are tuned to different radio stations or realities. Though the

Chapter Six

radio waves are everywhere and there are infinite stations to tune into, these two people are only tuned into two opposite stations, one positive and one negative, because of their position on the karmic wheel.

Imagine the one who is tuned into the positive station. He feels whole, has a great sense of purpose and finds life fulfilling. Everything is as it should be and he is grateful for all he has. He has a compassionate link to all living things, flows with life and all the challenges and changes it throws up at him and finds great enrichment from the experience. He is accepting of others and comfortable about how he looks and his relationships with others are about sharing and intimacy. He has no need to be powerful, to control others or be famous unless he wanted the creative challenges they offer. He accepts death as a natural part of life and dies peacefully when his time comes.

The other poor person, tuned to the negative station, feels incomplete, empty, needy and inferior to everyone around him or alternatively superior, vain and judgemental of himself and others. He thirsts for power to fulfil his endless needs and sense of emptiness, is drawn to addictions like alcohol, drugs, gambling and pornography and is assailed by violent hateful thoughts towards himself and others. He is full of fears, especially about death, and obsessed with the idea of eternal youth. When death comes for him he dies in abject terror. He spends his life envying others for what they've got, no matter how much he has.

Beings of Light can see how people are influenced and don't judge them. They understand they are going through negative or positive circles. Beings of Light, though, are wary of those who 'get off' on the negative influence and enjoy trying to drag others into it too.

Remember the interlinking cogs or wheels of karma? Well, all the people connected to you in your life, especially your direct family, are the cogs linked to you and influence your life. Your ego is linked psychically to your family and friends and is being influenced by their needs and desires. This is one reason why people can be full of conflicting needs and emotions. If you are in your negative phase of karma all those around you will influence your psyche into viewing the world in a fearful, negative way. It's their job to undermine you, degrade you, cheat on you, tempt you into self destructive or reckless actions, make you feel unworthy of love, stupid, selfish and a bad person. Everything is turned into an argument, all your views and beliefs are attacked and undermined, and any personal projects are sabotaged.

When a person moves into the positive aspect of the wheels of karma they will no longer feel comfortable around people reinforcing a negative view of them and will move away, change jobs, stop seeing old friends and family. People and partners will come into their life who reinforce a positive view of them and who are very supportive of their beliefs and desires.

Another facet of karma is the way we are made to experience a situation over and over until we have some sort of understanding of it. The movie "Groundhog Day", with Bill Murray, is a demonstration of karma. Remarkably in the movie Bill is in love with a certain girl who doesn't like him and wakes up to the same day over and over again. He at first tries to manipulate the situation, but fails to get the girl. Next he despairs and becomes self destructive and even finds ways to kill himself, but no matter what he does he's back again to play out the same scenario over and over again. Eventually he accepts the situation and decides to use the time to better himself and he stops trying to manipulate the girl. In the end a very wise Bill wins the girl and is open to a very different and fulfilling life. He accepted the limitation imposed on him by karma and changed from being a very selfish, manipulative and destructive sort of guy, to a wise and caring one whom people wanted to be with.

That's the dichotomy of this limited plane or Lower Realms. If we try to control our situation and all those in our life we are doomed to failure. Even when Bill dishonestly got what he wanted, for example, it was worthless to him and he'd be left feeling despair. It's a negative idea of fulfilment, it's ego's idea that if you get exactly what you want you'll be happy.

Chapter Six

This is the Fallen's idea of happiness and, as you may have seen in Lucifer's story, there's usually only one outcome. It is interesting to note that Lucifer in his lonely powerless life on Earth found greater peace and fulfilment than he ever did as the most powerful character of the Lower Realms. That was because Lucifer accepted the limitation of his very hard life on Earth and learned about true love, self-acceptance, and generosity of spirit. Even his aggressive warrior nature of old could be used for something so selfless as saving a dog.

To know true power we have to accept our powerlessness or limitations and in so doing, we connect with our souls, with the infinite, with God and know true power and freedom, because now we are infinite and eternal.

CAUSE and EFFECT

Normally people aren't aware of karma, especially in Western cultures. Most people don't remember their past lifetimes. Understandably they feel confused when random misfortune keeps on singling them out. When this happens they naturally feel unlucky, cursed, or even damned by God. Another facet of karma is 'cause and effect'; an action will have a corresponding reaction, if you do a negative action, for example, there will be a negative reaction.

Logical isn't it? But sadly you can have lifetimes on top of lifetimes of backlogged karma, especially if you are not a particularly aware person. This is where karma can be cruel and inefficient and why Beings of Light try to make people aware that their own actions are causing them such suffering. By understanding this they can be free of this endless burden.

But first you have to accept the limitation that is forced on you. Next, start to become aware how this negativity came about [why you have negative wheels in your life] and you'll actually understand how you, personally, created it and that nothing is singling you out. A person who's aware can transform, say poverty for example, into a loving experience.

Even though this person has little money, they will still find life fulfilling and fruitful and find great understanding and humility in being aware that they are meant to be poor. They created this poverty by their previous actions. With understanding comes enrichment [wisdom]. On the other hand, they could feel bitter and 'hard done by' and consequently have to keep going through their 'Groundhog Day' over and over again until they accept they are creating their own misery.

The big moment for Lucifer was when he accepted what he had truly become and that he had misused his power in the Lower Realms. The opposite affect had to be created for him, that is powerlessness and poverty. His love of war and the need to always seem heroic was counter balanced by his experience of World War One, where most so called heroes were blown to pieces in the trenches and their lives were no better than insects and the whole thing seemed mad and pointless.

Lucifer also had great power over women, especially his sex-slaves, so in his life on Earth he was completely ignored, abandoned or denied by them, especially by his mother and his daughter. Can you see the 'cause and effect' working here? The reason Gabriel told me the story of Lucifer was to understand that if someone as evil and hated as Lucifer can learn to accept that his direct actions created the circumstances in his life of hardship and loneliness, so can I. Lucifer found peace and enlightenment through acceptance. You or I can find hope in this and know we can find love, peace, wisdom, fulfilment and enlightenment too, no matter how unworthy we may feel. This is especially so when we grow up spiritually and take responsibility for our actions and are willing to face the reactions.

Some may question why didn't Gabriel rescue his own son from Satan and The Devil when he was quite capable of doing so? Didn't this awful experience push Lucifer down his vengeful path? To answer this question it is essential to understand that this universe is quite new. Gabriel mentioned that this is the thirteenth time it has come into being and Lucifer has had many lifetimes. Lucifer started

Chapter Six

out each time as a God Realm Angel [with the powers of a god] and each time took the same path of vengeance due to an injustice that was committed against him. He also imprisoned Satan and The Devil wrongly in a past incarnation.

So God told Gabriel he wasn't allowed to interfere in Lucifer's karma. It was hoped he'd learn his lesson, and in the end, he did. Gabriel mentioned that Lucifer was given the chance to take vengeance on The Devil or return to God. Lucifer had lost all interest in harming The Devil. He understood how pointless vengeance is and how it locks you into an endless karmic circle with that person and robs you of living a free life. You'll see in a later chapter how karma brought these three [Lucifer, Satan and The Devil] together to give them the chance to love, or at least understand, each other [in chapter seven].

Gabriel told me the hardest people to help in this world are the ones who believe they are righteous. They can't accept that they may have a dark secret, or they may be harming others psychically, even though they seem such good, spiritual people. They read all the right books and know all the right things to say, but it doesn't change the fact that, karma-wise, one day there has to be a reckoning. You have to face the ugly, well-hidden side that your ego doesn't want to face.

If you are wondering why bad things are happening in your life, all you have to do is ask God to show you why, and you will be shown. But most people don't want to know. They might find out they were a Lucifer and it doesn't fit with the ego's nice shiny illusion of itself. Your ego too may have to take some responsibility for its past actions, and believe me, most peoples egos don't want to do that.

BEINGS OF LIGHT

It may interest you to know that Beings of Light live amongst us. They don't found religions, lead armies, run countries, or huge multi-national companies and they aren't film stars, or elite athletes. They are average looking people doing average jobs who may move around a bit. You may work with one at your factory, bank, office or building site. They try to avoid work places that pander to addictions like bars and casinos. They are the people that have a kind word for someone when they're down, or point out that vengeance is a waste of time and only harms you, or try to help you see yourself, or another, in a more positive light. Most people will take this person for granted until they move on to another job or another town.

When the Being of Light moves on, his fellow workers may experience a sense of loss, a feeling that a certain joy or light has left their lives, or they may realise that an opportunity was wasted. If a true desire grows within their heart to see this person again and take the opportunity to know him or her more intimately, they will always meet again. Beings of Light usually offer three opportunities, but if you reject them more times than that, they will disappear from your life and probably never cross your path again, no matter how hard you try.

Beings of Light work hard at trying to help people stand on their own feet and make their own connection to God. They will usually leave this person before they can become too attached or dependent on them because the Being of Light would then become part of the problem, not the solution. [A negative being, on the other hand, likes you to believe you can't live without it, so you will be enslaved to its will and fulfil its needs].

Beings of Light each have their own way of doing things, of course. Gabriel is probably a bit more straight-forward, or blunt, with people he helps. He's often given the harder cases. Some people are more suited to this blunt approach. Myself for example, I've always liked the direct truth, so I don't miss the point. But of course there are a lot more sensitive and subtle people around whom the blunt approach wouldn't suit. Gabriel came into my life because I asked for help from God and was willing to face the truth of my past actions. He comes to me in the form of soul. I haven't had the honour of meeting him in the flesh yet.

Chapter Six

Gabriel told me an interesting fact that may offend people obsessed with the idea of miracles and divine saints, gurus, mystics, or beings with god-like powers. Beings of Light never perform miracles. It would go against what they are trying to help us understand. Miracles play right into the negative ego's idea of how to be happy in life. Ego would love to be granted super powers by God for being such a great and noble person so it can remove all obstacles from its life that cause it suffering and maybe even save a few people on the way.

Lucifer had such powers and by following the needy path of ego he used them to create the world he lived in and have complete control over everything in it. At first Lucifer was a very honest, self-sacrificing and humble person. But really he was only a child, and like most children when allowed to have all they can take, he became very selfish and dangerous. Our egos are like such children and, as Hindu masters will tell you, they make terrible masters but good servants to our souls. Beings of Light aren't going to do anything that plays into the hands of our egos. From personal experience I can say they have a tactful way of always stepping around ego and speaking directly to your soul.

It is interesting to note that many gurus and spiritual masters become famous because they can manifest miracles and people flock to them hoping they will help them or teach them how to become a miracle worker also. But you hear many disturbing stories of misuse of trust by many of these so-called saints on the lines of sexual abuse, embezzlement and fraud. Having psychic gifts doesn't mean you are a saint or God realised. The Fallen have incredible psychic gifts and many of them like to take on the persona of saint, guru, messiah, or messenger of God and that's why Beings of Light walk a far more honest and humble road.

Miracles play into the hands of ego because, if you have such gifts, your ego will convince you that you are the next messiah, that you are chosen by God, or you are God-like and can do no wrong. In another, if you lack these gifts, you maybe under the misconception you are less favoured by God or unworthy in someway and this may lead you to enslaving yourself to another you deem more worthy. Nothing could be further from the truth. Psychic gifts, wealth, power and good fortune only mean you are going through your positive aspect of karma. It is an irony that often it's during the negative phase of our karmic circle that many people turn their focus within and also reach out for guidance from God.

This is why the limitations of Earth are regarded by the Beings of Light as the best school for souls. That's the other side of duality; power and its opposite, powerlessness. That's what karma manages so perfectly, it creates your opposite over and over again and makes you face it.

There are places where a Being of Light may not be able to contact you directly. They can use another to be their mouthpiece for them. Some great pearl of wisdom or insight may come from their usually ignorant lips to aid another in their hour of need. You therefore don't need to have a shiny angel appear next to you, which would be lovely, but would also terrify a lot of people.

Beings of Light can use the flow of life and work within it. They may make you aware, unnoticed, of the words to a song on the radio [which answers a prayer or question you may have asked of God], a billboard, or documentary on television. A book may jump out at you and you just have to read it, or, a common technique used by the Beings of Light, you may be steered into the path of someone mirroring a negative trait of yours. That trait is often easier to see in another than it is in our selves. We may even be given the chance to see the outcome of the other person's actions and, if we understand how it mirrors our own actions, we may be saved from having to play out the karma that comes with it.

Beings of Light help us become aware of all that happens in our life and how it isn't chance, but appropriate for our needs. We stop feeling like victims of fate and realise we create the world around us by our past actions.

To me the thing that Beings of Light do that is a true miracle, and they do it all the time, is heal hearts and minds. Often people are so wounded by a loss or grief that

Chapter Six

it makes them incapable of being able to view a situation rationally. They also have entities [negative dark beings] feeding off the pain and deliberately stopping them from being able to let go or heal. Beings of Light remove them. [I will explain more about entities later on and why the Fallen created them]. But you have to ask for help, it is a law the Beings of Light have to respect. They can't do anything if you don't want them to. They have to leave you to karma. It may surprise you to know a lot of people actually enjoy or desire, suffering and misery. Beings of Light respect this and leave them to it.

A History of Angels

Chapter Seven

THE DEVIL ON EARTH

When Gabriel first told me of The Devil, Lucifer and Satan being brought together at the beginning of the 1900s, I didn't quite understand the relevance of the story. But I realised it was a karmic example of the many lifetimes these three had had together to give them an opportunity to let go of the karmic attachments they had for each other.

The Devil was reborn in the end of the 1800s to a prostitute mother in London who abandoned her on the doorstep of an orphanage. Life was harsh in the orphanage and the children were treated as if they were evil and unclean in someway because most were illegitimate. The interesting thing about this was that The Devil was the master of undermining people psychically and verbally and making them feel unworthy of love so she could take control of them.

For example, if the Devil was interested in possessing you she would focus her whole will on you. Generally she would do this if she thought you could fulfil the emptiness within her, as she believed Lucifer could. You would start to have inner thoughts that made you doubt everything about yourself. If you were dressing to go out, you would be assailed by doubts about your appearance, or if you were talking to someone you'd feel they didn't like you, or that what you were saying was stupid or arrogant. If you did something nice for someone you'd doubt your good intentions. If you wanted to start a new project you'd be assailed by doubt and despair. You'd also always worry about money and feel as if everyone was trying to cheat you. Whenever you had to show courage, fear and doubt would grip you.

It is hard to describe how destructive this is to a person's self belief and how this distracts them from knowing their own true feelings, until in the end they are unable to make the most simple decision. They feel no one wants them around because they are so horrible, ugly, unlovable, stupid and incompetent. There is no love in this at all. The Devil wouldn't accept that another may not love her, or loves another. She only knows she wants this person and doesn't care that she is destroying them in the process of taking control of them.

The Fallen can handle this sort of psychic and verbal attack. They have great natural psychic protection, especially if they are aware that another is attacking them. That is how The Devil is so cunning. She can subtly infiltrate another's psyche and make them believe her thoughts are their own inner thoughts until she completely takes over their thought processes. This is what I mean by possession. Karma will match up people with similar psychic gifts and abilities so that these powerful people will nullify and also be mirrors for each other, in the hope they will see in one another what they are unwilling to look at within themselves.

The orphanage people treated Rose [The Devil] exactly as she had treated others, they undermined her and made her feel unworthy of love and that she was somehow evil. For all her psychic gifts and powers Rose never once felt worthy of love and respect.

When Rose was about fifteen years old she was put to work at a local factory. Unlike a lot of the girls she worked with, she wasn't the least bit interested in the boys around at the time. She wanted to wait for someone special, someone whose soul could fill her great emptiness.

When she was eighteen years old she went to a Saturday night dance and spied a large strong lad across the room who instantly caught her eye. Usually Rose could psychically read a person but this young man was impenetrable. He even seemed aware of her probing and turned and looked right at her. Rose learnt that this young man was called Bill [Lucifer], that he too worked in a local factory and that he had an invalid father at home whom he cared for.

Already karma was at work bringing these two together. Even though Lucifer hated The Devil with a passion that

Chapter Seven

verged on madness, karma attracted him to Rose in the hope that he'd let go of his need for revenge against her. Lucifer [Bill] would psychically possess women by making them believe they couldn't live without him so they'd fulfil his own emptiness. The Devil and Lucifer were perfect mirrors for each other. Also, because of their own gifts, they would find it near impossible to possess each other.

People often ask Gabriel how such dangerous beings, with immense psychic powers [who can possess normal humans at will], are allowed to live amongst us. The truth is Fallen aren't the least bit interested in average human beings because such people have nothing they truly need or desire. The Fallen are usually locked in psychic struggles with their own kind, like The Devil and Lucifer were in this lifetime. Also karma didn't offer them any opportunity to have control or power over others. It made sure they were poor, powerless factory workers, not rich powerful rulers of vast empires and armies.

Within a year Rose and Bill were married and living at Bill's humble abode. Bill's father David [Satan] was a bed-ridden invalid. He used to be a huge, strong, arrogant, bully of a man, an alcoholic who had frequently beaten his wife and had driven to an early grave. So karma brought The Devil, Lucifer and Satan together all under the same roof.

David [Satan] had misused his vast physical strength to dominate others and enslave them to his will and he despised weakness. But now karma had made him an invalid. He was completely dependant on Bill's kindness and care to survive. Karma was offering Satan an opportunity to have compassion for those less physically fortunate than himself. This situation also offered Satan the chance to let go of his long-standing hatred of Lucifer.

Rose and Bill lived happily together for many years, even though they were poor and life was a struggle. But their time together was cut short by the outbreak of World War One. Bill joined up with all his fellow factory workers and was sent off to fight in the trenches of France. He saw this as an opportunity to be a hero but soon learned that he'd walked into a living hell. Men were being slaughtered en masse by

A History of Angels

shelling, machine guns, and gas, and rats feasted on their corpses. The rare time Bill actually saw his enemy, fighting was bitter and men used bayonets, spades and knives as well as guns to kill each other.

Rose was devastated when Bill was called up and she missed him dreadfully when he was gone. Her life became an unhappy drudgery of working at the factory and caring for an ungrateful David, who never had a kind word for her. Rose couldn't imagine life without Bill around to love her. Lucifer and The Devil had had many lifetimes together. The Devil always hoped Lucifer would fill her emptiness caused by the loss of her connection to her own soul. But when we rely on another for what we should find within ourselves, and also believe we can't live without them, we have to lose them. That's how karma works.

One night Rose had a vision of Bill crouching in a muddy trench. Shells were erupting all around. Suddenly Bill looked up at the sound of an incoming shell. He knew it was falling directly on him. Just before it landed he looked towards Rose and smiled. Rose screamed in horror and despair. Life had stolen Lucifer from her again.

This war finally convinced Lucifer he'd had enough of being the warrior/hero. He dreamed of a peaceful humble life and also of letting go of his hatred of The Devil. This is the positive side of karma.

Rose didn't want to live without Bill so she committed suicide. She hoped she could rejoin him in the here after. David too, a broken man, passed away in his sleep. This is where karma can seem cruel and unjust. Unlike Lucifer, who learnt great life-changing lessons from this lifetime, The Devil and Satan didn't grasp the opportunities offered. Satan is still lacking in any sort of understanding or compassion for those physically weaker than him. The Devil is still trying to possess those she feels can fill her emptiness. They have had hundreds of similar lifetimes in the hope they may learn a more loving and compassionate view of others and themselves but all to no avail.

Chapter Eight

ATLANTIS

To be able to tell you what brought The Devil and other Fallen to Earth, not as normal people but as gods and goddesses, and why those who came here were despised by Fallen and angels alike, I have to tell you about how these Fallen became vampires of peoples' souls or life force, so that they could stay down in the Lower Realms way past the permitted time. Once an angel cuts itself off from God and becomes a Fallen, it is running on borrowed time. It is using up its life force like a car battery and will eventually need to connect to the infinite again or cease to exist.

When the Devil fled Lucifer's wrath, she hid in a cave for many years in a state of madness. She finally healed enough to know she needed to move on and find somewhere to exist, far from Lucifer's long reach, with other Fallen. She created and travelled through many portals to other realms and soon found a realm where many enemies of Lucifer had created new kingdoms and subjugated the beings there. She was welcomed amongst Fallen there because of their mutual fear and hatred of Lucifer.

It's interesting to note that before Lucifer arrived these same Fallen were amongst the oldest and most powerful of the Fallen in the Lower Realms. They had completely invested into ego and were all very vain, power obsessed, and materialistic. They should have returned long ago to God but did everything in their power to avoid it. Then Lucifer came along and their world was swept away irrevocably. Karma is remarkable. If you hang onto something too tight, you'll lose it. As you read earlier, Lucifer fell looking for

A History of Angels

revenge against The Devil and Satan and wasn't the least bit interested in harming anyone else. Certain Fallen decided Lucifer was a threat, but he wasn't their enemy until they attacked him [cause and effect]. They barely escaped with the clothes on their backs.

The Devil, to her surprise, found her sister Jill amongst the Fallen hiding in this realm and both were glad to be reunited. [Jill will be known later as Death]. Jill had a husband named Leo and the two of them were glad to take The Devil in.

These Fallen, unlike most, were united and worked together on many projects to make up for lack of numbers. They decided to look for a beautiful realm and create a city, where they could all live and work on their many projects together. A tropical paradise was found with crystal clear warm oceans, white beaches, huge lush forests, and an amazing array of exotic flora and fauna. It was perfect. Over the next few years they built the most beautiful white city from the local stone that sparkled in the bright sunlight as if it had flecks of diamonds in it. They built villas for themselves, meeting halls, theatres and a library.

In this paradise, rich in exotic fruits and food of all types, the Fallen, not bothered by the usual conflicts of other Fallen, and cared for by many slaves, had time on their hands. They could indulge in artistic pursuits, hunting the huge dinosaur creatures in the forests, taking hallucinogenic drugs and having affairs and orgies. They also became amazingly vain and wore the most outrageous and revealing clothes and strutted around like exotic birds and spent the day endlessly preening themselves. They were in Fallen paradise.

Four years went by before the first hiccup occurred. A tiny parasite started to infect their slaves which attacked their hearts and they died en mass. The Fallen had their bodies dumped in the forest to be devoured by the many predators there. Soon they had no servants and slaves. It had been a very long time since these old Fallen had had to look after themselves. It was a major crisis.

Chapter Eight

They needed to find a new source of slaves who were immune to the parasite. Hunting parties were sent out into the jungles and forests to find any local humanoids who might be appropriate. It didn't take the Fallen long to locate small brown skinned people who hid in caves and seemed to have no weapons to protect themselves against the endless predators, and used only the most basic tools. They were a very languid, dreamy people who seemed to eat a daily intake of some type of drug that grew in the jungle. They then lay unmoving for days.

When the native people saw the Fallen in their exotic costumes, pale skin, great height and beauty, they thought the gods had truly arrived. They saw the Fallen weren't the least bit frightened of the huge dinosaur predators that roamed about. They seemed to find it amusing to kill them as easily as squashing a bug. So the natives were curious and willing to follow the Fallen back to their marvellous sparkling city. The Fallen noticed that some of the huge predators also followed them at a safe distance and waited outside the city when the natives entered.

Unknown to the Fallen, these little people had a gift. The drug they took helped their spirit leave their body and possess the weaker mind of the huge predators, which they used to protect them from other predators and catch food for them. They also lived off their very strong life force. The natives were parasites or vampires. Even from a very young age children were taught how to leave their body in a trance-induced state and locate a younger weak-willed predator and take control of it. This is why the natives didn't need weapons to defend themselves and lay around all day. Their bodies and their spirits were well fed and protected. This is also why a large number of predators followed the Fallen and natives back to the city.

It didn't take long for the natives to adapt to their new roles as servants. They seemed to have a gift of reading the desires and will of the Fallen and carried out tasks without even being asked. At first the natives tried to possess the Fallen but found their wills and spirits too immense. But the natives were hungry for something else the Fallen had,

A History of Angels

knowledge. Natives flocked to the city. It was as if they had all heard telepathically about the city of the gods and all the knowledge that could be gained there if you were willing to serve them.

This comfortable arrangement went on for at least ten years. The Fallen became even more debauched, if possible, and the natives became a lot wiser. Then a major calamity happened to the Fallen, for the first time in their existence they were growing old and they didn't like it. A solution had to be found urgently. They saw that their servants stayed young and healthy over the years. The Fallen wandered how they accomplished this remarkable feat. So the Fallen possessed the natives, whom they thought of as lower life forms, and discovered that they were parasites or vampires living off the life force of lesser beings.

The Fallen originally had vast life forces that would take thousands of years to run down. The Fallen needed life-forces of many natives, who only have a small life forces, to recharge their empty ones. When one steals the life-force of another, that person dies. Sadly, but karmically, the little vampires met their match in the Fallen and all in the end were sacrificed to fill the huge hunger of the Fallen for eternal youth and immortality. When the last native's life force was stolen the Fallen realised they were in trouble. They needed far vaster amounts of life force if they wanted to stay in the Lower Realms. The dinosaurs' life force was tried but the energy was far too crude for them and useless. They needed humanoids.

Fallen can leave their bodies in a ethereal body, as angels do. Angels complete many of their missions in their ethereal body, which they use to visit and guide people in the Lower Realms, track and locate enemies, spy and collect information. The ethereal body is invisible to the average human but angels and Fallen can sense or see them and may attack them in their own ethereal body. If the ethereal body is slain, the person's body dies, too, without a mark on it. But also your ethereal body can be trapped and used to feed an enemy. The victim's body will lie in a coma then eventually die. Lucifer used to spy on and hunt down his

Chapter Eight

enemies in his ethereal body. He was very good at going undetected.

The Atlantian Fallen decided they needed to find a place full of humanoid life forms that was unprotected by both angels and Fallen alike. With this in mind they sent their ethereal bodies forth and looked far and wide for a possible place, but it was dangerous work and many ran foul of an ever-vigilant Lucifer and were slain in their ethereal bodies and their bodies died. They became scared to venture out, but they grew ever more desperate. There was no one to care for the city of Atlantis anymore and it became covered in filth and weeds. The Fallen, too, became shabby because there was no one to wash and care for them and their clothes.

Fallen started to gang up on other unwary Fallen and kidnap them. These gangs would then, with their combined wills, over-power the victim and possess them, then slowly drain them of their life force. No one could be trusted anymore. Atlantis became a haunted terrifying place. People only ventured out well armed in groups or very warily in case they were spied and hunted. Paradise had become a living hell.

A particularly brave Fallen named Bret found a world teeming with unprotected humans, and far from Lucifer. This place was Earth. He told his two brothers and their spouses and they decided to flee through a portal away from Atlantis. The only trouble with Earth was it seemed to have a natural barrier or protection against portals so they could only visit it in their ethereal bodies. This also created problems for them in the stealing of life force. So far no one was capable of vampiring in their ethereal body.

Bret's brother John was out in his ethereal body one day when he found a vast dark realm created by a Senior Fallen. This Senior Fallen was known as the Empress of the Spiderpeople, and she sensed an intruder in her realm. She swooped on the Junior Fallen's ethereal body and captured him with ease. Normally a Senior Fallen wouldn't take much notice of a junior, but this one was different. She could see he was full the life forces of other Fallen and humans. This was the first Junior Fallen vampire she'd ever met.

A History of Angels

Even though Senior Fallen have immense life forces and create huge realms with them, they also run out of life force over the eons and must return to God. But the Empress didn't want to return. She created beings known as the Spiderpeople that in spirit form attach themselves to the back of humanoids and live off extreme emotions like fear, hatred, revenge and love. But it is hard to force a being to feel love. Fear is a lot easier to create in another.

The Empress created the Scorpion warriors who invaded other realms through portals and captured humanoids and brought them back to huge farms where they were shackled and fitted with a Spiderperson [who later would be known as dark or negative entities] and these poor wretches were tortured and abused so they were in a constant state of fear and hate. This strong emotion fed the entities, who were all linked psychically to the Empress, and fed her ever diminishing life force, and help prolong her life in the Lower Realms.

John never knew true fear until he met the Empress. She radiated fear and hatred, like a black sun, of the millions of beings that fed her. She looked at John as if he were an interesting bug. She was like a huge bloated spider with all her victims caught in her vast web as she was slowly sucked the life out of her prey. The Empress had a problem though. The angels had imprisoned her in her realm recently, for her crimes against humanity, and her Scorpion warriors were unable to venture out and replenish her stock of victims. She saw an opportunity for another source through John and his family. The Empress made John explain how he stole life force and he mentioned how they were in a bind now, even though they'd found a vast resource of humans on Earth. Though the Empress couldn't leave her realm even in spirit form, her entities could.

The Empress explained that John and his family only had to possess her spider entities then attach them [while in spirit form] to unsuspecting humans en mass on Earth and live off their emotions like she did with her victims. John was keen on the idea but he was no fool, he wanted to know what she got from the deal. She said she would

Chapter Eight

take half of the whole life force they stole from everyone. John thought half of something is better than nothing, so he agreed. The Empress was pleased too because she was going to be very well fed indeed, without any of the effort or risk she usually had to take.

John returned to his family and told them the good news and how they could have as many entities as they needed, all they had to do was go and collect them in their ethereal bodies.

A History of Angels

Chapter Nine

GODS and GODDESSES of EARTH

John's family hatched a plan to take on the persona of divine beings while in their ethereal body and subjugate humans to their will. It meant living nearly ninety-nine per cent of their lives in their ethereal body, which left the body open to attack and vampiring by enemies and family alike. John and his family hid their bodies in the deepest darkest caverns they could find, in the most remote lifeless realms, sealed themselves in and never shared the location with anyone and only ventured out in their ethereal body.

The Fallen began appearing to the masses on Earth and took on forms that would impress and bend them to their will. Such as many armed beings, animal headed humans, monsters, huge beasts, demons, divine beings glowing like the sun, or even winged Archangel forms. When they first arrived Earth was very primitive and people lived in small tribes and were quite peaceful. This didn't serve the needs of the Fallen one bit. They needed mass control of humans and mass misery. Two tools were used; war and religion. The gods and goddesses possessed certain people and had them become political leaders and priests and created vast kingdoms through conquest and control of people's beliefs. They taught their subjects how to build, wage war, craft weapons and tools out of metals and develop agriculture, so they could feed masses of people in large towns and cities where it was easier to control them. So came into being our earliest civilisations and religions. They also introduced human sacrifice, torture, slavery, mass murder and rape, so humanity became very materialistic and looked outside themselves for spiritual answers.

A History of Angels

Back in Atlantis things had become so untenable that all had fled, many back to relatives and old friends. It soon became apparent to the normal Fallen that there was something very wrong about Atlantians. They could feel all the stolen life forces within them making them a weird collective of other people's souls and personalities. They were viewed as abominations and shunned. The Fallen did an unheard of thing, they asked the angels for help to get rid of them. The Atlantians fled. Atlantis was only spoken of with horror after that and none would visit there and eventually the jungle reclaimed its crumpling stone walls and it disappeared from history.

Lucifer and other Fallen would slay Atlantians on sight, so would Christ Realm Angels. On Earth, Fallen and angels alike were repelled by them and still have this urge to kill them on the spot. Atlantians have a habit of starting up extreme religions and sects with themselves as the guru, master, high priestess, saint, or messiah and may even talk people into suicide rather than loosen their grip on them.

The Devil and two female friends from Atlantis fled via many portals that they collapsed as they went so that no one could follow. They hid in a dark cavern for a while but they realised, like John and his family, that they needed another source of life force to exist in the Lower Realms. The Devil had noted that John's family had fled early from Atlantis but none of them had appeared amongst the Fallen again. She suspected they must have found a new source of life forces and a safe haven. So the three of them used their vast psychic gifts and ethereal bodies to try and pick up a trail or hint of their whereabouts. It took them about a year but they found them playing gods on Earth and looking very well fed and youthful too. They weren't the only ones to notice John's family's early departure. Karma draws certain people together. So it was with the Atlantians. They all found their way to Earth and the battle between the gods began for control of its humans.

The Devil and her friends split up and they too hid their bodies in deep dark caverns, then returned to each other

Chapter Nine

in their ethereal bodies and warily set off for Earth and tried not to attract the other Atlantian gods' attention.

When The Devil and her two friends arrived on Earth they noted that Bret, John and their family were well set up around Egypt. So they made the wise decision to move far away to somewhere yet untapped. They choose the huge dark cold forests of Europe.

As yet the three didn't know how they were going to vampire in their ethereal bodies. They were hoping to psychically steal the secret undetected, but didn't have to bother. A very ugly little spider-looking black entity found them and brought them an offer. The entity was one of many given to John's family in Egypt by the Empress of the Spiderpeople so they could vampire their subjects. But it was obvious that the Empress still had full control of her entities, even when possessed by other Fallen, which meant she possessed the Egyptian Atlantians through their psychic connection to her entities. The three declined the offer.

They discovered another way. If beings willingly sacrificed themselves to you on an alter, in ritual suicide, in battle and in the act of sex, they gave you their life force. So all three chose their own peoples and became mother-like goddess figures, and set in motion fertility rites to themselves, which led to animal sacrifice, and eventually to human sacrifice. The Devil chose the persona of a beautiful tall slim dark haired woman with rams horns on her head, another, a wise old lady with a crow on her shoulder, and the third a big voluptuous mother. This was the beginning of the Earth mother goddesses and the witches and priestesses who honoured them and were possessed by these goddesses. They played on humanity's natural trust in mothers and the strong need to be nurtured.

The Devil realised they were still not able to harvest as much life force as she'd like. She spent her spare time trying to understand this odd planet and why it was protected from direct interference from outside by some invisible barrier that made the use of portals impossible.

The Devil could sense huge forces at work that controlled all facets of life. She felt karma working overtime. She also realised karma had drawn them all into a trap. She asked her two friends if they had visited their bodies since they'd journeyed here in spirit. Both said no. The Devil tried to venture away from the planet but ran into an invisible barrier, which was impenetrable. She also realised that more and more Atlantians were arriving every day. They were literally tripping over each other in competition for the life forces here. Also whatever blocked them in, allowed the entities to arrived from the Empress unimpeded. She felt the spectre of the fear and horror of Atlantis coming back to haunt them and be re-enacted all over again. This neediness of humans bothered her too. It reminded her of the natives of Atlantis. She was one of the few who realised they were on a planet of vampires!

She felt very bitter and became something of a recluse. She began to wander the planet in the bodies of humans she had possessed and tried to find a weakness in the trap. She felt intuitively it was held in human form somehow.

It was about this time the battle between ex- Atlantians, who were now the gods of Earth, began. A titanic struggle erupted and many of the older gods were defeated and slain and new gods took over. Even The Devil's friends were involved and were defeated and slain, but The Devil was not interested in the petty squabbles of her fellow Atantians which she suspected was all a waste of time. For all the energy they stole they seemed to lose the same amount. She realised their human followers were also living off the Atlantians' needs for their followers' adoration.

There was a book published the early 1980s called *The Celestine Prophecies*. One of the major points it made and quite accurately described was how humans all stole energy from each other psychically. Living off another's life force is vampiring and Gabriel said over ninety per cent of people on Earth do it.

What an irony. The Devil actually laughed at the foolishness of it all, and also the brilliance. She would have been proud to have lured her enemies into such an elaborate trap. All the other gods were completely oblivious to their predicament. She noted that no matter how much life force

Chapter Nine

they stole, something seemed to steal it back. It was like they were water vessels with a hole in the bottom, no matter how much water they collected, it always ran dry.

The Devil knew there was a symbol for Earth that she had never taken much notice of before. It was a serpent endlessly going around and around devouring its own tail. She bitterly acknowledged how appropriate that analogy was, because she certainly felt she was endlessly chasing her own tail. No matter how much life force she devoured, she was never sated. This epiphany was a great moment for The Devil. She understood the pointlessness of ego and how it left you unfulfillable. She was in her 'Groundhog Day'.

Most would have let go of their ego here, but The Devil had no intention of returning to God. She liked to be the boss of her own world far too much. Unknown to most Fallen, all of them have to have an incarnate body on Earth so they can experience what it is like to be a humble, powerless human. It is hoped that by sharing the plight of humans Fallen may grow to have greater understanding and compassion for them. This would also help Fallen let go of their need for power and eventually they might even let go of their ego.

It was about this time that The Devil ran into a human incarnation of herself while travelling within the body of a human she had possessed. The human incarnation, though ignorant of being 'The Devil' in the Fallen world, was very attracted to the person that The Devil had possessed. It didn't take long for this self to become aware of its true self, with the Devil's help. Now The Devil had two aware selves. They realised if there was a human Devil wandering around ignorant of being a god and powerless, then there must be Atlantian gods in human form wandering around everywhere all ignorant of their true Fallen, god-like selves and very vulnerable to possession. They went about psychically trying to ferret them out. Over the next five hundred years The Devil tracked down and possessed over two hundred ex Atlantians and stole their life forces via their very vulnerable human incarnations. She became very powerful indeed and also extremely psychotic because of the myriad of different selves and personalities she had absorbed.

A History of Angels

The first god to suspect that something was wrong was The Devil's equally perceptive sister, Jill. She had found another way to claim people's life force by becoming the Angel of Death. She claimed the spirits of those unaligned to any particular beliefs when they were vulnerable after death and willing to follow her and be absorbed by her. Death came across the Devil one day while both were travelling in their ethereal bodies and was surprised at how powerful and truly complex she'd become. Death realised her sister was full of the life forces of the gods who had mysteriously died. Death flattered The Devil and told her how great she was to outwit all those fellow gods. The Devil, in her pride, confided to her sister the secret of how she possessed the vulnerable human incarnation of the gods and stole their life force. Death was amazed by The Devil's brilliance but also noted that by taking on such strong personalities she had became quite insane. Also she could feel the hatred the different souls within her had for The Devil. She was going to stick to her weaker willed humans so she could control her inner self. The two parted on good terms.

Death warned her fellow gods that The Devil was hunting their vulnerable human selves and possessing them in order to steal their life force. This news shook the gods' world. The Devil became the most feared Fallen since Lucifer. Even to this day, both their names are feared by all the gods' and despised on Earth. Lucifer had found out the secret of their hidden bodies and tried to ferret them out and destroy them. The irony was, Lucifer's hatred of The Devil tied him karmically to her where she was trapped on Earth. So he had to have incarnations with her here until he let his hatred for her go, even though he wasn't a vampire, like the other Fallen trapped on Earth.

The gods desperately searched for their human selves to make them aware of their other Fallen/god-like selves so they could psychically protected themselves from possible attack. To do this, especially if you are an angel or Fallen, all you have to do is be aware of it happening then you can take steps to put psychic barriers up. This also started a secret war between the gods to track down and possess

Chapter Nine

each other. The sad fallout to all this is these human selves became very egotistical when aware of their god-like selves and missed out on the true karmic experience of humility and humanity. Being human is far more important in soul's journey than most people will ever realise.

You may ask what impact the coming of beings like Buddha and Jesus had on the gods [more on Jesus in chapter eleven]. Many of these gods claimed they alone were the One God, but of course they were all lying. Many humans turned from the old gods because of Buddha and Jesus, so many of the old gods faded into non-existence as their ritual connections were severed and they lost their source of life force. It was about this time Gabriel and other Archangels started to visit the gods and offer them help to let their ego selves go and return to God. There were literally thousands of gods taking up all the ethers around Earth. Out of all these thousands only about one hundred and twenty returned to God and only one hundred and ninety still exist today. All the rest faded into non-existence.

The coming of Buddha and Jesus had no impact on The Devil at all. She wasn't interested in the masses, her prey were fellow gods. But Gabriel visited her as well as the rest and made her the same offer. He was impressed by her intelligence and how perceptive she was in her more lucid moments. Then she'd revert back to her paranoid self and become fearful and suspicious that Gabriel was trying to lead her into a trap. Sometimes all the different personalities imprisoned inside her would take control and make conversation quite impossible. Over the years the Devil, with her vast will power, learnt to meld or incorporate all the different personalities into her own. But it makes her a complex and extremely needy character. The Devil made it quite clear that she wasn't the least bit interested in God. Gabriel explained to The Devil she had a karmic debt to all she had absorbed and that she would have to spend countless lifetimes paying her debt unless she acknowledged her crimes. She was unwilling to do so and used all her guile and gifts to try and avoid Gabriel's visits [he always found her] and she also tried to keep ahead of her karmic debts.

A History of Angels

Very recently The Devil started to fade into non-existence as there were no easy gods to prey on anymore. Gabriel visited her again and offered her the same help. Again she refused, still not wanting to have anything to do with God. So the infamous Devil's Fallen self dissolved into the nothing. All the life forces she stole returned to their original owners. There's a weak human Devil now, harmless and lacking all her psychic gifts. She has to reincarnate over and over again until she pays back all her karmic debts. Her life is marked by a great sense of pointlessness and despair, but it is one she chose; one without God and without hope.

Chapter Ten

HOW THE GODS IMPACT ON US

In my earlier vision I saw thousands of gods floating around the Earth. They were in all their outlandish guises and their eyes were turned to Earth. Gabriel never tells you a story unless it has direct relevance to you. Why did he tell me about all these Fallen characters who later became gods of Earth? I realised it wasn't just a history lesson. He was offering me an opportunity to understand myself and my role on Earth.

Remember the big and small cogs of karma? The gods make up some of the big cogs that influence you, as does your country of birth, and your direct family. When your soul comes to Earth it borrows an ego psychically connected to the very strong characters of certain gods that help influence the karmic role you play. When Shakespeare, in his play *As You Like It* said, "All the world's a stage. And all the men and women merely players. They have their exits and their entrances; And one man in his time plays many parts.....," he was speaking a profound truth. We are given a role to play in every lifetime, each very different from the last. That's why Beings of Light don't judge people. They know their borrowed egos are influencing them to play out all sorts of negative roles.

When I was about fifteen years old I became very interested in Carl Jung the psychologist. He was fascinated by the mythology of the early gods and how humanity seemed to have a collective consciousness that drew on the very strong archetypal characters of the gods and how they resonated with all of us and seemed to symbolise different facets of our sub-conscious and made up our egos. The only difference between races was that they seemed to be connected to the original myths of their ancestors. For example, an African American, who may never have been to Africa, would still have a subconscious connection to their original ancestral origins as well as being influenced by their country of birth.

How does this work? Karma chooses all the cogs that make up you and your reality. It uses the gods' egos to help you play out your karmic role. Not that long ago humans were no more than animals. The psychic connection to the gods has helped humanity develop into the sophisticated and intelligent beings we are today. The gods have immense knowledge of science, physics, building, electronics, the arts, and medicine. They are also emotionally complex beings. This connection to them is slowly transforming us, because remember these selfsame beings once were angels too. We've been offered the opportunity to know what it is like to be angelic and Fallen. You can see in the world today an acceleration of knowledge, especially around technology, of which the Fallen are masters, but also the sad consequences of such a materialistic and shallow existence which alienates people from their true selves and each other. This is the Fallens' influence over us. On the other hand there seems to be a great awakening of spiritual knowledge and an interest in compassion, which would be how angels influence us.

Recently I realised how much I was influenced by my karmic connections to these highly sophisticated and complicated Fallen. They led me into a very dark period of my life when I was twenty-eight years old. At this time I was filled with great despair and hopelessness. I felt all my dreams would turn to dust and that I'd live a fruitless and unfulfilling life. I went to a Jungian Astrologer. The interesting thing about astrology if it is done well is that it shows you all the karmic influences and different phases we move into. Jungian Astrology also helps you understand what characteristics you have and how they effect you and what you are trying to learn karmically from having these characteristics in the makeup of your ego. The woman who examined my chart looked dismayed at what she saw there. She showed me how it dipped right down into a very dark negative phase in my life. She said it meant I was going

Chapter Ten

into a 'Hell phase'. She'd never seen it before, and tried to reassure me by saying hell doesn't really exist, it was just symbolic of a negative phase in my life and it would last till I was in my forties. She was surprised at how well I took the news, it just reaffirmed a terrible premonition I'd had.

At this time I lived in a bungalow at the back of my parents' place. At night my whole room would pulsate with darkness. I'd feel my bed sinking down through the floor as I fell asleep but I'd always wake in time to stop the descent. The walls ran with black water and, half awake, I'd get up and move my bed away from the walls. In the morning they were always dry. I thought my roof was leaking and would ask my carpenter step-father if he'd have a look for me. He kindly did but couldn't find anything wrong. I started to dread sleeping in my room and started to drink more alcohol when I went out which was a mistake because I'd see the most hellishly deformed and diseased people leering at me in my sleep. I'd be woken up by ancient warriors tugging on my arm, trying to drag me off to some awful battle. I'd stare at them in wide-eyed disbelief and they'd soon disappear like smoke.

My mother sensed the darkness in my room and told me I should move down into the house. But I knew it was no use running from it. I'd dream of being a huge rock in the middle of a stormy sea. No matter how fierce the storm raged I was unmoved by it and wasn't swept away. I felt the rock was my soul and the darkness the storm. This is when I started to be assailed by violent and suicidal thoughts and self-loathing. With every task I tried to complete, no matter how small, I would be flooded by a sense of despair and hopelessness and find it almost impossible to complete. In a world where your self-worth comes from how good you are at something, it was devastating to my self-esteem. I also started to feel dishonest, as if I was a thief, or my intentions with girls were sleazy, and that I might die of some sort of horrible disease. I played hockey at the time and the playing field became a battlefield to me and I became a very tough player and was regularly injured.

A History of Angels

It was about this time I had a beautiful experience. One afternoon I suddenly felt that familiar displaced feeling and barely made it to my bed and collapsed there. I had a large window and it was open. I felt a gale force wind start to blow through it. I staggered to the window and slid it shut, but the wind was blowing even harder now and I was blown back to my bed and pinned there. The wind seemed to blow me within myself and I started to fall or be sucked into a huge white vortex where I kept being drawn deeper and deeper within myself. Finally I arrived at an infinite white nothing. I felt peaceful for the first time in my life. I knew I was in the heart of God. My hand appeared in front of my face and started to change into all sorts of different periods in history, sometimes male sometimes female, the changes happened with blinding speed and went on for a long time. I realised I'd had many lifetimes and I was feeling very weary of it all. I awoke on my bed and, from that time on viewed all that happened to me from the perspective of my soul and felt a sort of non-attachment to all the negativity I was going through and no longer struggled against it but let it wash over me.

It was truly like one of those old cartoons with the main character having the devil on one shoulder and an angel on the other. Something gave me the space within myself to choose and not just act on impulse. When Gabriel came into my life I faced my negative impulses in a loving way. Rather then catch an infectious disease, I worked in a hospital; rather than become insane, I worked voluntarily in a psych ward rather than experience jail, I worked for the justice department with people out of jail. Rather than fight in a war, I played medieval role playing games for a while. I still had to go through my negative phase, but Gabriel helped transform it into a positive and enriching experience. I learned to understand the terrible influences many are under and I have nothing but compassion for them, because it's truly an awful experience and one many can't bear alone.

How does this tie in with the story of all the Fallen and their lives? Gabriel said every character in my story was psychically trying to influence me to be like them. They were the cogs of my karmic wheel. They are still there, of course,

Chapter Ten

but it's as if I'm walking through an electrical appliance store full of big and small television sets all playing different shows at once. I know I'm not in the television show anymore, I'm just someone passing through on my journey of life and only casually take an interest in the crap they are showing.

I asked Gabriel, what was the point of me having to have karmic links to these very negative beings, feeling all they did and perceive the world as they do? His answer was obvious I guess. He said, karma. That for many life times I've judged all these people, especially The Devil. So karmically that ties me to them until I understand what motivates them and stop judging them. I can understand more clearly, now that I can separate myself from their feelings, that it would be awful to be The Devil. She has a terrible fear of abandonment. All her schemes and manipulations are for the sole purpose of having complete control over all those she loves so that they will always be there to fill her emptiness. I felt this small screwed up child within her that is always looking for someone to make her feel loved and safe all the time. But this child demands love only on her terms. It's a very ego based idea of love. It's so conditional. No wonder it always goes wrong for her.

I assumed that I must have been a warrior for many lifetimes and asked Gabriel. He agreed. He said I had very different motivations to Lucifer and found him very egotistical and vain. After feeling him, I realised how lonely he was. He hoped by being the best warrior, the hero, people would admire and love him for it. But, as happens with karma, it just made people jealous of him, scared, and hate him. So his skill as a warrior actually alienated him from those who he hoped would love him. It was also a very childish and ego-based idea of how to be loved; the classic over achiever. In his last lifetime as humble Tom, Lucifer faced his ultimate fear of being unloved and alone and just got by the best he could. In the end this humble old guy, who was a nobody, was very much loved and respected by all, when he'd given up hope he'd ever be loved again. He died at peace with himself and the world.

A History of Angels

Chapter Eleven

JESUS and MARY MAGDALENE

I was curious about Buddha and Jesus and asked Gabriel who they were. He said they were both Christ Realm Angels and actually knew each other and had very similar beliefs and ideas. There are some quite accurate accounts of Siddhartha's [Buddha] life, Gabriel said, and he had nothing to add to it. Only that Buddha was female in the Christ Realms but decided to incarnate to Earth as a male because she recognised how hard it would be to convey her message as a woman, especially in ancient India. The story of Jesus has been tampered with quite badly, Gabriel said, and if told properly it would have been quite similar to Buddha's story in showing the enlightenment of both of them and the similar messages they both wanted to convey.

It is important to understand ancient holy texts written about divine or holy people would have them born on an auspicious day [25 December was common], the mother would be visited by divine beings or messengers and holy men or astrologers would predict the coming of a king of kings or god on earth. Other elements included a virgin birth and powerful people and divine beings present at the birth. As a child the chosen one would show knowledge way beyond their years and at about 12 or 13 would give a lecture to all the most knowledgeable holy men, priests, and Pharisees of the time and amaze them. They would go on to perform miracles, be murdered or put to death in a public execution, then rise from the dead. Believe it or not nearly all cultures speak of holy people or divine beings living such extraordinary lives.

A History of Angels

When writing a holy text, ancient peoples would accord this special person with all these attributes. It doesn't mean it actually happened. By showing the similarities between one great person and another, a person in ancient times understood that this individual was divine. So when people try to use the bible or any holy text as fact they are making a sad mistake. In literalising their lives, we lose the true message and greatness of people like Jesus and Buddha who lived very real and in many ways ordinary lives. Many stories from the Old Testament came originally from Egyptian myths and beliefs. The Ten Commandments came from the Egyptian Book of the Dead. If the Bible or any holy text was a myth, does that mean that God doesn't exist? Some people are terrified of this. Do we need any holy text to know or understand God? Actually, no. There are people of all walks of life who have a deep connection and knowledge of God. They may even be illiterate, be born in the deepest darkest jungle or may never have laid eyes on any holy texts. It doesn't matter. All that is required is an honest desire to know God.

Angels have no churches or temples to God. They don't sit around reading ancient holy texts looking for hidden clues to find God in a maze of myth, hearsay, propaganda and truth. Angels have a very personal connection and relationship with God, and one that they enjoy discovering and developing over many eons. Jesus and Buddha both tried to open people to this inner connection to the divine and free people from enslavement to the idea of an outer ego idea of an 'all powerful wrathful Divine Being'. This enslavement is ego's idea of what it thinks God wants, but it is actually what ego desires, to enslave soul to its will.

With this in mind, Gabriel told me the story of Jesus. Jesus was a strong, independent angel with strong convictions. He was concerned that so many beings on Earth were created into suffering, ignorance and slavery by the Senior Fallen, and also, preyed on mercilessly by the Junior Fallen, in the guise of gods. He believed they were not being offered help to be part of God's Realms. He asked to be born among humans in Purgatory [Earth] and guide those with a longing for God.

Chapter Eleven

When Jesus took his proposal to the Archangels and the [Angelic] Elders they explained to him that he had a limited, though compassionate understanding, of those suffering on Earth. All the beings on Earth were there because of karmic lessons that had to be played out. They told him that the minor beings there were extensions of their Senior Fallen creators and all would return to them one day and be whole in the natural karmic cycle. What was happening to all these helpless beings was actually impacting on their creators [in a way they were their creators]. They were all one being. This is what Beings of Light mean by 'The Big Picture'.

Jesus argued that all these beings had their own consciousness and deserved the right to be independent and follow their own path of evolution and spiritual discovery. Gabriel pointed out that they were created so that the Fallen could express themselves more fully and all these independent individuals were just facets of a great whole. Jesus and a few of his friends could not accept this. They believed these individuals deserved the same chances as the angels had.

Gabriel explained that all of these beings did have the same opportunities as angels when it was their karmic turn and were offered the chance to be part of God's Realms and even be angels if they want to be. Gabriel realised Jesus's conviction was pure and so was his compassion for those suffering in ignorance on Earth, but he and his companions knew from long experience that there was usually only one outcome to this ideology. Those being helped would just turn the teachings into a new ego-based religion and would eventually be no closer to the truth, as long as the larger being [that they were part of] wasn't interested in the truth and God.

All angels are free to choose their life's path, so Jesus and his friends were offered all the assistance they needed for their venture. One friend was willing to incarnate with him onto Earth, another three would help them remember their true selves by guiding them in their ethereal bodies.

A History of Angels

When next Jesus and Gabriel spoke they disagreed about how Jesus should spread his teachings. As explained earlier, Beings of Light usually work quietly amongst the Lower Realm beings, subtly guiding them and showing them a path to God. But Jesus wanted to do something more dramatic and far reaching. He wanted to help as many people as possible. At this moment Gabriel looked very sad. He sensed the ultimate tragedy of the course Jesus chose. He also knew God didn't want him to interfere in Jesus's spiritual journey. "So be it," Gabriel thought.

It wasn't only Gabriel who disagreed with Jesus's approach to spreading his ideals, his friend Mary [Magdalene], who was the one incarnating with him onto Earth, wanted him to choose a more subtle path, a quieter one, so that they could pass their message to people over many decades and in many countries. But Jesus was determined.

Mary went to her father Gabriel. She was his oldest and dearest daughter, a famous healer, teacher, writer, historian, and musician. Unlike many of her sister's, she was no warrior. Gabriel loved her humility, her vast inner strength and great loving heart. They were very close. Gabriel asked her to reconsider her decision to join Jesus on Earth. Mary felt in her heart she needed to go, no matter what the outcome. As stated before, no angel will interfere in another angel's freedom to choose their own path. With a sigh, he accepted her position and promised to keep an eye on her if she wished. He was relieved when she agreed to this.

Gabriel knew his daughter was too pure and gentle for Earth but understood her soul was drawn there because it was time for her to experience the Lower Realms. He also knew she had a naive idea of healing some of her Fallen brothers and sisters in their human incarnations there so they'd return home. Gabriel pointed out you can't heal someone if they don't want to be healed and added that Beings of Light, Archangels and the Elders of the Christ Realms had been trying to do just that for eons and had greater resources at their command than hers. They call it healing through the back door. [Often, the more humble human incarnate of a Fallen was more open to their help,

Chapter Eleven

while suffering on Earth, then their god-like selves]. Mary understood what Gabriel was telling her yet felt compelled to make her own contribution. Gabriel kissed her on the cheek and walked away. He felt strangely emotional today, but he had to respect her wishes; that was the angel way.

Before Jesus and Mary incarnated to Earth, Jesus was granted a great blessing: The Christ. The Christ is Divine Compassion, the creative expression of God. This meant Jesus was very powerful indeed. But power in the Realms of God is a very different thing to the way we understand it in the Lower Realms. The whole of creation is made with it and also can be unmade with it. The Archangels have it and are guided by it. It makes them the most powerful beings in existence. The Archangels and Elders hoped Jesus would be guided by it too. But it is never easy to keep a clear connection to the divine in the Lower Realms when so many negative forces are at work to make you forget your true self. When the Fallen or gods of Earth became aware of the powerful new player in their game, they weren't happy and many worked together to try and disconnect Jesus from God but they failed because Jesus never lost his desire to serve God.

I sensed an uneasiness in Gabriel when I first asked him about Jesus. I asked him about this and he was quiet for such a long time, I thought I might have over stepped my bounds. But when he spoke he sounded thoughtful and a bit sad. This is what Gabriel said.

What made Jesus Jesus was his courage, his great conviction, his passion, and his indomitable will and these traits were also his downfall. The negative forces used his strengths against him.

I was shocked and asked if Gabriel was implying that Jesus fell?

This is why Gabriel was uneasy. He said Jesus's message and intent were beautiful, but his decision to go public, to attack the Pharisees [priests] of the time and his later decision to have himself crucified, when he was advised by his friends in their ethereal bodies that the Beings of Light and Elders were concerned about this, led to a great misunderstanding of how best to serve God. This misconception haunts us today. It is one of almost suicidal sacrifice and debasing oneself to God, which led to an idea of servitude or enslavement to God. This is abhorrent to God and Beings of Light. God tries to set people free through love of the self so we can become a free creative expression of God, not grovelling, self-debasing slaves who are easily led astray by corrupt priests down the path of ignorance, bigotry, inquisitions, and war, all in the name of God.

Gabriel explained why the brutal torture and the eventual crucifixion of Jesus was misunderstood in times when the peoples of Earth worshipped cruel and corrupt gods who demanded the sacrifice of people's lives and that they endure terrible torture or hardships to prove their subservience to the will of the gods. God would never ask this because it breeds self-hatred and also submission to the will of another.

Gabriel went on to say that in the story of Jehovah demanding that Abraham sacrifice his only son to him, to prove his loyalty to Jehovah, he demanded that Abraham deny what he felt in his heart and submit to Jehovah's will. Beings of Light would point out that in this story the character of poor old Abraham wasn't listening to his true higher self. No Archangel would ever serve a being that asked us to betray the trust our children put in us, when our job is to love and protect them. That Jehovah let Abraham off the hook only shows that Jehovah recognised that he would have eventually lost Abraham's trust over this criminal act.

What sort of god would callously make a bet with The Devil that Job would stay loyal, said Gabriel, even if he destroyed all Job held dear? If I remember the story right, Job breaks out in boils, his family is enslaved and murdered, his cattle are all stolen and his house burnt down. That a divine being would make such a bet with The Devil in the first place is unforgivable, in my book, and makes this divine being no better than The Devil.

Gabriel went on to explain that if all this had happened to Job because in the past he had murdered or enslaved someone's family, stolen his cattle, burnt his house down

Chapter Eleven

and cursed him with boils, then karmically, he'd be given the chance to understand the grief and loss the victim of his malice felt and hopefully learn by the experience. But what was described in the story of Job bares no resemblance at all to a karmic tale.

Gabriel said he has to deal with these hateful, egotistical, and self-serving so called 'divine beings' every day, and they are definitely not God. That is why he felt uneasy. Why, to this day, poor Jesus can't find peace. His intentions were pure, but his message was distorted. [Gabriel explains in detail what he meant by this statement later in the chapter].

Gabriel returned to the story of Jesus and Mary incarnating to Earth. Jesus was born to humble parents. His father was a carpenter and Jesus had two older brothers. Jesus's birth was not a Virgin Birth. This myth was added later by those who hoped to convey Jesus's divinity. It was common amongst pagan religions to claim divine beings were incarnated to the Earth by Virgin Birth. This claim was made later to impress pagans of Jesus's divinity. It was also claimed that Jesus was a direct descendant of King David and Abraham to reinforce this idea of his divinity. But none of this was true, said Gabriel.

In medieval Europe royal families claimed they were direct descendants of Jesus and would have family trees made up to prove it, to endorse their so-called divine right to rule. How would being related to Jesus make you divine? Was Joseph the carpenter divine? If this was true it defeats Jesus's whole message that God is everybody's birthright no matter what position in life they are born into. Jesus actually implied that the rich and powerful are the least likely to find God. It was Jesus's love of and personal connection to God that made him divine, not some imagined family lineage. There was a very good reason why Jesus chose to be born into the family of a humble carpenter rather than choosing a Caesar or Herod as his parent? Jesus wanted to show that the humble will inherit the earth. That's you and me, not because we are of divine or royal lineage. We also have free will to choose if we want to be part of God's kingdom or not. If Jesus had had a child, he or she would have had to make the same choice.

A History of Angels

Jesus was obviously an extraordinary man. Compassion radiated from his heart. People loved to be around him and felt true peace for the first time in their lives. Jesus came into his own when he spoke. The Christ [Divine Compassion] poured forth from his mouth to the multitudes, his words touching each person's heart and awakening the dormant seeds of their own divine compassion.

Like all beings born on Earth Jesus didn't remember his origins. But when he was a boy he would wander off on his own and go within and his sense of his true self and purpose on Earth began to awaken. Jesus was known as a good boy but he could show an unbending will when he felt strongly about something.

When Jesus was about thirty years old he journeyed to Egypt and studied there. He learnt about eastern religions and philosophies. This was the first time he heard of the teachings of Buddha. They struck a chord deep within him as they were very close to his own convictions. Especially the story of Siddhartha and how he was willing to walk away from being a prince and, no matter how much his father tried to lure him back, still followed his own heart, leaving his wealth and power behind. His willingness to face all sorts of worldly temptations and let go of all attachments to them, fascinated Jesus. That he did this through compassion for himself and all living things was something Jesus believed in deeply also. With a desire to face his own inner demons [ego] Jesus opened up to his own true self, to his own divine compassion, and eventually he accepted The Christ that lay dormant within him all these years.

Gabriel pointed out that if you read the Gospels you'll be struck by how, at one moment, it is Jesus the man talking. At other times The Christ speaks straight through him. In fact Jesus had two selves, the higher and lower selves, soul and ego, God and Jesus. When you incarnate to Earth you are given an ego, which can make it quite hard to keep a clear connection to your higher self. Jesus's ego was obsessed with the idea of a goal. His passion for his beliefs, his strong will, his fearlessness and his self-righteousness made it difficult for him to hear the more subtle and gentle

Chapter Eleven

promptings of The Christ. But The Christ always came to the fore when Jesus spoke in public.

You might be surprised that Jesus could ignore the guidance of The Christ, but when one is caught up in an ideal, a goal, one can easily miss subtle warnings. The Christ or God won't interfere with your free will, no matter how devoted you are, and Jesus was very devoted. You still have to want the guidance. At times this guidance pulls back when you choose an ego path. When we grow too attached to an outcome we choose the ego path, no matter how well meaning we are, and no one could be more well meaning than the compassionate Jesus. This is why Jesus felt forsaken by God many times but it was Jesus who had forgotten to listen and who pushed ahead with his plans.

JOHN the BAPTIST

Gabriel said that it was unfortunate for Jesus that he was influenced by John the Baptist. John was a very angry and frustrated man. He was once an angel and had fallen. He was still devoted to God but no longer listened to the softer more compassionate urgings within himself, which were his connection to God. He wanted revenge on Jehovah and his followers. Jehovah had already beaten him in a battle of wills when John and Jehovah, in their Fallen/god-like selves, fought for control over the people of this region. After this battle John incarnated to Earth and felt broken and powerless. He especially hated the Pharisees for their corruption and greed.

When Jesus met John and spoke with him, John's frustrations rubbed off on Jesus. John convinced Jesus that something dramatic needed to be done to shake people out of their dark ways.

The anger that John felt towards the powers that be and the corruption of the Pharisees led him to attack Herod and his family whom he judged evil, and so he brought about his own destruction. John would have achieved more by offering Herod's family a more compassionate alternative to the way they were living. By judging and damning them he alienated them. Who knows if they would have listened to his message, but it's surprising what fruit is born by planting a small seed of hope. John's desire for their destruction brought about his own. Karma. This is the forerunner to the path Jesus took.

Beings of Light don't like to use a confrontational, self-righteous approach, Gabriel added. It breeds resentment, fear and resistance. When people feel threatened they'll try to destroy you, it's their most basic instinct. We would like them to open up willingly to something more loving and far more fulfilling.

Gabriel said when he had to be more confronting, more forceful, it's usually with beings that should know better and already have an understanding of karma, as the Fallen all do. They were all angels once and lived and honoured a very strict code which all of them understood. Most of the people Jesus and John dealt with didn't know any better. They lived in a very harsh 'dog eat dog' world where 'might was right'. To be weak was to be enslaved or die. So, with this in mind, Beings of Light need to be patient.

Gabriel said John lacked patience. Peoples' ignorance and confusion over his message seemed to completely invalidate him. It made John wonder if his old connections to God, his whole reason for existing, might be an illusion. That's why he attacked people of the time so forcibly. He was actually terrified he'd forget who he truly was and would cease to exist. He felt lost in the darkness and abandoned by God. He had indeed forgotten his true compassionate self long ago and had stopped listening to his heart, which is what makes an angel an angel and connects them to God. He became obsessed with an outer [ego] idea of God and God's will. He thought God's will was his will. And so John was arrested by Herod and imprisoned.

After the execution of John, Mary Magdalene and many other helpers worked hard to promote Jesus's loving and compassionate message in a quiet way. People were more open to it than they had expected. Jesus began to talk to larger and larger crowds. He gave them hope. He told them

Chapter Eleven

they didn't need to be rich, powerful or divine to be chosen by God, to be part of his kingdom. This love was even offered to the deranged, the possessed, and the diseased. But Mary Magdalene started to feel uneasy at all the attention Jesus was attracting, especially from the authorities.

Jesus was greatly saddened by the death of John. It also reinforced in him a sense of impending doom. The reality of the path he had chosen that may lead to his own death hit home for the first time. But he hardened his resolve and pushed forward with renewed purpose.

Jesus began to openly attack the Pharisees of the Temple and created powerful enemies. They felt their whole world being threatened. The Romans were only slightly bemused by the rantings of just one more holy man in a land infested with them.

Pontius Pilate, the Roman governor at the time, had a wife from Gaul who was deeply moved by Jesus and asked Pilate to leave him alone. Pilate realised Jesus wasn't attacking Rome or starting a revolution, so he ignored him. But the Pharisees feared that if people believed Jesus's message, they wouldn't need or honour them and the Temple any more. They weren't willing to give up all the power and prestige they had without a fight. Jesus had become very popular by this time. He had little interest in the rich and powerful. He felt they liked the status quo too much to be interested in what he had to say.

Jesus realised most people were trapped by the fear of death into living their lives in survival mode. They sacrificed all compassion for themselves and others, making them live like animals and easy to manipulate and enslave. This is when Jesus came upon the idea of a dramatic Phoenix-like moment where he would show the masses that death was only an illusion and that soul was eternal. Beings of Light realised earlier on that the path Jesus had chosen would lead him to make such a dramatic choice and tried to forewarn him, but to no avail. If Mary had known what he was going to do from the start she properly wouldn't have supported him. But Jesus only made this choice after John's death.

A History of Angels

The reason Jesus raised Lazarus from the dead was an attempt to demonstrate that death was only an illusion, soul was eternal. People misinterpreted this act. They didn't see that their souls were eternal but that Jesus had the powers of a great sorcerer or god and could sweep away all their ills. Jesus was becoming the problem not the cure. No longer did people look inside themselves for the kingdom of heaven, which is the message Jesus was hoping to convey, but outwardly to this divine being.

When Jesus healed a leper by helping him believe that if he surrender to God's will he would be healed, he opened this person to his higher self and so he healed himself. It was a beautiful moment. But the masses didn't see it that way. All they saw was Jesus perform a miracle. 'Why would I heal myself when Jesus can do it for me?' This is the path of ego. This is the trap Beings of Light try to avoid. Jesus knew this and Mary was concerned.

Gabriel said, imagine a person has cancer. To Beings of Light there is a good karmic reason why this is so. They see it as an opportunity, a chance for people to free themselves of their fear of illness and death. Often people who contract cancer have a very controlling idea of life. The illness and their imminent death robs them of any control over their own lives. It is taken out of their hands. At first they are angry and scared. 'Why me, what have I done to deserve this?' Beings of Light try to help this person understand how they karmically created the cancer. If they can accept it and not fight it, they will find great inner peace.

They would also be free of the fear of death, which enslaves us to ego. Of course a person should still go and see a doctor and try to have it healed. Often when a person accepts the cancer and treatment they no longer karmically need it. They have faced their fear and have let go of the need to control their life. If and when the time comes to die, this person would die in peace. They would have embraced life for the first time and flowed with it.

Imagine Jesus took the cancer away? Wouldn't that person just go straight on living in the same negative way? What was learnt? That every time something goes wrong

Chapter Eleven

I want a divine being to come along and take it away and never look at how I created the problem in the first place? I hope you can see why we have issues with the way the well meaning Jesus chose to open the masses to the eternal within, Gabriel explained.

For Mary and many Beings of Light, what happened next made them deeply sad, said Gabriel, and also destroyed a few people who were vital to Jesus's tragic plans. First there was Pontius Pilate. Much pressure was applied to him to get rid of Jesus by the powerful Pharisees. But because Pilate loved his wife he ignored them. He also had a grudging respect for Jesus. Secretly Pilate was quite curious about God. Pilate spoke to Jesus on three different occasions warning him of the forces arrayed against him and telling him how they wanted his death. Pilate offered to help Jesus slip away to safety out of Judea. Jesus declined, thus tying Pontius's hands.

When Mary heard of these offers of help from Pilate she had her first real argument with Jesus. She couldn't understand why he didn't accept so that they could go on teaching quietly in other countries. She could feel another much more subtle road being offered by God now. But Jesus was adamant. He also stopped listening to the subtle pleas of his angel friends in ethereal bodies guiding him.

Next Jesus put pressure on his most devoted helper, Judas, to betray him to the authorities. Judas had his Abraham moment, Gabriel said with sadness in his voice. Judas should have followed his heart and refused Jesus's order and even walked away. Beings of Light are always tested to see if they are truly listening to their heart so as not to become tools for the negative powers. If they are asked to do something that compromises their own convictions, we'll even refuse God's will. They realise God does this to test us sometimes, just to make sure they're not just puppets.

But Jesus was very persuasive. We as Beings of Light, said Gabriel, ask ourselves how did Jesus help Judas? Judas hung himself after Jesus's death. How was asking Judas to betray someone he loved and respected over all others any sort of help to Judas? How did this act help

A History of Angels

Judas find love and compassion for himself and a link to God? Judas damned himself to Hell and he's still there. We keep visiting him but he can't let go of his guilt.

Pilate was tragically affected by Jesus's actions also. He was used as the tool of Jesus's own destruction, even though he didn't want this outcome for Jesus. He even hoped by offering to pardon one of his prisoners that Jesus would be chosen, but a thief and murderer was picked instead, much to Pilate's disgust and surprise. After the crucifixion Pilate's wife left him. He was always haunted by Jesus's death and felt used by the Pharisees, whom he despised. He felt a coward and a failure. How did this outcome help Pilate find love and compassion for himself? As Beings of Light we have to consider the impact our actions have on others.

When Jesus was crucified there was a powerful moment just before his death when he realised God wasn't with him. It was the first time he truly felt alone. Of course God hadn't forsaken him, but it also wasn't God's will that Jesus sacrifice himself in this way. God left him to his choice. Who forsook whom? But God also showed the love he had for Jesus. Quite dramatically The Christ left Jesus as he died, unleashing a huge storm.

When Jesus died and was taken down from the cross he was entombed. Like Buddha, he didn't want people to become attached to his outer form. He would have hated all the statues that were later made in his likeness for people to worship like a pagan god, especially of the crucifixion. He left instructions that his followers secretly remove his body and bury it in an unmarked grave.

Jesus would have been horrified by the stories that arose later on about the resurrection of his corpse. They defeated the whole purpose of the crucifixion. After his death Jesus visited, in his ethereal body, all his followers to show that the soul is eternal and the body is finite and passes away. The belief that your body can rise from the dead perpetuates an obsession with defeating death. There's no love and acceptance in this. It's an attachment to something impermanent. That's the road of ego and suffering. Gabriel stated strongly that Jesus knew this, and it is tragic that his

Chapter Eleven

message was so distorted in later years.

Jesus spoke about karma and reincarnation but later on powerful people, like the emperor Constantine, had these texts removed from the Gospels. Constantine, who wasn't a Christian, was impressed by how bravely Christians faced death when they were being persecuted. He realised what a powerful tool it would be to have subjects who could combine this devotion with serving the state. This is when he began to perpetuate the lie that he and the church leaders were divinely chosen. This is also why he didn't want people to believe in karma, which taught that the humble and poor would also have their turn at being powerful. By doing this political and religious leaders changed the whole meaning of Jesus's main teachings that we are all equal, that we can all find the kingdom of heaven within and become sons and daughters of God.

The real message of Jesus's crucifixion, according to Gabriel, was a Phoenix analogy. He wanted to show that by letting go, or by destroying the lower self [ego], the Phoenix [higher self] rises from the ashes. That Jesus was tortured and crucified bothers Beings of Light because it plays into the hands of the negative powers. These negative powers play on peoples' self-hatred and despair, pushing them to self-mutilation and abasement or even a suicidal self-destructiveness in an attempt to sacrifice themselves on God's altar. This of course has nothing to do with self-love, acceptance and compassion. It breeds self-hatred and fear, which enslaves people.

At the time of Jesus's death, his early followers were very different to the way Christians became later on. These first followers were equal. They had no priests controlling them. Jesus's teachings were left to people's own interpretation. Men and women were equal. Mary Magdalene's teachings were also highly thought of. So were Judas's. Early Christians didn't focus on the crucifixion or any sort of resurrection but more on finding self-love and the eternal within. They never spoke of the miracles either. Jesus would have been very proud of them.

A History of Angels

Hundreds of years later a patriarchal society decided to discard any teachings that didn't serve its purpose. The leaders copied the structure of Pharisees and the Temple. They discarded Mary Magdalene's writings and reduced women to a minor servile role. They kept people ignorant by mediating between them and God.

When Judea rebelled against Rome, in later years, early Christians in Rome decided to cut themselves off from Judea and the Jewish people, even though most Christians were originally of Jewish decent. They didn't want to be persecuted along with the Jews. They decided to use Judas as a scape-goat.

Mary Magdalene was later presented as a prostitute. Many believe she was an apostle but was later written out of the story. There are rumours she was Jesus's wife or lover but Gabriel said that wasn't true. Jesus would have been happy to marry her but Mary refused because of the confrontational path he had chosen.

Jesus would not have liked the way the Old Testament and New Testament were joined as one book: the Bible. The Old Testament has nothing to do with Jesus's teachings of love, compassion, forgiveness and finding the eternal within. It is full of the old vengeful, wrathful god raining destruction on his enemies and helping his followers enslave and destroy their many enemies. It perpetuates the idea of redemption through sacrifice and divine punishment. People are crippled by the idea of sin and guilt, which enslaves them in fear. It's interesting to note that fundamentalist Christians always quote the Old Testament when they want to fight a war or punish someone. These teachings have nothing to do with Jesus's teachings. Karma isn't about punishment and redemption. It's about cause and effect. It's an opportunity to have a greater understanding of a situation that may be causing suffering to ourselves and others.

In later years when Christians were trying to convert pagans they started to focus on the resurrection and miracles of Jesus. But all cultures have stories of people accomplishing both these things. Christianity transferred early pagan rites from Fallen gods to Jesus. They used

Chapter Eleven

Mary, his mother, to fill the earth mother role, so important to western cultures at the time.

Gabriel explained that Christianity turned Jesus and Mary [his mother] into pagan gods. This is why Jesus has no peace. He has tried to fulfil this role and even competes with the old gods in the hope of freeing people enslaved by them, so that people can serve God. According to the laws of karma, you become what you hate. In his frustration at the gods, Jesus became one and is now trapped by all his followers' needs and prayers. He would love to be free of this burden, but how? By people doing what he always wanted them to do, commune directly with God.

So what happened to Mary Magdalene after Jesus's death? Gabriel said she went on quietly spreading the teachings until her later years just as she hoped Jesus would have done if he'd chosen a quieter path.

A History of Angels

Chapter Twelve

ARCHANGEL GABRIEL

ANGEL GABRIEL

GABRIEL

I asked Gabriel to tell me more about himself. He was happy to do so. He said there were three versions of Gabriel all serving God in three very different ways but all shared the one soul. These were his different selves. Gabriel related the story of the three Gabriels, starting with Gabriel the man.

I was incarnated to Earth about the same time you were born here. I was raised by harsh, materialistic parents, went to school and was a mediocre student and afterwards did lowly paid casual work. I was unemployed many times and was looked on by my family as a failure. I drifted from town to town and had a few relationships that didn't last. I only lived in rental properties and drove an old car. What possible reason could I have for living such a life?

Well, when you, and many others, moved into their negative phase of karma, I did too. I shared the experience with you all, stood in the unemployment lines, worked in the factories for abusive bosses, had needy and demanding partners, undermining parents, no close friends and was poor. To many I seemed a failure. But while you were linked to dark negative beings, you were also linked to me. I helped you understand why you were going through all this limitation and to see the wisdom in the experience and then find love for yourself. Your analogy of feeling you had a devil on one shoulder and an angel on the other was more accurate than you know.

A History of Angels

When Lucifer [Bill] was in the trenches in World War One, I was in the medical corps. You also were in WWI as a pilot. I helped you, and at least one hundred others just like you, to see the pointlessness of it all and the madness. Lucifer only died recently as he completed his Tom lifetime. He was a lot older than you are, but I helped him just the same. That was his last lifetime before he chose to be absorbed into God.

You observed one day that you were amazed that three of your close friends were going through exactly the same troubles as you were. Well, I was helping your friends just as I was helping you. It was hoped that by you all [karmically] coming together you could be mirrors for each other. Did you notice that all your friends are secretly quite spiritual? They also felt me [Gabriel] by their side, but not all were as interested in my help as you were.

When you started to use your art to better understand yourself spiritually, I also started to paint. I'm also writing this book with you, but you are listening so well to your soul now, and to me, that I leave the actual writing to you and only guide you now and then. Essentially all the answers are coming from within you and I help you when the negative forces try to cut off your connection to your higher self and to God.

You are probably noticing our relationship is changing. For a while it was as if I was part of you and I helped transform all the negativity assailing you into something enriching and positive. But now that you have distanced yourself from your karmic ties our relationship has developed into more of a friendship and we are sharing the journey together.

ANGEL GABRIEL

Angel Gabriel has been mentioned in the story of Lucifer and Isolte and even Jesus and Mary. I have a self that lives amongst the Christ Realm Angels. I'm happily married to Isolte there and we have two beautiful children. We have a son who's sixteen years old and a daughter who's five

Chapter Twelve

years old. We live in a cabin I built in a wood not far from a community. Angels mainly live in small communities. We have centres with libraries and higher education, but on the whole, we are scattered far and wide in our vast realms and love living amongst nature and using our hands. We had to build a military academy because of the Dark Angel threat. I'm an advisor and teacher there.

The Elders know who I truly am, but they keep my secret and I play my humble role well. The Elders are amongst the oldest angels and commune directly with Beings of Light and Archangels when any major decisions are made, especially if these decisions impact on the Lower Realms. We live under strict rules of non-interference with the Lower Realms and have to clear anything we do there with God. I appear in my Archangel ethereal body at these meetings, even while my angel self is present.

My main angel role is as a scout and spy. I keep an eye on the more destructive Fallen, usually while in my ethereal body. I'm very good at going unnoticed. I visit those who call my name, especially if they are the more arrogant Fallen. I specialise in impossible cases and try to help them return to God. Many of these Fallen remember me from when they were angels and respected me, especially the more war-like ones who knew me at the military academy. Also some Fallen are old family members, friends or lovers from my different angel selves who have passed away now. But I haven't forgotten any of them. They are still in their same form, sometimes for thousands of years and are now mentally very complicated and hard to help.

I've also been a commander in some of the wars in different angel realms against the Dark Angels and even against Senior Fallen. I've also died in many battles over eons just like any other angel. I'm usually called on when dark beings arrive that are far too powerful for the average angel soldier to handle. I'm highly regarded amongst the military.

Back home in the peaceful communities the angels don't take much interest in the fighting and only notice I'm absent a lot. They think I'm a negligent husband and father. This makes Isolte very cross. She wants to remind them that beings like me allow them to live the peaceful life they do.

The Christ Realm Angels don't really understand that they are in a way part of the very dangerous and violent Lower Realms. We're still part of the karmic wheel and are affected by all that happens in the Lower Realms. A lot of angels believe they can only be happy if they hide their heads in the sand like an ostrich in denial. I remind them of a more dark and dangerous existence and they resent me being around because of it.

My son is a bit like this. He enjoys his peaceful angelic life and doesn't take his military training serious. He'll be drawn [karmically] into the fray soon whether he likes it or not, and will have missed out on an opportunity to have my guidance and training. Isolte knows better than most what a shock war will be to our son. She fought in many. Karma always makes you face your opposite. The Christ Realms are very much part of karma.

The outer ideal of peace, of Utopia, is an illusion that can be snatched away easily, even for angels. Peace is an inner connection to the eternal peace of your soul and is permanent and unperturbed by the storms that blow around it. You are also seeing again why angels fall, to face their opposite. Also the Dark Ocean analogy is relevant here because it explains why angels, especially those angels with an outer idea of peace and harmony, will be drawn karmically to the opposite of this down in the violent Lower Realms.

ARCHANGEL GABRIEL

To describe my Archangel self is quite difficult. You may as well ask me to describe God. I'm an infinite expression or facet of God. I'm one of God's many guises. When people are drawn to me they are really drawn to God. When they are repelled by my presence, it means they've chosen the road of ego and aren't interested in God. A being like the Devil would be drawn to me for my outer power but she'd hate my soul and my connection to God.

Chapter Twelve

One of my main jobs on Earth is to help people connect to their higher self and to God. It's a hard job because most people have such an ego idea of God and spirituality. When you were growing up, Rod, you had the opportunity to be around all sorts of religious and spiritual people. But as you have said to me in the past, you saw yourself as a spiritual fence sitter. There was an emptiness about it all that disturbed you.

In your life you've had the opportunity to meet gurus, healers, religious intellectuals, psychologists, astrologers, numerologists, psychics, practitioners of natural medicine, yoga teachers, practitioners of magic, priests and spiritual writers. When we look to another for answers we are instantly drawn away from our true self and down the road of ego where we need others to fulfil our needs and heal us and guide us. This leads us further and further away from our inner self and truth.

As explained earlier in the book, the way Beings of Light operate in the Lower Realms is that they try to help people stand on their own two feet and find answers within themselves so that they learn to listen and follow their heart and soul. A Being of Light will try to point out how we truly feel about something so we can make a decision from the standpoint of our soul. When we start being more aware and are able to know our own true feelings, even in the most clumsy way, the Being of Light will pull out of our life and only work with you on the inner. You are forced to find the answers within yourself.

Of course it's hard and many negative forces are at work to cut us off and mislead us but any little truth found within oneself is worth a world of knowledge. If Beings of Light hangs around in human form they play into the hands of ego and people will become reliant on their guidance and lose all trust in their own truth. Beings of Light then become the problem not the cure. This was our point with Jesus. He was compassionate and well-meaning and tried so hard to help people find their own inner truth, the kingdom of heaven within, but he was soon turned into an ego icon, a talisman or charm against peoples' fears,

A History of Angels

and ego idea of a god [one outside ourselves], especially after his death.

I help people on the inner. There's no use making an idol of me to worship, I don't answer to ego. I leave that sort of worship to pagan gods. I'm not here to fix your problems, but I will help you understand why you are having them and transform a negative experience into a positive one. If I take away a problem you miss out on the chance to learn its karmic lesson and it will come back even more intensely next time.

Imagine you are unable to swim and fall into the ocean. I could pull you out, but what about the next time you fall in and I'm not around? What I do is jump into the water with you and help you float, and when your fear subsides and you know I'm there for you, I begin to teach you how to swim. When you are competent enough, I get out of the water and instruct you from the shore. Then I leave you to your own journey and pop back every now and then and see how you are going. This sort of support doesn't appeal to a lot of people. They'd like a nursemaid for the whole of their lives to take care of all their problems. People may not want to hear this. They suffer from huge misconceptions about the role of angels. However if people want true help and guidance, I'm there for them.

Another more obscure job I have is to do with time. There are beings with the ability to manipulate time to their own advantage. Archangels sense the interference and how it is impacting on the outcome of the future, we track down the disturbance and the culprit and make adjustments so that the future is played out karmically as it should be.

Two whole existences ago there were divine beings of great power who fell and who are excellent at manipulating time to their advantage and avoiding karma. They will go back in time and murder an enemy who beat them in the now or manipulate a situation with fore-knowledge so they are the most powerful person in the game, or are able to get rid of rivals for someone they love. When you have this sort of power it's very tempting to break and

Chapter Twelve

manipulate the rules. God has lost patience with them and I usually have to dispatch them if they don't mend their ways.

With our ability to read the pathways of time and the possible outcome from any action and the way it impacts on time, we advise the Elders of the angels whenever they want to interfere in some way in the Lower Realms. We can tell them if their action will change the course of history and possible karmic outcomes and lessons. We can also see the karmic pathways that lead off any individual and the outcome of choosing that path. When a person first begins to listen to their heart and soul, and not just to their ego, many possible pathways open up around them and sadly soon close down when someone chooses ego over soul.

When you listen to ego blindly, there's usually only one karmic path, like a railway track, you can't change direction or make different life choices. When people make this choice, and most do of course, it's very easy for us to tell them what the future holds for them, especially if they don't change their ways.

Lucifer surprised us. We expected him to travel down the same destructive negative path for many more lifetimes. He made a spiritual back flip that we very rarely see amongst the Fallen. At first he only had one outcome to his future, then pathways opened up all around him when he started listening to his soul.

With you, Rod, we knew you'd die in your late thirties if you didn't start listening to your soul. It was a sort of fail-safe so you wouldn't karmically waste your life. You would die and have another opportunity, quite quickly, to listen to your soul. You already had the desire to know God. It was just a matter of looking within yourself to find your old connections again.

A History of Angels

Chapter Thirteen

AWARENESS

Why is awareness so important? Most people just get by in life. They don't know why they make the decisions they do or why they react to situations the way they do. At the end of their life they have a sense of resignation, defeat or maybe felt they were just swept along by a tide that dumped them at there last stop, death. Most people feel that most of their true desires are unfulfilled.

When a psychiatrist or psychologist tries to help a person in distress, the first thing they do is look for clues about some habit or thought pattern that might be triggering negative emotions and actions. It is very hard for the patient to have the detachment to observe themselves rationally. In spiritual terms Beings of Light understand that negative forces are at work to block you from understanding what causes you grief.

When I worked at the Justice Department it was known that sending people to prison didn't stop them from acting in a negative way. Chances were they would keep re-offending. I especially remember the men who were offered anger management. They were all in trouble for aggravated assault. Observing and dealing with them I realised they had emotional buttons that were very easy to push and they'd always respond in the same violent way and most regretted their actions afterwards. This fed self-hatred and low self esteem. Of course there were the darker ones who seemed to get off on the violence like a drug and saw themselves as heroic. They were the deluded ones, the psychopaths; the hardest ones to help.

With the ones who regretted their actions, I was always surprised at how honest they were. They made no excuses and truly seemed to feel honest regret. Some of them had even been in prison for murder. They all had moments in their lives when they wished they could go back and change the situation and act in a more rational and positive way. No one understands better than these men how just one action affected their lives and the lives of everyone around them. How does a counsellor help such men?

First they look at their emotional buttons and what triggers them. Next, what created the emotional buttons in the first place, say in childhood. Did they have a violent parent, for example?

Gradually these men are observing themselves. They start to get some sort of perspective on what moulded or shaped them into the men they are now. They stop judging themselves so harshly and see that emotional land mines have been planted all over them. They gain some insight into the damage done to them that set them on a constant negative cycle of abuse. What shocks these men is the realisation that they've become what they hated, their abusive parent. They are the violent adult now.

This is the moment of choice. Does the individual want to go on being like their abusive parent? Nearly all of these men say no. From this moment every time someone pushes their emotional buttons they can choose how they are going to act. At first it is hard to break the habit of a lifetime, but whenever they pull back enough to make a choice they find that the moment is gone. They don't act on the violent impulse.

What I've written here is obvious, that it's easy to see what perhaps has shaped and motivated these extreme men. My point is we all have emotional landmines planted in us which can shape our lives and force us down a path just as narrow as the path that took these men to prison. One day we'll look back on our lives and wonder why we went down such an unfulfilling, loveless road? We were basically programmed to take this road. I call it being 'railroaded' in life.

The way to change this is through awareness. This is not about blaming your parents for all that went wrong

Chapter Thirteen

in your life. They too were programmed. It's about choice. Some people say we have too many choices now in modern day life. I'm not referring to the many materialistic choices we have on offer now, I'm talking about how you want to feel about yourself and your life. Do you want to go down the road of ego or soul? I spoke earlier about the men who get off on violence, how they love it, and see themselves as heroic and are completely deluded about what people really think of them. They don't care what people think of them as long as they get what they want.

I'm sure we've all had bosses like that. I have. They want to be in a position of power so they can get what they want and don't care who they hurt getting it. They'll delude themselves into thinking people actually respect them and want to be like them, even desire them. The only people who actually respect them are other psychopaths. These people never look back at the trail of destruction they leave in their wake. They completely disengage from humanity so they don't feel remorse or pity, because it would get in the way of their obsession to fulfil all their needs.

In a way we are all minor psychopaths. We all try to disconnect from those around us because we don't want to think too deeply about the effects of our actions. When Gabriel tried to help Lucifer he made him emotionally connect with all the humble people around him. Lucifer was shocked at how strong and beautiful humble people can be. Suddenly he saw how his actions affected those around him, he felt their pain and was filled with remorse. He also saw how he was being manipulated to play out the deluded heroic psychopath character for hundreds of years. He truly felt what his heart and soul wanted - peace. He didn't want to harm or control anyone, he just wanted a quiet life, to get to know his heart and soul again.

Also humanity interested Lucifer. He started to observe people around him. He didn't judge them, he was just curious. He saw himself mirrored in everyone he met. He noticed how people seemed unaware of why they did what they did and were then surprised at how unhappy they were. It all seemed to be about ignoring others and trying to get away with as much as possible before anyone challenged them. Then they either tried to destroy the person who challenged them, deny it, or flee. He realised it was an ugly and loveless way to live. He was observing ego at work. If everyone is competing for the same things [love, power, fame] then it's a very 'dog eat dog world.' People learn complex and dishonest ways of getting what they want. Because Lucifer had been powerful enough to get what he wanted he lacked any understanding of how complicated this game was among humble people. His soul wanted him to take a humble path so he could experience and understand how these people lived and what motivated them. Lucifer's ego found it hard to accept his powerless position in life now though, and he fell into a deep despair. This was about the same time I felt Lucifer in my life.

When I was about 28 years old I felt my karmic path ahead. It was an ego path. I sensed negative forces were pushing me down a road I'd been down many times before. I felt I'd wasted many lifetimes endlessly trying to find and fulfil the same needs with all the same unfulfilling outcomes. I watched my friends and those around me going after these same things that in the past I strove for and that I knew would only have one sad outcome - disillusionment. I started to feel quite suicidal. Gabriel mentioned once to me that I had a fail-safe inside me that if I didn't connect with my soul by my late thirties I would have happily passed away.

I had no desire to go down the well worn path of my ego. This opened me up to help from Beings of Light like Gabriel. That's all I needed. I was already becoming all too aware of the emotional buttons that were pushing me down a narrow path not of my choosing. I used to dream of being swept away and drowned by tidal waves. These tidal waves were full of the extreme emotions from my family. These emotions made it impossible for me to know how I truly felt about anything. I kept hoping love would come into my life, or a career, that would change everything. But after a while I dreamed I was just surfing these emotional tidal waves and would turn around and ride the next one in. I became aware. I stopped

Chapter Thirteen

reacting. I started to choose how I wanted to feel. Of course I couldn't change my outer life much but I began to change inside. Life and everyone around me started to interest me. It wasn't about achieving goals, success, fame, respect from others, wealth, a love in my life. It was something far more personal and something that couldn't be swept away by outer events. No matter what life threw at me I became curious. I began to feel the complexity and brilliance of how God works in our lives and that nothing is 'just an accident'.

If you choose the ego path you don't want to notice the signposts all around. They just get in the way of what you are endlessly striving for. What if your heart and soul don't really want what you are willing to sacrifice everything for? What if your soul thought it a waste of time? Most people don't ask these questions of themselves. They want to believe a soulmate will come into their life and make everything all right. But what if that soulmate leaves or dies or even worse, falls in love with someone else? This illusion of happiness can be easily taken away and I promise you it will be. Even if you stay together till the day you die there's always the slow loss of what you originally had, which at times feels crueller than losing this person all together.

Am I saying don't waste your time in relationships? Of course not! But your soul and karma views relationships very differently to the way ego does. Someone you are madly in love with today may have been your greatest enemy lifetimes ago. We are brought together for many varied reasons, none of them are to do with finding a soulmate. That would mean we are incapable of being whole. We'd always need to find this same person. That's a lie of ego and one of the main reasons people choose the ego path over soul. They want this outer idea of love over and over again with always the same unfulfilling outcomes. Remember The Devil's reason for the path she chose. She was always looking for this exact outer idea of love all the time.

Next time you are madly attracted to someone, take the time to consider why? Be aware. You could save yourself a lot of heartache and the trouble of going down that very narrow path again that you've trodden many lifetimes before. We

A History of Angels

lose our neediness for people, when we can observe ourselves and them with some detachment. You'll find that a deeper, more fulfilling love for yourself and them can come out of it, if they are right for you, or you can understand the karmic lesson of being in an unfulfilling relationship. Both types of relationships would hold an inner enrichment for you and wouldn't just be a waste of time. You will start becoming the emotional surfer, not someone swept away by the emotion of it all and drowned.

We all know the saying, 'love is blind.' When ego finds love, it is only aware of what it wants and that this person maybe the one who can supply it. This is generally when we become little psychopaths and don't really listen to the person we think we are in love with, really take a good look at them and listen to the quiet warnings of our soul. We just see them through the 'rose coloured glasses' of love - through ego. We lose our awareness in this moment and repeat old patterns. If you believe you can only be with someone at the cost of being truly aware of their feelings and your own, there is no true love in the situation. You are just caught up in the emotional wave of your needs at the time. Ego robs you of choice and will only lead you down a well-worn path to suffering.

Chapter Fourteen

SIGNPOSTS

Every living thing is offered the chance to become aware of itself and its part in the universe. To assist it on its journey, your soul leaves certain signs or markers throughout your life, not unlike the escape button on a computer. Your soul understands its karmic path but also knows that the ego, especially one being controlled by spirit [a collective of entities or perverted ego], can take complete control, leaving the soul stuck playing out the same scenario over and over again and nothing is learnt. That's why a soul may eventually leave a person and return to God. A perverted ego is a collective of other beings' egos and dark entities trying to maintain their existence by living off your soul. They will do this by possessing your ego. I'll explain in more detail later.

  Most of the ancient indigenous cultures believe in these signposts and go to great lengths to find and honour them. An example of a signpost is déjà vu. This is our soul warning us we are making a choice that is leading us down a well warn and fruitless path. That feeling of being in the moment, or that you have experienced something like it before, means that it's a 'Ground Hog Day' warning. It helps if you believe in reincarnation, but if you don't, you've probably played out this same situation many times in your lifetime already. It's like a friend pointing out that you always pick the same sort of person to have a relationship with and you usually have the same negative outcome. This friend is a signpost. You have a choice. Do you start to question why you keep choosing the same sort of partner, or do you laugh it off and tell your friend to mind his or her own business?

A History of Angels

You may still choose this partner but start to think about what your friend said. You question your motives. Is this person like one of your parents, for example? You start to become aware. You may still go through with the relationship but you notice how this partner seems to manipulate you just like that parent did. Where once you had your emotional buttons easily pushed, now you observe the situation and notice how very familiar it all is. Whenever this attempt to manipulate you comes up, for some reason, the moment has a great clarity about it. Soul has highlighted the situation, or signposted it, so you will take note of all that happens.

Even more interesting than your partner's manipulations is when you catch yourself as the manipulator also. Soul doesn't need to change another person to be happy, or the world for that matter, but it can work on itself. This is self-empowerment. Most people realise they can't change their parents or their partner, so why do they keep trying when it's really themselves that they should be looking at?

Everyone is locked in an endless struggle for control of those around them, hoping by changing these people they will be happy. That's perverted ego's outer, and near impossible, idea of happiness. 'If everyone gives me what I want I'll be happy.' Realistically, how likely is it that you'll ever have the power to make everyone do and act the way you want? Do you think Lucifer was happy? He realised in the end he only needed and wanted basic and simple things. These needs didn't involve control over someone or something to be fulfilled. You don't need to control someone to love them. If you feel a need to change a person, do you truly love them? Are you truly listening to your heart and soul? That's what a perverted ego does. It takes over your life and makes you fulfil all its needs and also get everyone around you to play along.

If you would like to learn how to listen to soul, start to notice when out-of-the-ordinary things happen in your life. Say you are going to a job interview and you are late and rush out to your car and the front left tyre is flat and, to your horror, you never had the puncture in the spare tyre fixed. To me this is a signpost moment. Why did it happen today

Chapter Fourteen

of all days? What is it about this job I'm not looking at? Even that I'm rushing to it blindly in a state of panic would ring warning bells. What should I do? Well, I'd phone the people interviewing me and tell them of my situation, and if they agree, see them another day. I'd then go inside and sit down and think about the situation as if I were analysing a dream.

Cars to me are a symbol of our mode through life, our ego. [If you dreamt about your car, take note if someone else is behind the steering wheel, is controlling the car, or if you have passengers. This usually means you've got a perverted ego running your life; they are driving your car, your way through life]. You've probably noticed that the cars people choose to drive say a lot about them. The left front tyre would be first thing I'd look at. The left side is soul and the right ego. You steer with the front wheels. They indicate what direction you choose to take. My front left tyre is flat. Something about this job is going against the choice or direction my soul wants me to take. This job opportunity is probably a possible 'Ground Hog Day' choice by perverted ego. Does soul still want me to go through with the job interview? I'd suspect, it didn't, because my spare tyre is flat also. I've been through this situation before and had the same outcome and didn't deal with it back then.

While I sat there I'd probably notice a whole set of needs and fears making me panic about missing the job opportunity of a lifetime. This is usually the perverted ego manipulating your ego [mind] to take the job. I try not to act on these fears and notice that I feel detached from them, as if they're not my own. I feel like my parents are in the room pushing all my emotional buttons and telling me how my self-worth depended on me getting this job and being the sort of person they've always wanted me to be. Do I want to be the person they want me to be? If yes, I'd go to the job interview; if no, I'd cancel the appointment. The signpost from soul gave me choice.

How is this different from superstition you may ask? Perverted ego [spirit] looks for signs in life also. But what it looks for is warnings of karma catching up with it. It spends its time trying to avoid karma, so that it can keep on going after what it wants, like a little psychopath, with no regard for your original ego and soul's chosen path or even your health and wellbeing. Perverted ego doesn't want to pay for or learn from its negative actions. It gets quite paranoid after awhile and takes on very childish rituals to protect itself from possible retribution. People like this often turn to extreme fundamentalism or spiritualism in the hope they can ward off this possible outcome. The last thing a perverted ego wants to do is face or understand what it fears.

Psychologists understand the power of the unconscious and subconscious in helping people face fears they spend their lives running away from. That's why they use dream analogy. The unconscious mind [soul] tries to slip warnings or signposts to the conscious mind [ego] in the form of symbols. It knows the subconscious mind [perverted ego] will try to censor or block the conscious mind [ego] from recognising these warnings.

The subconscious [perverted ego] is full of all those unfulfilled needs and fears that run our lives and, in some ways, are borrowed or inherited from our families and other dark beings and entities. They stop us looking at our true feelings and the fears that lie buried deep within us. The symbols or signposts are usually charged with great feeling when they appear in a dream so we know to take note. They are a clue or key to unlock our unconscious mind [soul] so that it becomes part of our waking conscious life. No longer do we need to just analyse our dreams. Every moment is imbued with the possibility of connection with our unconscious mind [soul]. We can became like the indigenous peoples of old and feel a great connection to our inner self, to the natural world, to all humanity and to the Great Spirit, God.

I'll try to explain the difference between ego, spirit [perverted ego] and soul in more detail in a later chapter. But a simple way to look at ego [mind] is it is like a dog. If guided well by soul, it can be a very fulfilling relationship. Soul needs ego to play a specific role in this lifetime then discards it when it dies and moves onto its next reincarnation.

Chapter Fourteen

Spirit [perverted ego] tries to hook onto someone's ego and bend it to spirit's will and change ego's [mind's] karmic role in life and also try to maintain spirit's control from one reincarnation to the next. It does this by avoiding going to the light after death. Another analogy for spirit or perverted ego is a bucket of muddy water in between soul and ego trying to confuse ego [mind]. Spirit tries to block or censor any messages from soul.

Imagine you are looking at a stage with a dog sitting off to the left. It is waiting for guidance and reassurance from its master, soul, off to the far right. Master looks like a person made of white light. In between the dog [ego] and its master [soul] is a crowd of people [spirit, perverted ego] jostling each other and trying to take control of the group so their needs will be fulfilled. Dog can't see soul standing off to the right. Soul tries to guide and direct the dog but the crowd is in the way and they keep on shouting out their own commands to the dog. Dog tries to hear its master's instructions but is soon confused and obeying the crowd's loud and insistent demands. Ego, spirit, soul.

A History of Angels

Chapter Fifteen

THE FOUR HALLS OF THE DEAD

I asked Gabriel what happens to someone when they die? He said it is quite complicated on Earth because of interference by the gods. If you are unaligned to God you are vulnerable when you die. There are four main gods who try to convince you that they are either the 'one true god' or it's their job to claim you for God. They will try to lead you back to their Hall of the Dead so they can hang onto your soul after you reincarnate and slowly drain it like a battery or energy source.

The Angel of Death is one such being. She was also known as Anubis [the jackal-headed god in Egypt]. Hades of the Greek gods is another [also known as Pluto]. Genesha the elephant headed god of India is another. Jahweh of Old Testament fame, also known as Osiris of the Egyptian gods, is also a god who fooled the unsuspecting into believing he was 'the one god'.

All have Hall's of the Dead where they take you back and try to fool you into believing you are in the place you deserve to be. If you say 'no,' they have to release you to be claimed by angels. Believe me, the angels will come and get you and won't be denied. But everyone has the right to choose. Some people fear their karma and want to avoid the angels, they are usually the ones scooped up by the four gods of death. These halls can seem like heavenly places too. The gods try to supply what you think you deserve. If you think you are good, the hall looks heavenly, but if you are drawn to a darker place, they create that too. It's all an illusion, of course.

A History of Angels

In my original long vision I saw Gabriel visiting a hall of death and asking a powerful king to give Lucifer's soul back to him because Lucifer wanted to return to God. There were twenty evil looking warriors on each side of the king who leapt forward to slay Gabriel, but he just smiled and they all froze, their swords pointed at their own throats. They looked truly terrified. Gabriel told them, whatever they intended to do to him they would do to themselves. It was like a lesson in karma. The king was petrified with fear and instantly agreed to hand over Lucifer's soul. Gabriel said this king was Jahweh and he had fooled Lucifer when he was on Earth into believing he was 'the one god' so Lucifer naively handed his soul over to him.

I told Gabriel I saw tanks or pools of glowing water full of awful hellish fish and serpent-like creatures that filled the pools. Gabriel said this was hard to explain. The glowing pools were the stolen or trapped souls the god Jahweh was living off. He had deliberately placed beings in the pools who some people thought were guides and who turned to them in life for guidance. But it is their job to cut you off from your true self. These so-called guides [perverted ego] become your thoughts and feelings and lead you away from your true self. They exist in your subconscious. They also stop you from having the opportunity of true guidance between lifetimes by the Beings of Light.

Beings of Light will help prepare you for your next reincarnation on Earth and free you of the interference of these dark guides who want to keep you ignorant because they live off your life force, just as their boss does. As soon as you become aware that your soul is in the wrong place, all you have to do is ask for help from God. Someone like Gabriel will come and free you and take you back to where you should be and see that you are healed of the damage done by these parasitic beings who prey on the unwary.

This is also another reason why Beings of Light don't judge people when they are behaving badly. Often it's these same dark guides [perverted ego] who are completely running this person's life and slowly destroying any sense they might have of the true self trapped within. Sadly enough, this is most people on Earth.

Chapter Fifteen

This pooled water brought back vivid memories to me. I told Gabriel I had reoccurring dreams, always about four fish tanks, and how a person was worried they'd forgotten to feed the fish in the tanks and clean the water and glass, but everything seemed to be surviving anyway. As I grew older and went into that dark period in my life the fish became more aggressive and preyed on each other and only the hellish monstrous fish and serpents survived and grew very large and took up more space in the tanks. In recent years I've dreamt of empty fish tanks full of crystal clear water.

Gabriel said this was my soul trying to warn me that it had selves trapped in the four halls of death. These selves were full of dark guides who were keeping the different selves ignorant of my soul. But my longing to return to God was strong and Gabriel came and freed these selves from the four gods.

The fact that I seemed to be in all four halls of the dead confused me. I asked how was that possible? Gabriel laughed and said I'd become aware of an important fact. My soul, which has always been claimed by Beings of Light, realised it had no understanding what happens to other people who are claimed by the four gods of death. It allowed different selves it had created to be claimed after death by all four of these beings. I've even experienced returning to Valhalla, the halls for the dead warriors of the Germanic and Nordic peoples. When these people became Christian these halls slowly disappeared. My soul asked Gabriel to come and release my different selves from all these halls when I felt I had understood the experience of being part of them. He's kept an eye on me ever since.

THE KARMIC PLANES

Not all people who are unaligned to God are snared by these gods of death. Many who don't believe in the 'hereafter' and God are drawn into the realms of karma and given an opportunity to understand their negative habits and the fruitlessness of playing them out lifetime after lifetime.

A History of Angels

The brilliance of karma stuns me. When people, who don't believe in a 'hereafter,' die they find themselves waiting in a line of people at an airport terminal with their ticket and passport in hand. In the past this queue might have been at a train station, or a seaport, or caravan crossing the desert, or boat across a river.

The people in the queue think they are alive and well and their journey seems quite natural and right. Most will have blocked their recent death from their memory. If they were particularly perceptive they would notice that the people in their line were very similar to them. Say, for example, if someone was a ruthless corporate wheeler and dealer and multi-millionaire, this person would notice others very like themselves. They might even recognise someone they had known in real life who had died recently. An underworld hood or thief, for example, would be in a line full of thieves and hoods just like them. Even an extreme fundamentalist/religious person would be in a line of people as pious as themselves.

On the surface this would seem a wonderful thing. To be with people just like yourself. But this is where karma is brilliant. It is offering you a thousand mirrors of yourself so you can truly see and understand how a way of life that you've probably played out endlessly before is stopping you from listening to your true heart and soul and leading you farther down the fruitless and loveless path of perverted ego. I've listed a few varied paths perverted ego can take in life just as examples.

Let us return to the ruthless multi-millionaires. They fly out on a flight, in first class of course, heading to a luxury island resort. When they arrive, they are impressed by the beautiful resort with its white beaches, crystal clear swimming pool and large fashionable rooms full of modern conveniences. A sumptuous buffet is laid out, but there seems to be no staff. At first they take little notice, but these are people used to underlings jumping to their beck and call and they soon start to complain. Some are infuriated at the lack of service and decide to leave. But the aeroplane has gone. There is no way off the island. It dawns on them they

Chapter Fifteen

are stuck till the next flight. Some won't accept this and wander around the island fruitlessly looking for people and maybe a boat they can hire. But the only thing on the island is the resort and all the multi-millionaires.

These multi-millionaires have got where they are in life by being ruthless, unscrupulous and bullies. Now the only people to try to trick into giving them what they want are people just as cunning and ruthless as they are. Arguments and fights break out and all try to get their own way. Things begin to deteriorate badly on the resort. Washing piles up. There's no one to cook. The pool water turns slimy green. But everything the multi-millionaires need to survive is there for them. There is plenty of food and water and even cleaning products.

Some people adjust better than others. They begin to work together and cook meals and clean the rooms and wash their dirty laundry. These same people begin to notice how ugly some of the other multi-millionaires are in the way they get what they want. They try to make the more responsible ones their servants. The responsible ones refuse, of course. The more ruthless ones even gang together and try intimidation, beating and even murdering others.

The moment when things become truly ugly, some of the people begin to realise that they are no better than sophisticated thugs. Their perverted egos fooled them into believing that they were somehow better than everyone else and that others admired them and wanted to be like them. But what they see now is something so raw and ugly, it shocks them to their core. Some point this out to the others, but most refuse to see themselves in this light. These ruthless people want to destroy the more honest and perceptive ones so that they won't have to look at the truth about themselves.

A strange thing starts to happen. The perceptive ones find themselves on a flight off the island. They return home greatly changed and go to bed exhausted. When they next wake they have reincarnated back to Earth a lot wiser. They have distanced themselves from their perverted egos.

A History of Angels

What about the more ruthless ones left on the island? They create their own living hell of a 'dog eat dog world.' The resort has become a murderous battle zone between rivals for supremacy. The only thing that starts to make these people realise that all isn't as it should be is that murdered people keep returning healed and ready for revenge. In the end even the most pigheaded see how pointless their endless striving and bullying is. They just lie down exhausted and wait for death. They die and are reincarnate back to Earth.

Their perverted egos, which is what is driving these people to try to fulfil their needs the same way over and over, has taken a huge battering and these people usually have a world-weariness about them. This can be a moment in someone's life when their ego [mind], that has been possessed all this time, remembers its original role on Earth. You often see rich, famous and powerful people walk away from their old lives and live humble quiet ones, which was what their soul wanted from the start.

The recently dead thief mentioned earlier might arrive in a tough city with mean streets and alleyways full of gangsters. At first he or she will love the fact there are no police and they can get away with any crime and hang out with people just like themselves. But in this city there are no honest, defenceless, gullible people. Everyone is a predator on the prowl. The only people they can prey on are other thieves and thugs. Their world is suddenly very dangerous. Also no one is actually making or producing anything. Basics are in very short supply so competition is even fiercer. Life becomes one huge struggle. No one trusts anyone. Friends are willing to betray each other for short-term gain. You can see how people would soon tire of this, especially when they feel the pointlessness of it all. People they once admired don't seem like heroic outcasts of society anymore and are no better than dangerous self-serving children. These aware people are ready to reincarnate back to Earth as the rest pointlessly struggle on.

Why did I use deeply religious people as an example? These poor people can live lifetime after lifetime under an extreme perverted ego view that they will find some sort of

Chapter Fifteen

ever-lasting peace and be honoured by God by how severely they denied their heart and soul's more loving and softer view of life. They will be convinced they are sacrificing themselves to God, but are really sacrificing themselves to a Senior Fallen. These people arrive at a religious community full of the most pious people who compete to prove who is the most faithful and honoured by God. These so-called holy people are surprisingly harsh and extremely judgemental of each other. Any perceived lapse in ritual, dress and behaviour is attacked vehemently.

There are no people of so-called low moral character to focus on in this community. Only the righteous and pious live here. Life deteriorates into one big witch-hunt. These so-called loving people lack compassion for each other. Those judged are dealt with harshly, even executed, but keep returning even though they should be dead.

Some start to notice that there is an amazing lack of basic humanity in these extreme beliefs. This humanity is what makes life worth living. They seem to be turning their love for God into an excuse to control the thoughts and lives of others and never really have an honest look at how ruthless and ugly it has all become. The more perceptive might point this out and may be persecuted or even executed for their trouble. When they wake up they have reincarnated to Earth with a very different view of how to honour themselves and God.

If someone is always trying to play out the same identical character lifetime after lifetime, as Lucifer did as the heroic warrior, it's usually a sign they are possessed by a perverted ego. This is when soul is trapped in 'Groundhog Day' scenarios. Karma will deliberately set up situations that frustrate and exhaust the perverted ego so it will give up control, hoping ego [mind] and soul will know how to fulfil it. But once soul takes control it will distance ego [mind] from the perverted ego and teach ego how to recognise the difference between soul communicating with ego [mind], compared to perverted ego. Eventually perverted ego will look elsewhere for fulfilment. If a person asks for help from God these perverted egos are usually removed and destroyed.

GHOSTS

I asked Gabriel if there were ghosts and lost souls on Earth? Gabriel said, yes, far more than the living, especially in old cities. There are many quite accurate films and television shows about these lost spirits. *Sixth Sense,* a 1999 film starring Bruce Willis, as an example, was a very accurate film. Even the opportunity offered to the dead psychiatrist in the film to help the boy was accurate. Most ghosts are an example of perverted ego's [spirit's] attachment to a person, place or way of life and a complete refusal to let go of these things after death. This perverted ego, which has attached itself to soul by possessing ego [mind], may eventually be left behind to slowly fade away over many centuries. This happens especially if soul goes to the light after death where Beings of Light prepare it for its next reincarnation or to return to the God Realms. Once ego is discarded, the perverted ego has no hold on soul anymore.

The spirit or perverted ego [ghost] no longer has any real link to the soul and tries to maintain itself separately by living off the life force of the living, especially loved ones who are grieving. It is important to understand that this shadow of your lost loved one isn't really them. It's one of those parasitic collections of dark guides that make up the spirit that probably ran your loved one's life. Australian Aborigines move away or even burn down their home so the ghost has to move on. They also won't mention the deceased family member's name for over a year, then they have a ceremony to say goodbye.

If someone had a particularly violent or sudden death this person may be confused and believe they are still alive and wonder why everyone is ignoring them. These people usually don't believe in the hereafter. Also concern for a loved one may prompt a person to try to hang on after death or even out of a sense of guilt. Sadly these are forms of attachment and spirit's way of making the deceased exist in a sort of pointless void.

Chapter Fifteen

If a person let's go of life and allows angels to take them to where they are suppose to be, the angels will also help the deceased watch over their loved ones, but they won't interfere in karma. They also won't help the deceased become a parasite, which is what a ghost becomes. If you feel a loved one, or even a strange ghost around you, ask God to move this being on. Let angels sort out what's best for you and your family. Even if the ghost is trying to communicate with you, it's not always for as loving a reason as you might think.

THE WAY OF THE LIGHT

When Lucifer agreed to die he was drawn to the light. He woke in a hospital bed feeling very weary. His heart ached. His father Gabriel was standing at his bedside. Gabriel explained to his son that much damage had been done to Lucifer's heart by parasitic dark guides and that healers were going to repair it for him. Lucifer went into a sort of operating theatre where Beings of Light waited for him. As they worked on his heart, Lucifer felt the great love and compassion the healers had for him. He had a vision of a huge computer circuit board from horizon to horizon with an angel flying across disconnecting it from Lucifer's heart. The healers were disconnecting him from the negative programming the dark guides had put in place to cut him off from his true self and soul.

When Lucifer woke he was sitting in a huge hospital waiting area. He had a bandage around his chest and head. He noticed people being rushed in through a white light portal into emergency. Many of them had half their bodies missing. They were in great agony. Gabriel sat quietly next to him. He explained that dark beings had completely cut these poor people off from their lower halves by possessing ego, so they could live off their souls. Ego is our connection to Earth and the Lower Realms. It would take a while but angels would retrieve all that was lost of them so they could be made whole again.

A History of Angels

That night Lucifer had a vision of thousands of people all converging on the place where he was born. He realised they were all his different selves over many lifetimes and planes of existence all returning to be one within himself. He also noticed ex-lover's, especially The Devil, trying to hide amongst his different selves and sneak back inside him. But angels walked amongst the crowd and always spotted the intruders and took them away. The ex-lovers were very angry and abusive to the angels. For a while Lucifer felt like Frankenstein sewn all together with different human parts, but of course, it was just all his various selves merging.

When Lucifer felt better he was asked to return to his old high school. The classes were full of people Lucifer remembered from his warrior days. They were like cocky arrogant teenage boys hooked on the idea of being heroes. Lucifer had to take many different classes on compassion, karma, gratitude, non-attachment, loss, grief and sadness and how to transform all this into wisdom and self-love. He did well in them all except one class, which he failed endlessly; letting go of his attachment to being a warrior. He realised he had failed this same class over many lifetimes and if he didn't pass it this time he would have to reincarnate again, which he dreaded.

The other young guys in his class were pretty taken with Lucifer. They knew him by reputation. He also seemed more mature and wise. They noticed he never bragged and wandered off on his own if they started bragging. He sighed a lot in class when they gave cheek to the patient teachers and once walked out in disgust when a student threatened one of the teachers.

Lucifer sat in the courtyard feeling great despair. He felt trapped with these immature so-called heroes. Everything about them annoyed him. He even felt like bashing a bit of sense and respect into them. Couldn't they see how compassionate the teachers were being with them? The teachers could just let them reincarnate again, even though these same 'heroes' had asked for this help from God, just as he had.

Chapter Fifteen

Gabriel approached Lucifer as he sat lost in thought. Lucifer looked up at his father and realised he was ten years old again and sitting in his primary school uniform. He suddenly had the strongest déjà vu. He remembered this exact moment as a boy sitting alone at school. Gabriel had appeared to him and it was like time stopped and all the movement and noise of the schoolyard ceased. This was definitely a signpost moment. Gabriel lent down and smiled lovingly at his son.

"Do you remember this moment Lucifer, when I appeared to you at school and asked you if you wanted to be a warrior again?" Gabriel inquired.

Lucifer said, "I do father, and I said I was so sick of war and only wanted a peaceful life."

"And I said that you would have to have a lonely, humble life at first, where no one honours or admires you and you would probably die penniless, unloved, and even forget I'm your father. But no matter what, I'd always be by your side." Gabriel said with great sadness in his voice.

"I understand, father. I can't do this anymore. I'm truly sick of the way I've lived my lifetimes. I'm willing to have this unhappy life to be free of the grief that burdens my heart." Lucifer said, with great conviction and sounding far wiser than his ten years of age.

Gabriel felt so proud of his son in that moment. He realised this karmic loop or 'Ground Hog Day' that Lucifer was stuck in was finally coming to an end.

Time means nothing to Beings of Light. They can bring you back to the exact moment, if you truly desire it, that led you down the perverted ego path and offer you another chance to choose again. Remember it's all an illusion anyway; life, death, the whole thing. In this moment Lucifer was free of it all and returned to God.

This is the beauty of choosing the path of light when you die. Any regret, any wrong that you feel needs to be righted, you'll be given the chance to do so. That's why I said the opportunity offered to the psychiatrist in the film *Sixth Sense* was quite accurate. His heart, his soul couldn't find peace till he righted a wrong he believed he had committed,

A History of Angels

so the Beings of Light helped him. Like Lucifer, he wasn't aware that he'd already died when he made that choice to return and help the boy. He wasn't allowed to interfere in the life of his widow though.

People ask what happens when you die. As you can see someone you love and trust, who's chosen the path of light, will be there to meet you and be your guide. Your surroundings will be familiar and reassuring. The hospital was something Lucifer recognised as a place of healing, and his old school a place of learning.

Chapter Sixteen

EGO
[Conscious Mind – Lower Self – Primal Self]

Ego is a like a primal animal made from the Void. It is pre-programmed by karma to help soul play a role on Earth. It allows soul to experience what it is like to be human and part of the Lower Realms. Human beings are just sophisticated animals running on base, primal, survival instincts. This is our lower self. When we die, ego is absorbed back into the Void because soul doesn't need it anymore. Ego was never meant to be a permanent entity. Karma will choose for soul a new persona, a new role, for its next existence.

In Buddhism they believe if we just run on primal instinct, on survival mode, on fear and attachment, we will reincarnate back as an animal. I asked Gabriel about this. He said, that there was no need to reincarnate back as an animal because a person just living on pure survival mode, the path of ego, was already an animal.

The path of survival also makes us competitive and when we run on this energy we stop listening to our heart and soul. Ego is attached to the idea that things outside itself in life will make it happy. It even views love like that. To ego it has to possess, own and control the object of its desires. It makes ego ruthless and competitive. This attachment to the idea that controlling or possessing the object of its desire causes nearly all its suffering. Also it makes ego goal-based. Meaning it is always trying to achieve gaols that it thinks will finally make it happy, but that happiness is allusive. It is always in the future or just around the corner.

A History of Angels

While I was writing this chapter I visited my neighbour Frank. We sat on his doorstep and he told me he was feeling very unhappy and confused. I said to Frank that he reminded me of a beautiful old tree whose roots sank deep into the earth and branches reached far into the sky. It hit a real note with him. I felt his beautiful wise soul delving deep into the suffering of this world and the rich fruit of wisdom he was bringing forth from it. I said there is this mythical animal in Dr. Doolittle that has a head at both ends and is always trying to go two different ways at once, so ends up going nowhere. It is called the 'Push-me-pull-you.' I said that is your ego and soul with two very different ideas about how to find happiness from the same things. And that the turmoil he was going through at the moment was a very special moment [a signpost moment] when you are aware of the struggle going on within, to see if you follow either ego [mind] or soul.

We walked around the back of his house so I could borrow his mower. He has a muscly eager young dog, named Tiger, who was so excited to see us he jumped all over us, scratching us and knocking us over. He then started banging into our shins with a stick so we'd throw it for him. Frank had a world-weary look about him as he refused to throw the stick unless Tiger would let go of it first and not try to snatch it back, biting our fingers. He told him to sit down and wait for us to throw the stick. When we threw it, Tiger would tear off after it and smash into things breaking them and hurting himself in his eagerness to fetch it. He'd then race back and smash into our shins again so we'd throw it again. I quickly learnt to fend him off with my foot and made Tiger obey the rules Frank had laid down for him, before I threw it again.

You can't help but love Tiger, he's such a happy dog and would do anything for your attention. Watching him I had another signpost moment. I noticed how Tiger looked like a little demon when he wanted something. If you asked him to tear a child to pieces he'd do it, if he thought you'd give him attention. It wouldn't even cross his mind that it was a horrible crime. He just wouldn't understand what was upsetting everyone as long as you were pleased.

Chapter Sixteen

I also saw how Tiger's obsession with us throwing the stick for him was just like ego and its goals. No matter how many times we threw it, Tiger was never satisfied and just wanted more.

I saw how big intelligent gentle Frank was soul and Tiger was his ego [mind] and soul and ego loved to have a relationship together but it only worked if soul set ground rules and boundaries for ego. Ego is very much apart of nature. It is a wild lovable animal but, as in the wild, utterly ruthless about getting what it feels it needs to survive and where life wasn't so complicated. You lived where you trusted your instincts and your fears were very real and you were equipped to face them.

Animals accept death as an everyday possibility. They have to kill to survive, there's a sort of ruthless purity to it. They also expect no compassion or pity from any other animal. In civilisation there are numerous rules that have to be adhered to just to get the slightest bit of acceptance into a very large and complex pack of egos that is the modern world.

When our soul decides to incarnate to Earth it needs this wild little animal called ego to help it truly understand what it is like to be human. Humans are part of nature. All indigenous cultures understand that. We are just another complex and successful animal and very much part of this world. When we are at our most primal we are solely about survival. This is the little psychopath in us all. It is just like Tiger the dog. But soul can offer this little animal in us a very rewarding and loving experience, which it has never experienced before. It can feel part of something bigger, more eternal, more fulfilling and free itself of this endless quest to cheat death and come out on top in the food chain.

But if the ego runs the show the soul is enslaved to ego's ignorant and primal ideas of fulfilment. We see it with celebrities all the time, especially when they first become famous and ego takes over. They turn into selfish ruthless children and use everyone around them for their own pleasure. But life becomes very empty and unfulfilling for these people and they start to feel lonely, unloved and used by the people around them. But this feeling comes from their soul. It feels prostituted to the ruthless and childish needs of ego. Ego will turn to soul like a naughty child and demand love. Soul won't give it unless ego starts to respect soul. Ego may turn to drugs, sex, gambling, anything that fulfilled it in the past. But soul is not there to enjoy it with ego this time and it all feels empty and worthless. Many people feel suicidal in this moment. It's their ego realising it is incapable of fulfilling itself. Ego could go back to running on pure primal survival again but it has had a taste of nirvana now, of the Holy Grail. The old primal ways aren't fulfilling anymore.

Many people turn to religion or holy people at this moment to give them this nirvana, peace and fulfilment. It doesn't work, even though for a while it felt good to be around people who respect their souls. But ego doesn't want to give in to its own soul, it wants to keep control, so it looks for someone with soul to give it to them. Ego will look for a lover with soul and hope to control this person and have access to their soul or even have children for the same reason. This is why Gabriel said Earth is a vampire planet. The very nature of ego is to feed off another to survive. That's why relationships are so complicated and full of suffering and heartbreak on Earth. Our egos don't want soul running the show. They want to feel loved and still be the boss.

I was a member of a club once. At this club there was a woman who nearly tore the club apart because she wasn't getting her own way. She even tried to change the laws of the club in the hope of getting her own way. The club was once a lovely collection of friends. This woman had to stand down as president and felt hurt and confused that people were rude to her and didn't listen to her. I sat with her once at a meeting and was shocked at how she spoke to people and ordered them around and how surprised and angry she was that they would ignore her or bitch about her behind her back. Her husband had had enough and left her after thirty years of marriage. She was devastated. She couldn't understand why life was so cruel. She had no idea she had created her woes. I felt very sad for her. That's ego for you,

Chapter Sixteen

a terrible master, but a lovely servant. Ego has no self-reflection or self-awareness. It is just a cunning and pushy animal willing to do anything to get what it wants and can end up very lonely, especially as it grows older.

PERVERTED EGO
[Spirit – Subconscious – Collective of Dark Entities – Ghost]

Remember the story of the Scorpion and the Fox? The Scorpion asked the Fox to let it ride on his back when it swam across a river. But the Fox was very reluctant. He said, "You'll just sting me and I'll die." The Scorpion said, "That would be crazy, if I sting you while you are carrying me across the river, I'll drown." The Fox saw the sense in that so he let the Scorpion climb on his back and began to swim, but about half way across the river, the Scorpion stung the Fox. The shocked and dying Fox asked, "Why did you sting me, we are both going to die now?" As they sank beneath the water the Scorpion replied, "Because that's my nature!"

What is a Perverted Ego? When a soul incarnates to Earth it is given an ego so it can play a role on Earth. But the Lower Realms were created by powerful beings known as Senior Fallen. To maintain their existence here, without returning to God, they have to steal other living beings' life forces. As mentioned in the story of the Atlantians, Senior Fallen like the Empress of the Spiderpeople, create entities, which they place on other living beings so they can drain their life force.

When a soul first comes to Earth it only has the ego karma gave it. The Senior Fallen wait and watch what strong needs and attachments someone develops while here. Senior Fallen attach to your ego a collection of dark entities, which are like hungry ghosts that heighten or exaggerate these needs. The strong negative emotions created by these attachments and needs create addictions and suffering which feed the dark entities, which in turn feed the Senior Fallen. The more obsessed a person becomes with fulfilling these attachments, the more they commit or invest their soul energy into the fulfilment of them. The more they invest, the more the Senior Fallen vampire away, until this person's soul will be completely possessed and absorbed into the Senior Fallen and no longer exists.

Have you heard of 'the carrot and the stick' analogy. In medieval times they used to tie a stick above a donkey's head. From the stick would dangle a carrot on a string before the donkey's eyes, and out of reach. The donkey would be spurred on by the prospect of eating the carrot to greater and greater efforts, but to no avail. He'd exhaust himself for nothing. Perverted ego does that to soul.

When I worked for the Justice Department many of the offenders were heroin addicts. I sadly noted over time, many of them became like empty shells, all the soul went out of their eyes. These unfortunate people would be completely possessed by these dark entities. Their whole reason for living was only to fulfil this addiction. Their soul would disappear and only this dark collection of entities would be left, which is what Gabriel calls a spirit, perverted ego or subconscious.

Have you ever known someone who is a lovely person until they drink alcohol? It's like their whole personality changes. That is the dark entities taking over and aggressively pushing this person to fulfil this addiction in an extreme way and maybe other dark desires while drunk also; like violence, or to have sex in a degrading way. The dark entities feed off the guilt, remorse and self-hatred the poor person feels the next day. They may even try to drive the person to suicide, so that the Senior Fallen can claim their soul while they feel they don't want to exist anymore.

When hypnotising or regressing people, therapists often tap into the collective memories of these dark entities that make up the subconscious mind [perverted ego]. These memories won't always match any experience your mind [ego] or soul has had. Someone could have therapy for many lifetimes and never be closer to understanding what true memories the mind and soul share.

The subconscious [perverted ego] would love all the focus and re-enforcement of itself as your true mind that all this

Chapter Sixteen

therapy would give it, which is why some people come away very unfulfilled by therapy and no closer to their true inner self. It would help the subconscious take over from your true ego [mind] and make you only listen to it.

Soul might recognise that its ego has been completely taken over or possessed by these entities. Soul may choose to end its life here early, return to the light and so discard the perverted ego along with its ego. The perverted ego becomes a ghost and will look for another host or soul to maintain its existence on Earth, otherwise it fades away over time. When soul reincarnates back to Earth, it is more aware and able to cope with the influences of these dark entities now. Buddhists call this detachment from your desires. This detachment allows soul to have choice in life and not become a puppet for the Senior Fallen. But some souls are more attracted to attachment than others and love losing themselves in the illusion of the Lower Realms. They are the ones who fall prey to the Senior Fallen.

The story of Frank and Tiger shows you the straightforward relationship between ego and soul. But when the perverted ego becomes a factor a person's life becomes very complicated. So how did the demise of Lucifer and the Devil come about? When they fell they both had very immature ideas of how to be happy. This immature self became their ego. The Senior Fallen take note of a person's needs and see if they can exploit them for their own gains. Lucifers need to be the heroic warrior was something that the Senior Fallen used as a way of possessing his ego and perverting it to their will in the hope he'd become their puppet and tool. But once Lucifer tired of being the heroic warrior he stopped listening to the spirit or perverted ego that actually made him Lucifer. He actually listened to his karmic ego, which was humble Tom. No longer was the spirit of Lucifer [the perverted ego] able to have its needs fulfilled by him. Tom was following his heart and his soul now.

The Devil, on the other hand, was unwilling, like Lucifer, to go back to school and get help so she could let go of her need for others to fulfil her emptiness. This meant that the Senior Fallen who possessed her was able to exploit this need and eventually absorb her into itself. That's karma at work also. The Devil wouldn't give up her need to possess others so she was eventually possessed and absorbed herself.

One night I went to a pub on my own to see a band play. I felt Gabriel's presence very strongly. It was like I viewed the room and people in it as Gabriel would see it. There were about two hundred people present, but most of them were just like shadows or ghosts. Only three people stood out to me. There was a shy girl who seemed out of place in the pub, but her soul shone so bright. I realised she must be one of these 'tourist' angels Gabriel mentioned before. The other two looked more worldly, cynical and smoked and drank heavily. They also had bright souls but it was like they were shrouded in thin black cloth. They were Fallen.

When I went home I kept thinking about all the people who were like ghosts. Doesn't everyone have a soul? I asked Gabriel about this.

He said, that most humans on Earth were created by the Senior Fallen, the original creators of these realms. Humans were created for a specific role that in some way serves their creator. All these beings rely on stealing life force from others to make up for the lack of a soul they have. They would be attracted to crowds, large sporting events and concerts, rallies and parades, or even going off to war, anywhere where there is mass emotion. This gives them a sense of having a soul. They also look for people with soul and try to have relationships with them so they can fill their emptiness. They are also tools to feed their original creators.

These soulless people, and ones who have had their soul drained away by a perverted ego, envy people with a soul. It makes them very hateful and destructive. This is where the Scorpion and the Fox story comes in. There is a sort of pointlessness to their existence. They may even hate God, thinking it is his fault. This also makes them self-destructive and attracts them to addictions, violence and self-hatred. They can also have a sense of wanting to have vengeance against the world, because it has been so cruel to them. These are the people Jesus and Buddha wanted to help and free from enslavement to the dark desires of their creators.

Chapter Sixteen

Soulless people are only ego with a perverted spirit in place of a soul. It is the very nature of ego to end; it is no different for perverted egos, except perverted egos would like to take a soul with it. The Scorpion [perverted ego] tricking the Fox [soul] into trusting it and then killing it so it would drown in the river [the Void] and, in so doing, destroying itself, is exactly what the perverted ego desires to do. If perverted ego succeeds in fooling you into destroying yourself, through attachment [to be absorbed by a Senior Fallen], it dies with you.

Why doesn't God doing something about this awful situation, you may ask? Well, God is. All the Senior Fallen were at first being forced to have another self incarnated to Earth to share in humanity's suffering, in the hope they might learn compassion for those they created. But sadly these selfish beings haven't learnt by it. So God is now phasing out their powerful god-like selves and making them exist only as average people on Earth. All the Realms they created are being taken over by God so people can live out their existences here as long as they desire to or be helped to leave and join the God Realms.

Just in case I've confused you with all these different definitions for the three aspects 'ego' 'spirit' and 'soul' discussed above, I'd like to list all the different names I've used below in three columns.

Ego	**Spirit**	**Soul**
Conscious mind	Subconscious mind	Unconscious mind
Lower self	Possessed	Higher self
Mind	Dark entities or guides	True self
Primal Self	Perverted ego	
	Collective of dark entities	
	Ghost	

A History of Angels

Chapter Seventeen

LOVE

Gabriel said it was about time we spoke of one of the most misunderstood words in the English language: Love. It is a word that strikes a deep note with all humanity but is also, like the word God, one of the most misused words. The word 'Love' is used to sell everything from Jesus Christ to pornography or even chocolate. People will even say they murdered a loved one out of love, because the loved one left them and they couldn't live without them. Most Beings of Light believe humanity has no real understanding of love. With parents and lovers it is a frequently used to mean 'if you do exactly what I say, when I say it, then you truly love me and I may love you in return.' On Earth we call this 'conditional love'. Beings of Light would say there's no love in it. Most people believe God's love is conditional. If I say and do the right thing, God will give me what I want.

I'm going to break love down into three sections: Ego's idea of love, Soul's idea of love, and God's idea of love.

EGO

I don't want you to think Beings of Light look upon Ego as evil. That would be a complete misunderstanding of the relationship between Soul and Ego. Ego is born out of a very tough environment and, as explained in the last chapter, is all about the survival and continuation of the species. Ego is eternally looking for security and for a mate. These are often one and the same thing. Nearly everything about humanity is driven by a primal desire to attract a suitable mate; what we wear, what car we drive, what we do, how we speak in public, our need for money, even to own a nice home.

We do this by appearing as attractive as possible, by looking good, being successful, sexy, famous, wealthy and powerful. A house, car, money and a good job are all symbols of our capacity to support and protect a mate. They represent ego's primal needs. In this sense it is just like any other animal on Earth.

That we've made the whole game very complicated doesn't change the driving force behind what motivates us. In a way Dr. Sigmund Freud's theories were based on the fact that humans are driven by the most basic urges from the moment they are born. They are nurtured by their mothers, then by their fathers and as adults want these same basic needs met. If our parents abandon us when we are babies, we die. Most people carry through to adulthood a great primal fear about being abandoned.

A baby needs to bond with its parents very early to ensure they don't desert it. This is when humans, and animals first psychically 'tap' into someone and try to make them meet their most basic needs to survive. The easiest way to do that is by making someone love you. But also the parents feel the need of the baby within themselves, which often transforms them into a softer and more vulnerable person. Many people, even the most hardened, can change drastically, especially emotionally, with the arrival of a baby. Suddenly all the parents' attention is on the wellbeing of the child. When this happens it means the baby has successfully bonded with its parents by a psychic chord. Many mothers are very aware of this chord.

Via this psychic cord babies take on the parents' fears and desires. It helps the baby know what it needs to avoid in life that my harm it, or what may fulfil its needs. It's a sort of osmosis. It's what gives humanity a survival edge over other animals. My mother has an intense fear of the water, which I carried with me until I was a teenager. As an adult I realised I love the water.

When a baby doesn't bond with one of its parents, we see the sad opposite. Say the mother had a particularly hard

Chapter Seventeen

labour and birth. She may even have nearly died giving birth, so had to face incredible pain, fear and even death because of the baby. So to the mother's ego, the baby nearly killed her. The mother may fear the baby now and won't let the baby bond with her. Also the father may be used to the mother, his lover, fulfilling his most basic needs to feel loved and secure, like his mother did. He may feel that the baby has stolen this attention away from him and will feel abandoned and, out of this primal fear, will refuse to bond with the baby also. On the same line of thought, especially if the baby is a girl, the mother may feel abandoned by the father when he bonds with his daughter. So from these simple examples you can see that the dynamics of a family may be anything but harmonious. But this story is common and is the way of this world.

We all want someone to give us the love and security we looked to our parents to provide. Most people did not bond with at least one of their parents. In macho societies the father is often a dominant, harsh, bullying character, especially to the son who is usurping his wife's love. The son then looks to other men to fill the void created by lack of fatherly love and will form close male friendships to make up for this loss. The son would literally kill for his friends because he has such great need for their love and support. These sort of men are attracted to the armed services, to street gangs, sporting clubs, bars, boys' schools, monasteries, anywhere women aren't welcome.

Often such men have a loving, long-suffering mother whom they respect and love above all others because she fulfilled their most basic need for survival. They would kill for her if they had to. So this macho male respects mothers and hates fathers. When this young man becomes interested in girls, he might treat the girl badly as a way of showing his friends that their love and respect is more important to him than the girl's is. He will probably dominate and bully this girl as long as he has his mother's love.

All this changes when such a man gets married and his wife falls pregnant. Suddenly she too is a mother. Naturally his real mother, who felt unloved by her macho husband

and looked to her son to fill the void, feels threatened. The daughter-in-law is usurping her place with her son, so she tries to cause trouble between him and his wife. If this child is a son, the macho guy will in turn feel threatened and the whole circle will start all over again.

This type of man thinks he can only keep his wife by dominating her and putting her down [just as his father did to his mother], although he relies on her for love and support. He takes it very badly if his wife leaves him. He needs her to be the heart he ignores within himself. He thinks it's a sign of weakness to acknowledge his feelings and is afraid of risking the loss of his male friends' respect, even to the extreme of murdering his wife to save face. The sad drama is all set up to play out again with the newest member of the family. If it's a boy the mother will turn to him for the love she craves from her husband. If it's a girl she may feel usurped by the daughter in her husband's affections.

With a dominant mother the dynamics are nearly the same. Such a woman would undermine and bully her husband and feel threatened by a daughter. She would even bully her and turn her into a dominant wife one day who, like the macho male, will bond closely with female friends to make up for the lack of love from her mother. She also needs the love and support of her husband and would become very destructive if he left her. Both male and female dominant partners would feel their very survival is at risk if abandoned by their partners or by the child they have turned to for love and support.

A Being of Light would ask, where is the love in any of this? Ego would be thrilled to find someone to make it feel as loved and secure as it was as a baby. It would be prepared to sacrifice anything to keep this and would fall into agonising despair if the object of its desire rejects it or is enticed away by rival.

The euphoria we feel when we think we've found someone to fulfil our desires is ego's idea of love. It completely ignores soul at this point, even discards it, because it thinks it has found someone it can manipulate into giving it what it wants. Ego will be very possessive and jealous of the love

Chapter Seventeen

of this person and will guard them against all rivals and even drive off their friends. It will try to bind the other to itself either by dominating them or enslaving itself to them. When ego is completely focused on the object of its desires it ignores the promptings of its heart and soul. This is the moment when any true love is sacrificed to the need for security and control. When love, desire and intimacy disappear, disillusionment sets in.

As the years go by, a great world-weariness can fall on this person. They may even start to age drastically and their health may fail. They might feel all their dreams have come to nothing, that their partner has failed to fulfil their desires, even though they sacrificed everything to be with them. They may feel deeply depressed, or even suicidal. Ego knows it invested everything it had into this one hope of happiness and fulfilment but it failed and is exhausted. Should it leave this partner and risk being alone? Should it look for a new person to fulfil its desires? Does this sound familiar to you?

These scenarios represent what many people hope for from God. When they fail to find fulfilment in their parents, lovers or children, they turn to God to fulfil their needs. Some try to enslave themselves [sacrifice] to what ego thinks God wants, [which is what we see in extreme religious practices]. Others might go as far as to murder people in God's name, or try to dominate others as a religious leader in the hope that this will give them some sort of control over God.

SOUL

The key word for Soul's idea of love is 'intimacy'. Soul loves an intimate relationship with God, with mind [ego] and with other living beings. That's the reason for its existence. Intimacy is the most misunderstood part of relationships. Ego despises it because it means a willingness to expose oneself to the scrutiny of soul, God and other living things. It makes ego very uncomfortable. Its very survival is threatened by it, especially if it is one of these perverted egos that only exist by fooling others into giving it what it wants. But our true ego, mind, loves the joy of self-discovery with soul, which also offers ego a connection to God. It gives mind a taste of the infinite and all its limitless possibilities. Mind is like a child in a lolly shop, excited by so many choices, when before it only had the narrow road of basic survival.

Often in my art I paint hundreds of eyes all over an object to symbolise the beautiful mind-expanding moments when we are able to view soul and God through the mirror of mind. Soul and God aren't self-reflective by nature, they just 'are'. That's why the relationship between mind, soul, and God is so fulfilling and hints at the reason for our very existence. We are reflections and extensions of God, just as mind is to soul. As in a hall of multifaceted mirrors, we and God, mind and soul, reflect each other infinitely.

But mirrors are cold; mind, soul and God feel. This feeling adds great depth and perception to any experience. This is what enriches us and why we exist, why soul is willing to come down and be part of such a painful and limited experience as life on earth. Soul and God find the challenges here very rewarding; so does mind. In order to become intimate with God, you need to listen to your feelings. This connects you to your soul. Your feelings are your soul's eyes, ears, touch and smell. They are the bridge between this world and God. When an angel speaks to you, he or she hears you through their heart and, because of this, understands what it is you are truly trying to say and how honest you are being.

Soul knows its own feelings. It helps mind know what it really wants and what it seeks to express in the world. Soul lives purely in the moment. It can sense possible outcomes to any of its desires and also outcomes from decisions forced on it by ego. It can decide whether it wants to be part of some action, or not, pull out of the body if unhappy, or, out of curiosity, support ego for a while in its quest.

Soul is willing to try anything once, just for the experience. It has a sort of naive innocence and Beings of Light monitor it so they can warn it that a particular choice might hold a dangerous and unforeseen trap. Gabriel pointed out to me that most young souls in human form are in relationships with very negative people. Soul is curious about what

Chapter Seventeen

makes these dark ego people tick. Also the dark ego person may be trying to recapture the sense of wonder, love of life and innocence it used to feel. One could say this is a true marriage of opposites. It could explain why some very nice people go out with such obvious arseholes. Curiosity.

When soul meets a person also full of soul, it finds that person very attractive. It sees in this other soul an opportunity to be able to express itself openly and honestly. Incredible desires well up within it that were unfulfilled while it had relationships with ego-based people. Ego-based people aren't the least bit interested in intimacy and truly getting to know and share with soul. They only want soul to fill its own emptiness. Gabriel said it is very common for women and some men to feel strongly attracted to him when they meet him in human form or ethereal body because of such unfulfilled desires. These souls feel they've finally found another soul who will acknowledge their existence, and may even be intimate with them.

One of the hardest things for a person to accept when existing in the Lower Realms and Earth is that we don't always get what we want. Can we accept that someone we love loves another? Great disillusionment can come from this situation. I once asked a girlfriend if she could love me if I lived overseas? She said yes. Could she love me if I was sick, disfigured or handicapped in someway? She said yes, and I believed her. I asked her if she could still love me if I loved another woman? Her face went very dark, brooding and angry. She said she couldn't love me if that happened. I asked her if that was true love then?

Do we only love those who give us what we want? This is the question Gabriel asked of me. He was trying to show me love without attachment. We can become obsessed with the fulfilment of our heart's desire and invest more and more of our energy into trying to capture and control the object of them. This is the road of ego and causes our soul great suffering. We learn greater love and compassion for ourselves and others the moment we accept that our dreams and desires may not be fulfilled in this lifetime. I remember my darkest hour when I felt completely thwarted in every attempt to fulfil my creative and romantic dreams. I started to have suicidal thoughts. I couldn't think of one reason to go on living. Life seemed so pointless and joyless.

I then heard a voice in my head asking if someone could find peace in a concentration camp. At the time there were very harrowing films showing the horror of the Jewish Holocaust. It raised many questions in me. Someone could become very disillusioned with God and humanity in such a situation. I realised if one could accept and see it as an opportunity for soul to experience powerlessness and horror and not look to try and control the situation, a person could still be at peace with themselves, humanity and God. To me this would be a Buddha moment. We learn more by not getting the object of our desires. If we accept this we are truly free.

When souls are attracted to Gabriel they may be very disappointed that he can't have a romantic relationship with them. Soul has to make a choice. Do I reject Gabriel because he is not giving me what I want or do I accept the love he is truly offering? This is the same question soul asks of itself with God. Do I reject God and life because I'm not getting what I want, or do I accept what is being offered and find true peace and happiness? Ego loves the idea, for example, that God, Gabriel, Jesus, Buddha or a lover, will finally fill its emptiness by fulfilling all its desires, not unlike Santa Claus or the Genie from Alladin.

So returning to the point when our soul meets another also full of soul. What if this person is already in a relationship which it is unwilling to end or compromise? Usually karma sets this impossible situation up so that ego can't get attached to the object of its desires. This is an opportunity for soul to love this person without attachment. Ego can't accept this. A tug-of-war begins between soul and ego. Ego will try to think of a way of winning this person and is willing to pay any price.

If soul wins it will become more aware of its suppressed desires and feelings. It realises it no longer needs to fulfil these desires to find inner peace and happiness. It will start to view itself and the world in a completely different way.

Chapter Seventeen

Where once ego viewed the world hungrily, always looking for possibilities to fulfil its desires but was continually thwarted and bitter with God, life and humanity, soul now knows peace. It will be willing to feel everyone around it and itself. It will truly become aware again. At first it may be shocked at what it sees with new clarity in people it thought it loved and couldn't live without. It may notice a lack of real love or intimacy. These people may need this soul but don't really know it, or want to get close to it, as long as it is there for them when they call.

Consequently soul begins to re-evaluate its relationship with itself and others. People may be hurt that this soul isn't willing to play the game by their rules anymore. Some will even become abusive and ugly and show their true nature as a nasty little ego willing to do anything to keep the object of its needs and desires. Soul doesn't want to hurt anyone but can no longer pretend it finds any true love or fulfilment in the situation. Soul realises it would rather be alone than compromise itself anymore.

Ego will be terrified to let go of attachments it thinks it needs to survive. Soul will ignore ego and know it is truly safe and fulfilled because it is listening to itself. It can see threats clearly now and also see which paths ahead are loving choices, even if they don't look like it to ego. Soul is on the road to true love and intimacy with itself, God and the world. Now when soul meets someone it will be able to read this person's heart and know their true intentions.

Ego's choices are so limited. It always turns to what it knows to survive, no matter how negative and unloving. Soul is always willing to embrace the unknown and find alternative paths to explore in life. Such courage is true love for the self. Soul won't accept a negative situation unless there is some lesson in it that it wants to explore and understand. Otherwise it will pack up and leave.

When soul meets someone it loves it will be honest and straightforward with this person about how it feels. This person may be surprised and put-off by such a direct approach, especially if their ego is in charge. It will feel threatened by this straight-forwardness. Soul doesn't mind if

A History of Angels

the object of its desire doesn't feel the same way, it just feels good to be honest and express itself to this person. It knows it has honoured its true feelings in that moment and feels fulfilled.

Powerful people in the world fear those who stand-up for what they believe in and defend what they love, fiercely and fearlessly. They don't fear death, only not honouring their heart. It's the most fulfilling way to live, no matter how short or brutal their life. This is what makes angels so courageous. The only thing they fear is not following their heart. Dark beings try to confuse soul about how it feels and manipulate it by what it loves. Soul doesn't feel emotions, that's what ego feels within the mind and these emotions are easily manipulated by dark beings and other egos. Emotions stifle your feelings and stop you having any insight about yourself, about life and those around you. You feel lost and alone in the dark. You miss the clarity and love of your soul, the direction and leadership it gives, and also your purpose for existing.

This is why the relationship with soul is the most loving relationship you can have. It is far more important than finding the romantic love of your life. You can't truly enjoy that relationship anyway without your soul being involved. It's like a blind person being given the most rare and beautiful painting. I don't know how I ever existed before I felt close to my soul. I feel loved and secure. I don't feel like I need anyone to make me happy as I used to, but I'll certainly enjoy my next relationship. It will have a clarity, intimacy and love about it I haven't felt for a long time. And when it ends, and it will end, I'll feel blessed by the experience and the opportunity to truly know another soul.

Chapter Eighteen

GOOD and EVIL

Good and Evil, like Love, are misunderstood concepts on Earth. There is ego's idea of Good and Evil and there is soul's idea. It is interesting that people in this age are confused about what they believe in and whether it is right or wrong. Where once we followed our leaders blindly and church and state worked together to rule all facets of our lives, people have felt betrayed by the many disastrous wars over the last century that accomplished little but death and suffering. Both sides saw themselves as Right and Good and their opponents as Wrong and Evil.

We are seeing in the U.S.A. at the moment young men and women going off to fight in Iraq in what many believe to be a holy war. The right wing fundamentalist Christians and people of the Bible Belt areas in America believe that Iraq had something to do with the September 11 suicide bombings of the Twin Towers, even though their own C.I.A. experts have said that Iraq had nothing to do with it. So these well meaning young people, who want to protect their loved ones and country, go off to war in Iraq to fight terrorists.

But when they arrive they see that the population of Iraq is being subjected to far worse terrorism than America ever was. Scores of innocent people are killed every day in bombings. Young soldiers are blown up by unseen enemies and shot at by assailants hiding in civilian areas. When they shoot back they inadvertently kill the innocent civilians they thought they were there to protect. Many Iraqis blame them for all their woes. Because of the Allied war in Iraq Islamic Fundamentalists from other countries are using Iraq as a battle zone. They see the Western Alliance as evil and are prepared to kill Western and local people alike in the name of God. These so-called terrorists are willing to die for God or kill for God. They believe their cause is just, that America is evil and the world needs to be free of its dominance.

When young soldiers return home to America they are seriously disturbed by the horror they have witnessed and were a part of and understandably they feel very disillusioned. What was it all for?

Nothing I've said here is new. Australia and Britain have troops in Iraq even though 80 percent of the population of both countries were against the war. Troops were sent regardless by leaders who felt they knew better. It was the same with the Vietnam War for American and Australia. For Russians it was the war in Afghanistan. The Russians were told they were there to help their communist comrades in their time of need but in the end the soldiers felt no better than terrorists.

In World War One, soldiers on both sides were told they were right and God was with them. But what was it all really about? Was it worth the loss of twenty million or more people? When the crusaders went to the Holy Land they were told by the Pope that killing Muslims wasn't murder. They arrived and slaughtered a whole town of Christians by mistake because they looked like local Muslims. They were also shamed by how truly honourable the enemy leader Saladdin was and how merciful he could be to the defenceless, even though he was a great warrior and a Muslim.

EGO

Ego has a very different idea of Good and Evil to soul. Our whole concept of Good and Evil is an ego concept and essentially an illusion. It is an Us and Them idea. Ego thinks anything is evil that threatens its security and survival. It can justify any act, no matter how brutal, if it feels threatened, even if this attack takes the form of someone contradicting or undermining a belief system it lives by, however wrong

Chapter Eighteen

or ludicrous their belief system might be. Ego is savage in driving off or destroying this threat because its survival and control over its soul is based on this illusion. You don't need a set of strict rules to guide your life if you follow soul and your heart. But ego does. It gives it a sense of control over itself and its environment.

Ego can only operate with what it knows. It isn't creative or adventurous. You see this in the wild with certain animals that have a particular environment and food source. Any sort of change to either can be catastrophic. Many egos are like this. They aren't equipped for change. They are attracted to strict moral and religious codes where all facets of their lives and those around them are controlled. Other egos are like rats. They can survive anywhere and come out on top no matter how catastrophic a situation. These egos see the misery of others as an opportunity to get ahead, to prosper.

In Germany in the late 1930s people were angry at the way France and Britain had bankrupted them after WWI Germans lived through such a terrible economic depression they felt their very survival as a race threatened. Then Hitler and the Nazi party emerged. Many of the unemployed soldiers from the war joined the party. Hitler gave them a reason for their woes; France, Britain and the Jews. Suddenly the German people had something to focus their fear and powerlessness on. The rest is history.

Most Germans thought what they did was just. There were those, however, who saw the horrific treatment of the Jews, the loss of free speech and invasion of other countries as wrong. These people prophesised a disastrous outcome for Germany. Many of them ended up in the same concentration camps as the Jews. They were viewed as evil traitors till the war started to go wrong for Germany and self-righteous Nazis started to doubt the course they had chosen. It gradually dawned on them that they had made a lot enemies by their brutal treatment of their opponents and could expect no better treatment in return.

The history of the world would be different if the Nazis had won. They would have been seen, in their own land, as saviours and heroes, and having the God-given right to

A History of Angels

rule because of their superiority to all other races. Ancient Romans felt this way. They destroyed and enslaved whole countries without mercy. Like the Nazis they were great racists. Ego is racist. It is always looking for a way to protect what it has won, or inherited, and will always try to define itself as superior.

The history of the world is built on conquering peoples subjugating indigenous people and viewing them as less than human. The conquerors even view the destruction of another's culture as a good thing. They see themselves as God's messengers bringing enlightenment and civilisation. No matter how hard the conquered people try to assimilate with the conquering culture they will always be viewed as inferior, as a threat, because their beliefs are alien.

Ego is a clan or tribal based animal. Its survival depends on loyalty to its own family or group. Its ideas about Right and Wrong, Good and Evil come out of this. Before a country goes to war, its government tries to whip up extreme nationalistic fever amongst its people, because ego has a pack mentality. People are often ashamed at how they were swept up by self-righteous zeal to commit the most horrendous crimes. It felt right at the time until judged at a later date by others.

This pack mentality comes out in sport and in the work place. The nicest person can became savage when he or she sees others achieving the goals and fame they crave for themselves. They feel justified using the most dirty and underhanded acts. If we didn't have umpires people would kill each other over a simple game. But it isn't just a game to ego, or to the fans that support their heroes.

Ego views everything like this. If a young attractive woman starts a new job many of the older women in the company may feel threatened by the attention the girl might attract from the males and the power this gives her. These women might band together against the young woman, finding fault with her to justify their harsh treatment in the hope of driving her away or destroying her. They may insinuate she is immoral. But also they don't want the men to know what they are doing because they know they would be repelled by this action.

Chapter Eighteen

I've seen this same scenario played out even amongst the most religious and spiritual people especially when they feel someone is receiving more attention then they are from a religious leader. They throw their beliefs out the window while they remove any perceived or imagined threat. They then whip back seamlessly into place afterwards without a moment of doubt or self-reflection. Ego would only be worried that people in the group might judge them or shun them if they found out. It has nothing to do with right and wrong.

Ego can and will justify any act so long as its position is safe and secure in the group, no matter how ruthlessly they dealt with the threat. The Catholic Church justified the horrific actions of the Inquisition because it felt its power base threatened by other beliefs. They accused people of heresy and sorcery, often wrongly, tortured false confessions out of them and burnt them to death, all in the name of Jesus, who taught compassion and love.

But ego doesn't see the hypocrisy in this. I find it ironic that even gangsters who murder and torture people wear crosses and go to church. They rely on the thought that all their criminal acts can be absolved in confession, or by a priest at their deathbed or, as in the case of the inquisitors, by doing it all in the name of Jesus. How convenient! There are also Buddhist countries that fight wars in the name of Buddha, the Being who taught people not to harm a living thing!

This is how ego judges Good and Evil: whatever is a threat is Evil and whatever helps in its quest for security and power is Good.

SOUL

Soul's concept of Good and Evil is very different. Good is all to do with heart, compassion and empathy for other living things. It doesn't matter what side a person is on, what religion or politics they follow, what race they are. Soul can sense when another has empathy and compassion for them, even if that person is part of a group that may harm or kill

A History of Angels

them. Soul finds it hard to use the word evil for someone but it recognises a complete lack of empathy in another and a desire to enslave or harm others for gain. Such is an ego-based person. Soul recognises when another is living in a criminal way, as perverted egos do, drawing on the life force of others. That's the ultimate in evil to soul.

Soul recognises that people go through karmic negative and positive phases in life and that outer appearances can be misleading. Gabriel allowed me to have an insight into this with a vision he gave me one night. Gabriel used the lawless and violent Wild West of America as an analogy to enable me to see how Beings of Light view good and evil. When Fallen tire of their time in the Lower Realms they can ask for help to return to God. Beings like Gabriel will find them and, if imprisoned, free them and take them back to the Higher Realms for help.

WILD WEST VISION

I saw Gabriel, in the role of ranger or marshal, visit towns [realms] in the Wild West on the judge's [God's] behalf. He would ride in alone and stop at the sheriff's office. In my vision, I dreamed that Gabriel rode into town and found the sheriff and his ten deputies. It was obvious they had all had dealings with him before. They respected his skill with a gun but most of the lawmen secretly hated and feared him and would use any excuse to kill him. Inside Gabriel I could feel him read their true intentions, even though the men who hated him most were the ones who laughed and joked with him and feigned friendship. I could also feel which lawmen had good hearts and were truly honest.

The sheriff and his deputies knew Gabriel would soon move on. They benefited from their position in the town and many, the sheriff included, misused their power to control most of the local business, gambling and commerce. Anyone who got in their way was branded an outlaw, dealt with harshly and ostracized by them and the law-abiding and religious towns people.

Chapter Eighteen

The good-hearted lawmen tried to deal fairly with people and were sympathetic to outlaws they thought had been unjustly branded. They wouldn't have any part of beating and torturing them when they were locked up. They were quick to defend anyone in need of help from them. But the dishonest lawmen were only interested in helping those who lined their pockets and supported them. They wouldn't tackle any gunslinger or bully if there wasn't anything in it for them. They would turn a blind eye when someone was raped or murdered, especially if that person had spoken out against corruption in the town.

In the sheriff's office, Gabriel asked if a certain man was being held in the cells. The sheriff, with a look of barely veiled hatred, admitted he was. Gabriel politely asked for him to be handed over to his care when he left town and said that this man would never trouble the sheriff or the town again. The sheriff wisely agreed to his request. So after shaking his hand Gabriel walked out into the street.

Gabriel then visited a bar where the local crime boss and all his gunslingers hung out. The other lawmen knew it was a very dangerous place to visit and avoided it. When Gabriel walked in all the gunslingers looked up warily from their card games and drinking. They knew how skilful the marshal was with a gun and that he was fair in his dealings, unlike the local sheriff. Gabriel didn't interfere in their business unless they were going to harm someone who asked for his protection. When this happened they knew he could be deadly. Many a gunslinger had died trying to harm Gabriel or the person under his protection. The gunslingers grudgingly respected him, unlike the self-righteous sheriff and his men who were no better than crooks, and the law-abiding citizens who were no better than sheep blindly following them.

The local crime boss looked remarkably like the sheriff. He could have been his brother. I saw they could switch roles seamlessly. Both were all about power; one got it through being a lawman and the other a criminal. Both were ruthless, but intelligent and perceptive enough to know nothing was to be gained by messing with Gabriel.

A History of Angels

They were polite to him, even friendly, in a cat-and-mouse sort of way.

When Gabriel sat down with the crime boss he saw the men around him were cunning guys who said the right things but secretly hated both their boss and Gabriel. But one guy looked bored. Gabriel smiled at him; this was the true reason Gabriel was visiting the bar, to see if this man was ready to return to God. He gave a world-weary smile in return. He had a good heart. He was one of those unfortunate people who'd been branded a criminal unjustly by the lawmen, even though he wouldn't deliberately harm another without good reason. He too was a very dangerous man with a gun, so the other men didn't try to force him to do anything he didn't approve of, like rape, murder and torturer. He'd happily put a bullet through the corrupt sheriffs heart if he had to, though. Gabriel felt that this man wasn't ready to leave this life yet. He would check on him in one year's time.

After his chat with the boss Gabriel wandered out into the street. A friendly tribe of Native Americans had just arrived to trade with the shopkeepers. One of their warriors lay wounded. He'd been shot while riding into town by settlers new to the West who didn't know that the indigenous people were friendly. They thought they were murderers and savages and might steal their cattle or harm them. Many of the warriors were great Braves, feared by the sheriff and his men who also despised them and talked to them like they were lower than animals. I sensed that the natives symbolised angels and lived by very similar codes of conduct.

But some of the natives who appeared to be brave and spiritual warriors didn't feel it in their hearts. They realised they lacked the connection the others had to all life and to nature and at the same time envied them and judged them harshly. I could see how they were like many of the self-righteous townsfolk.

Gabriel returned to the sheriff's office and collected the prisoner he'd come to set free and take back to the God Realms. He sensed that the sheriff and his men had a dark

Chapter Eighteen

secret. Three deputies were missing. As Gabriel rode out of town with the prisoner he suddenly turned off the road and asked the man to wait for him in a clump of bushes. Gabriel dismounted and snuck off in the direction of the road where he crept up behind the three missing deputies waiting in ambush for him. He drew his gun and asked if they were looking for him. They turned in surprise and tried to shoot him but he was faster and shot all three.

In this story I saw how Gabriel viewed people, how he saw good and evil in all different groups. But the good ones were more subtle and if you weren't connected to your heart you'd miss the fact that they felt empathy and compassion for others no matter who they rode with. But the ego-based people made quick, harsh judgements of others, especially if they weren't accepted into their group. They were quite happy to see harm come to them even though they hadn't wronged them in any way. Even someone being more respected or liked by the leader was enough reason to find fault with them and try and destroy them.

Gabriel asked me to imagine a minister or priest who was highly respected and admired in the community. He lived a life of celibacy, helped those less fortunate than himself, and had great spiritual insight and understanding of Scriptures. To ego this would be a Good Man, a Saint. But what of the true person who lay hidden within whom the public never saw? The corrupt pederast who knew the only way to fulfil his dark desires was to earn everyone's trust? Wouldn't he need to seem a saintly man to achieve his ego's goals?

I understood how all these different people had been on the opposite side of the fence in different lifetimes and had been members of the gangs and groups they hated and feared now. All had been lawmen, townsfolk, settlers, outlaws, and Native Americans at least once in past lives. The people who were being truly evil saw themselves as good. They could justify their actions and judge their enemies as evil without even knowing them or what truly lay in their hearts.

I saw how karma gave people the opportunity to live the life of those they hated and judged in order to come to understand they are the same under the skin, even lawmen

A History of Angels

or criminals. There are good and bad in every group. The purpose was to give people the chance to develop empathy and understanding for those they once hated and be able to connect to their hearts and the hearts of others.

Buddhists say it is harder to have compassion for the self than it is for another. Karma hopes that by us understanding others we will open up within to our own heart and have compassion for ourselves. Ego-based people have no compassion for themselves. If they did, they wouldn't need to harm others who mean them no harm and ignore their own heart and soul. Gabriel and all Beings of Light defend themselves and others if they are attacked but don't ever assume that someone has evil intentions just because they are, for example, a Dark Angel nor, on the other hand, do they assume that all angels have good intentions. I know that may shock some people but Dark Angels often decide to become angels and angels decide to Fall. If Dark Angels made the momentous decision to choose the path of God, it would be a travesty if a Being of Light assumed they were evil and killed them on sight.

Angels are all part of the karmic circle. They will reincarnate as Dark Angels one day and Angels of Light another. Those connected to their hearts understand and take to being an angel better than others. When they are Dark Angels they are loyal to the clan, loving to their families, brave and honourable and even respect angels in battle, even though they are their enemies. But most Dark Angels despise angels and are cruel and ruthless to them. When a Dark Angel is an angel and is still ego-driven, he or she only takes on the outer persona of angelness. They will obey all the laws strictly and do all that is asked of them but will be very judgemental of others, especially if they are Fallen and Dark Angels. They will lack true compassion and understanding, even though all his or her outward actions would be done strictly by the angel rules.

I have a very gentle, quiet and spiritual friend named Chris. He has a good heart. People like and trust him and unfortunately take advantage of his helpful nature. He's always stuck doing something for one ungrateful person

Chapter Eighteen

after another. One night we spoke of our pasts. He surprised me when he admitted that when he was a young man he was friendly with drug-dealers and gangsters. Looking back he still to this day can't say why he was friendly with these guys. I laughed when he told me and I said his soul must have wanted him to understand what motivated these men.

He said they were good to him and liked him around. They'd never known a nice gentle fellow like him before. He drank and took drugs with them, but they understood he wasn't interested in becoming involved in their drug dealing and other illegal pursuits. Chris knew from their stories that they'd beaten and even murdered rivals in the past. They also treated women badly, which bothered him and he'd warn women to stay away from his friends especially if they didn't realise how dangerous they were.

Then one day Chris had had enough. It was like he'd woken up from a bad dream. He couldn't hang out with them anymore and quietly drifted away. Chris finds that he hardly ever runs into them anymore, like he isn't meant to. He used to worry that he would, but as the years went by, it just never happened.

To look at Chris now it's hard to believe he was ever part of this world, but his life is not unlike my own. I look back in wonder at this other person I used to be and who I used to hang around with. Chris and I understand these lawless, wild people better now. I still find it easy to speak with tough guys and they know I can look after myself so they don't hassle me. I noticed the same with Chris. He can speak easily to the scariest guy in the bar and laugh with him and put him at his ease. Soul was just curious. I also remember some of these tough guys being very loyal and ready to help me in a pinch, unlike some of the more respectable and selfish friends I had.

PLAYING GOLF WITH THE DEVIL

While speaking to Gabriel about the Wild West vision, I remembered a dream I had when I started to go into that

A History of Angels

negative phase in my life that I spoke of earlier. I told Gabriel I dreamt that I was playing golf with The Devil, who looked like a tough, cunning older woman. We both had very different ideas of how to play the game.

It was a beautiful sunny day and I enjoyed being out on the golf course - the grass and trees and the birds that flew about and sang in the branches. I wasn't a particularly good golfer, but I enjoyed the challenge. Each shot offered me the opportunity to improve on the last and each was a very different challenge. I kept a tally of my shots and rolled my eyes in amusement at some of the bad shots I played and the trouble I'd got myself into in the rough. But it was always satisfying to play a good saving shot to get out of trouble.

I didn't take too much notice of The Devil but helped her find her ball when she lost it and said "good shot", or "well done" when she played well or "bad luck" when she miss hit. The game seemed far more serious to her than me and she would become very angry if one of her shots went astray. Also the scorecard seemed very important to her. She made sure I put the right score down on my score card and worried I might have forgotten a shot here or there, which I hadn't.

Whenever I played a shot, The Devil would try to distract me. She would laugh or make fun of me for any wayward shot I played and, to her annoyance, I'd laugh with her. It was all good fun for me. She watched me with hungry, wolfish, needy eyes, and glowed with jealousy whenever I played well. She also tried to hide any miss shots of hers from me and cheated with her scorecard. Winning to her was very important, it was like her life depended on it and she was willing to cheat and lie to win. To me golf was just an amusing game. I was playing against myself and I didn't really care if I won or lost to her, that wasn't the point. I liked the challenge of it.

But I realised in the end that she needed to feel superior to me so she could have some sort of control over me. She needed control over me to be happy. She just couldn't enjoy the challenge of playing against herself and the beautiful day and surroundings, the good company and laughing at all our missed shots. The day was long hard and hateful to

Chapter Eighteen

her, and I frustrated her because no matter what she did or said to put me off my game I still enjoyed myself. She also knew I was very aware she was cheating and that it seemed to amuse me because she was so obvious about it. It all seemed farcical to me watching her act so innocent whenever I caught her cheating and I'd joke about it. She always pretended her mind must be slipping now she was getting old and forgetful, even though she was as sharp as a tack.

Who won the golf game in the end? I don't know. It didn't seem important. Like I said, it was only a game. One of countless games I've played over many lifetimes. Soul found them all amusing and interesting in their own way.

A History of Angels

Chapter Nineteen

DEFENDING ONESELF

It might be appropriate now to speak of the difference between the way Ego defends itself compared to Soul. The last chapter gave a symbolic insight into one of the roles Gabriel plays, that of the law enforcer, and how this often brings him into conflict with others to the point of death.

When I asked Gabriel how he feels about taking the life of another, he said that life and death are a dance to him. He feels the hand of God in both and accepts that he could die just like his opponent. He shares the fear and hate his opponent feels which is why he has compassion for him. In his own heart he feels at peace, he knows this moment is meant to be, that the rest is in God's hands. So the dance of life and death begins. If he feels regret in his opponent's heart Gabriel will stop the fight and try to talk to him and see if he would like to make a different choice. But if only murder and revenge is in their heart, they will have a swift, brutal and loveless death that will feel pointless.

If we are fighting for something we love then death isn't pointless. We have been true to ourselves and soul will accept death happily as part of the dance of life. But if our death was for something as empty as revenge and hate, soul will despair at the final moment, because there is no acceptance. I've died many times, Gabriel said, and I've been fortunate in that I accepted my death as fulfilling a soul purpose, which makes death worthwhile and fruitful. Most people are horrified at the thought of how pointless death can be, and for good reason. Ego sees no point in death and is unwilling to accept it because it believes that nothing will be gained from its own death, except non-existence. To ego death is losing the most important game there is. Defeating death is the ultimate game.

EGO

Ego is like a desperate animal willing to make any compromise to survive. It only knows life. It has no sense of the infinite or of something after death except non-existence. The thought of its impending death is a very bitter pill indeed to ego, so it will do anything to forestall it. This defending itself from death can take many unexpected forms.

People are often surprised that a lovely gentle woman may choose a really tough aggressive male to be her partner; an alpha male. This would be this woman's ego's idea of how best to defend itself, just like any animal in the wild. Males often band together in gangs or clubs because their ego feels safer being part of a large pack in which it would expect the other males to be by its side when it needed defending. Male monkeys and chimpanzee do this.

Ego sees many things as important to its survival. Most are to do with personal power. Its idea of power over others can take many forms in its various relationships with lovers, family, work colleges and generally in life. What ego tries to do is use whatever skill it may have, no matter how minor, and exploit it for personal gain. You might say it is only natural to use a gift for personal gain. But ego uses its gifts to gain some sort of control over its environment for personal power in the hope its needs will be fulfilled.

If you were a computer geek who had no hope of defending yourself with brute force you would try to claim some sort of superiority at home and your workplace with your computer skills. If you were athletic you might try to prove yourself on the sporting field. If you were a good-looking person you may try to exert power over others by how much they desire you or even how skilled you were sexually. Even University academics can be brutal with each other and easily threatened by the arrival of a bright new intellect in their midst, even in the form of a student. They will attack the perceived threat with all the skills to hand and hope to win intellectual superiority.

Chapter Nineteen

Ego views this quest for superiority in any walk of life as crucial to its survival and explains why people can be so deceitful and ruthless. Ego doesn't care if it is unhappy or that it may be hurting others. It has tunnel-vision and is obsessed with goals, which are linked to its often very bizarre ideas of security and happiness.

What do I mean by bizarre ideas of security? Well this can take the form of alcohol and drug abuse. They offer ego a false sense of warmth and calm. Feeling high is a form of security. The odd thing about addictions is that addicts feel their very survival is at stake if they don't get their drugs. The drugs have become part of their reason for existing. Ironically the very thing they are addicted to could cause their death.

Ego clearly has a very broad, but very limited, idea of security. Also to ego there is only one life, so with this in mind, it often feels defeated in its quest for personal power and may turn in its despair to forms of escapism. The whole Western world is geared to fuelling this need for escapism because most people feel ill equipped to gain any personal power and fulfil their desires. They are made to feel like they have to be famous, rich, beautiful, or successful to be powerful in this world and ninety per cent of us aren't in this so-called elite bracket. Ego therefore feels helpless and a failure. It grows anxious and fearful and very powerless. It looks more to forms of escapism like television, film, video games, gambling, sex and drug abuse to give it fleeting feelings of empowerment.

Ego views death as the ultimate defeat, one it has dreaded and tried to forestall all its life. It is, however, one defeat it has to accept. Even the most powerful person on Earth cannot cheat death. This perceived defeat is a bitter pill for ego to swallow. Why me? Why should I have to die? This sense of bitterness breeds hate in the heart of ego and a need to have revenge against life. If ego believes someone has got in the way of its survival it hates them and wants to destroy them. It doesn't stop to think that maybe all its actions have led it to this fearful moment, this reckoning with death.

A History of Angels

Remember ego is a little psychopath. Ego will only wish it had some sort of foreknowledge so it could have made a better choice to avoid this bitter end. It may become angry, remorseful, beg, bargain, threaten, cajole, lie, fain remorse, anything - when it is cornered. And if you let ego off the hook it may seem so very grateful for a while but it will resent the perceived loss of personal power involved in begging and bargaining. It will always look for your destruction, because it could never feel safe as long as you are alive and could threaten it again.

Knowing this you can see the problems faced by Gabriel. He may have cornered someone who has been murdering, torturing and enslaving others, but in this person's ego-driven mind, it has all been necessary for its survival. It attacks others before they can harm it and cannot see how its actions may be wrong. Stalin was an example of this.

When meeting someone like this, Gabriel understands they lack that basic connection to humanity, that empathy we feel in our heart that shows the truth of our actions, and how unhappy we are making our soul. Also this 'us' and 'them' attitude alienates us from others because everything is perceived as a personal threat to ego, even a lover. The lover may turn against them or abandon them, which is a threat to its survival. This is why love can turn to hate so easily with ego-driven people.

When Gabriel talks to a person like this they are very dangerous. They feel cornered and desperate. Ego isn't interested in looking at its actions. It only wants to survive. At times like this Gabriel's hands are tied and there is only one conclusion to such an encounter. I feel for him because I know he doesn't like to hurt any living thing.

But luckily for us all, most people on the Earth have a lower and higher self, they aren't just listening to ego. Most people do have an innate sense of right and wrong. Again it's a bit like the old angel on one shoulder and the devil on the other. But of course your ego isn't a devil, it's a scared little animal that just needs strong compassionate guidance by your higher self.

Chapter Nineteen

SOUL

Soul doesn't hate but is no fool. It knows fear and recognises a dangerous person or situation. It will do what it has to do to survive but not at any cost. It doesn't allow fear to control its actions. If it has to sacrifice itself to survive it will gladly accept death. The story of Lucifer is a great example of this. Lucifer sacrificed more and more of his connection to his heart by being as tough and ruthless as he could in order to defeat his enemies. He sacrificed his connection to his soul and the guidance it could have given him to help navigate a way through his many trials.

In the end when fear no longer ruled his life, Lucifer was prepared to die rather than go back to his hard, brutal ways. His only reason for fighting on was his concern and love for his family. They were looking to him for deliverance from the multitude of enemies arrayed against them. To fight on in this situation was a loving act even though he was weary. He did not hate his enemies anymore and would gladly have accepted death as long as he could protect his family.

Do you see the huge difference here between, on one hand, hate and revenge or, on the other, protecting your loved ones? If Lucifer had died in battle he would have happily moved on to the light after death and not sought to be reborn amongst his enemies so he could have a chance at revenge. He freed his soul so that it could make loving choices, not be locked into a terrible karmic cycle with his enemies. He also accepted that his children had their own karma and choices to face.

Being connected to soul helps us understand a bigger picture. It helps us see that ultimately we have to let go of our family. This doesn't mean we don't love them, but we can get in the way of their growth. Lucifer finally came to realise this and gave more and more responsibility to his children. If he were honest with himself, he would have recognised that most of them were as strong and capable as he was. Only his ego clung on to the idea that he was indispensable to his family's survival.

A History of Angels

Lucifer's children and grand children blossomed into good independent people in their own right after his death. All of them learnt much by Lucifer's transformation in his twilight years into a caring, loving, gentle man. He was much more loved and respected then than when he was the terror of the Fallen world. Lucifer's old kingdom has broken up now and is run independently and justly by all his children. They aren't a major threat to the other Fallen rulers and are generally left alone. They are also very capable of dealing with any enemy who attacks them. But their lives are much happier now than in the old, hard, ruthless days of their father.

Soul draws a line at what it is willing to do to survive. There is more to life than survival and death is only a doorway. Soul would always choose death rather than do a great evil and live. Stalin is an example of someone who lost his connection to soul. He was willing to wipe out whole countries if he thought they were a threat. Stalin's wife spoke out against his policies so after her suicide he had her family murdered.

I explained earlier how soul will instantly know if someone is lacking the basic empathy that gives us humanity and compassion; a person with a black or twisted soul.

Earlier in the book Gabriel mentioned how The Devil needed others to fulfil her desires. She wasn't interested in finding fulfilment within herself. Her soul became stunted by this very immature idea of love. To Gabriel, dealing with The Devil is like dealing with a very gifted and dangerous child. At first this need is understandable and part of the learning curve of soul. As it develops it understands how unfulfilling and needy looking to others for fulfilment is. But some souls become twisted by this desire and focus their whole will on it. So they become obsessed with exerting personal power over others to make them fulfil this need. They also resent any interference by Beings of Light and avoid going to the light after death. They also try to maintain their control over others between lifetimes and when they reincarnate.

I guess it is all about attachment to an outer idea of power. Soul instantly recognises such stunted souls and is

Chapter Nineteen

repelled by them, especially in their human incarnations on Earth. Soul knows they live to enslave others to their will. Most Senior Fallen are very bitter lonely people on Earth and for good reason. They are completely ruthless about getting their own way and having power over others and find neither need fulfilled due to karma.

Lucifer too became obsessed with protecting himself at the cost of his soul. It was stunted into being like a small child in the dark always fighting unseen assailants. Rather than face the fear of the big bad world Lucifer just decided he wanted to be the toughest being in it, at any cost. This is why he challenged his own father Gabriel to a fight. Lucifer knew his father had been a better swordsman then he. The thought that someone could defeat him undermined Lucifer's belief in his own invincibility. It made him feel like that small scared boy in the dark again. In the end, after many lifetimes, he couldn't care less if he was the toughest warrior or not. The price was too high. Lucifer grew up.

This is why it is important when asking for help from God that we understand that God is very willing to help, but God would rather help you face your fears lovingly, than give you special powers to overcome them or take them away. That is a very immature idea of receiving help from God. Making Lucifer a greater warrior wouldn't have helped him face his fear. Being a humble lonely man on Earth did and Lucifer died at peace for the first time in eons. Next time you ask for help think about the opportunity the moment is offering you and the implications of running from your fears.

The Devil only had to ask for help and her childish need for others to fulfil her could have been healed and her loneliness and suffering could have ended. It is also interesting to know karma would have continually put The Devil with people as empty and as needy as herself so she would see how fruitless the endless struggle was. In the same way as Lucifer, after death, found himself in a schoolroom full of warriors with the same immature need to be heroes. How childish it all seemed to him in the end.

A History of Angels

Chapter Twenty

TIME

Time is one of the great illusions. In telling the story of Lucifer and the other Fallen it is hard to explain that their time on Earth could have a parallel on any number of multiple planes of existence. Your soul is part of the infinite and so its possibilities to experience any situation, at any given time, are infinite too.

We all ask ourselves what if we'd chosen a different path in life? Well, chances are your soul is living out those different paths right now on another plane that would be very similar to Earth as we know it now. You'd be born to the same parents and go to the same school but you'd make very different choices about your life's path. In the movie *Groundhog Day* Bill Murray's character has to live the same day over and over and in each he makes different choices. In the film these experiences happen one after the other. Soul doesn't need to do this. It can live all these different choices and life paths at once. Only the starting point is always the same.

This is where time is confusing. It doesn't run along on one continual line. If you were to look into your past lifetimes you would become very confused by all the different parallel realities you've lived during the same time in history. In each there would only be small differences to the environment, circumstances and people.

For example, if you journeyed to the old neighbourhood you grew up in, everything would seem both familiar and different. Other people in your neighbourhood could also have made different choices. Say the local grocer decided to travel the world and not live out his life at the end of your street, like he does in this life, how would that affect the world as you know it? People talk about how even the death of a butterfly will have a domino effect on everything around it and could even change the course of history.

Beings of Light don't like time to be meddled with because it affects karma, but they like soul to be able to fulfil its true potential. Multiple planes exist so that your soul can truly explore all facets of its time on Earth at this moment. We all regret certain choices we've made which hamper us getting on with our lives. Beings of Light created these extra planes so our souls can fulfil all its desires for that particular time, which would be impossible if there was only one reality.

I was madly in love with my first girlfriend and we broke up for a reason I didn't understand. I always wondered what my life would have been like if we'd stayed together. I remember having a very vivid dream where we met at a café many years later and, though things were uncomfortable, we spoke honestly about our time together and I understood how lost and in pain she was at that time and why she finished the relationship.

When I woke up I felt at peace about our time together. I felt like her soul and mine truly got together and finished something karmically between us. We both came away with a compassionate understanding of the other. I've never felt the need to see her again since then. Was it just a dream or did it really happen on another plane? I believe it did happen. What's real and what's illusion?

I also saw myself living with this ex-girlfriend in another life. I was a bit overweight, I rode a motorbike and we weren't particularly happy. The dream was boringly real and showed a quite unfulfilling relationship for both of us. Was that dream real? Did my soul explore that path? I believe it did happen on another similar plane.

Sometimes we have dreams that are amazingly realistic but there will always be a few things different to the world we know now. When you have dreams about these similar realities you are being given glimpses of your simultaneous multiple existences. Ego is repelled by this notion of

Chapter Twenty

multiple existences. It undermines its sense of control over its environment. Ego is terrified of the thought that this life we live right now might not be the only game in town. Ego wants you to invest your whole self into this one lifetime so it can maintain its existence when you reincarnate. In all these different realities soul would have a different ego that it would discard when it dies. That's why Beings of Light try to teach us not to become too attached to our ego or this lifetime. It is all just theatre for soul - an illusion. That's what is meant by impermanence.

Soul may have become very attached to a particular lifetime but was forced by circumstances, like sudden death, to move on before it felt ready to. It would feel it has unresolved issues. Karma may recognise that a soul is still too inexperienced to understand or deal with a situation so it makes soul move forward into new incarnations until it is wise enough to deal with this attachment. Grief or unrequited love, are two very common attachments.

So what can soul do about something that happened to it, say, five hundred years ago? It is all dead and gone now, isn't it? Sometimes it takes soul a lot of living and growing up before it is ready to face a particularly traumatic time all over again from the past. But when it is ready soul will be offered a chance to relive that moment over and over again in 'Groundhog Day' fashion. Karma will try to bring the same people together and recreate a similar situation but in modern times. But sometimes this doesn't work. The medieval world and mindset, for example, is a very different one to our modern day reality and sometimes an attachment can only be faced in that time frame.

So soul waits till the other souls who were part of this past drama, are ready and Beings of Light will create this situation and times again. Only the major players need be real, the rest will just be an illusion. Soul will have the same chance to face and heal some great grief, fear or loss or make a more loving and compassionate choice. In a way it is 'role playing' the past, but it is very real to the people involved in the drama and they can still go through all the trauma of pain, suffering and death again but this time hopefully all are wiser and will make different choices. But what if the other souls are unwilling to be part of this re-enactment? Do they actually need to be there? No, they could be part of the illusion also. But soul is still able to play out this drama and have the opportunity to make more loving choices.

Talking of time reminds me of how hard it is to describe what happens to someone after death. There are shared realities that soul might want to be part of, like the idea of heaven and hell within certain religions. Being a shared reality these places will exist and you can go there. So what is a 'shared reality'? They are realities or planes of existence that Senior Fallen created. Many souls are interested in visiting them and being part of their reality. If there is great interest in a certain reality, like Earth, then Beings of Light will create similar realities so all souls can experience it.

It is a hard concept to grasp that there is only 'the now' and that the so-called 'future' and 'past' all exist in the one moment. In theory you could dwell in ancient times while also living now and in the future. But are they really the past and future? You've seen how an illusion of the past can be recreated for soul if it needs it. But soul lives on a time line of its own. Its karmic path of cause and effect is shared with others around it that make up the components or wheels that affect each other as they share their time together. Time actually runs in a karmic circle. You rotate back to where your time began. If soul wants to, it can go through that same time line all over again but make different choices. This is the phoenix side of soul. It will rotate around growing old, wise and world weary, then will be absorbed completely back into God and be re-born, if it so desires. It incorporates all this wisdom into its renewed self and sets off on the karmic circle again. But the different choices soul makes will affect the outcome of the shared realities. Eventually soul will exhaust all possibilities and these realities will be absorbed back into the Infinite and whole new realities will be created.

Soul can experience ancient, modern and futuristic times at the same moment. Visiting different times is like playing different virtual reality games. We can choose to

Chapter Twenty

play in the past, present or future because they already exist on different planes. This Earth we live on now may never develop into a Star Trek-like futuristic civilization but there are realms where this exists now and your soul can experience it. Soul can visit any place in time on its karmic circle at exactly the same moment unless karma steps in and blocks it. Time is an illusion. It's all virtual reality to soul. But unlike our mind, soul can grasp and absorb infinite experiences at the same time, which it will assimilate and transform into wisdom when it returns to God. Beings of Light can help soul understand and assimilate experiences while living them, even before soul returns to God.

Souls being born now are very different from the souls that were being born when Gabriel came into being, so that's why they have their own timelines. Souls are developing and changing. A whole new existence is coming into being and there is always an overlap. One existence doesn't just end and another begins. Too much is lost that way. New souls can sense the difference and wisdom in old souls as well as limitations. They can learn from others' mistakes. As beings like Lucifer and The Devil bow out of existence these new souls may have a brush with them and learn from it. But that doesn't mean all old souls are phased out; most are re-born 'Phoenix like' and renewed, unless they became a particularly twisted soul like the Devil. These souls are 'unmade' and absorbed back into the infinite, never to be reborn.

Your soul is a creative entity. Besides these shared realities, soul creates its own fantasy realms where it loves to play, create and explore itself. Sometimes soul invites others to join its fantasy realm. If many start to share in it, then it becomes another reality for other souls to visit, experience and share. Some souls find working with other souls too testing and they choose to escape more and more into their own fantasy realms. These souls eventually fade into nonexistence because they invest their whole self into their fantasy. Many of them are drawn to escapism through drugs and virtual reality games. Their soul is karmically made to have a body here on Earth but they find this world too harsh and limiting and can't get used to not having complete control over their environment. These souls are known as the 'escapists' to angels and Beings of Light and are the hardest to help and guide.

All the different timelines of all the souls together create the most beautiful pattern, which has a sense of harmony and beauty that is hard to describe. It is like a sublime piece of classical music where many play their part in the divine song. But the song evolves and overlaps seamlessly into a new song.

Gabriel told me one of the hardest things for angels to study is the complexities of time and the illusion of time and reality. These realities are heavily linked to karma and the choices we make and how that affects our future.

Chapter Twenty-one

WHY IS EVIL ALLOWED TO EXIST?

One of the main reasons people turn away from God or don't believe in the existence of God is that God allows evil to exist. As mentioned before, ego and soul have a very different view of good and evil to each other. God and Beings of Light like Gabriel have yet another view.

When a soul is young there is no experience that doesn't interest it. In its naivety it wants to explore all facets of life. This often leads the soul into very destructive actions. On Earth we judge the actions of children and juveniles differently to adults. God and Beings of Light judge the actions of young souls differently to old souls. Older souls are dealt with far more harshly and swiftly than younger souls.

We've all probably had friends in life we love who were drawn to dangerous people and destructive ways of life. No matter how well they are brought up or how religious their up-bringing, certain people are attracted to the dark side. Even though they are sweet and innocent, they may choose a wild and dangerous partner, or hang out with people on the wrong side of the law. It will all seem fascinating and exciting for these young souls because this way of life is so different and new to them compared to the Realms of God. It is all a game and a young soul rarely considers the consequences of its actions in these early stages of its existence, not unlike children.

Some young souls allow Beings of Light to guide them while others want to be free to experience everything on their own without interference or censor. I mentioned earlier that I have a friend who, even though he is a nice, gentle,

A History of Angels

honest guy, was very attracted to certain gangster, drug-dealer types when he was younger. But something stopped him ever crossing the line and actually harming someone or becoming like these criminals. He allowed Beings of Light to show him this way of life without losing his sense of self and his connection to God.

Other souls would want to immerse themselves in this lifestyle and truly take on the role of a gangster. Some of these people walk away from this when they are older and wiser. Others can't imagine not being a gangster and will try to play this role out lifetime after lifetime until they've had their fill. This is when a soul invests completely into its ego in that lifetime and carries it with it when it reincarnates. This is also why karma will lock a person out from a certain time so it will let go off its attachment to this ego role it always wants to play. Lucifer couldn't play at medieval warrior in these modern times. Karma placed him here in the hope he'd let go of his obsession.

Gabriel allowed me to see Lucifer through his eyes. To Gabriel and all Beings of Light, Lucifer was just a young soul who didn't know any better. But after a while Lucifer was willing to listen to God and Beings of Light, even though at first he didn't understand what they were trying to teach him. He had to be guided and shown, after much suffering, that there was a more loving and fulfilling way to live.

When I had my vision of Gabriel speaking to The Devil I saw a young teenager a bit older than Lucifer but still inexperienced. Her view of life and how to find fulfilment was a very young soul's idea. She acted very much like the petulant, unhappy teenage girl that all parents find difficult. She felt completely let down and disillusioned with her parents [God and the Beings of Light], that they didn't give her the love and fulfilment she craved. She was trying to punish them and the world in general all because she didn't get her own way. That no one could really give her the sort of fulfilment she wanted didn't matter to her, she just wanted her own way and was willing to do anything to get it.

Gabriel was so patient with The Devil. It was obvious she loved him and Gabriel felt love and compassion for her, but

Chapter Twenty-one

because Gabriel wasn't willing to dedicate his whole life to fulfilling her every wish she also hated him. While they were talking, she continually tried to destroy him psychically. Gabriel was very aware of what was going on and looked bemused, sad and a little fed-up with her attitude, but also unconcerned. Nothing she could do would truly harm him.

I remember Gabriel comparing souls to dogs. When a soul is immature, it is like a puppy running around getting into all sorts of mischief. It is very vulnerable to danger and death because it doesn't know any better. A puppy can be amusing and affectionate in its innocence but is also very needy and scared when left alone. Young souls too look for the same love and protection in life they used to have in the Realms of God. But life in the Lower Realms is much harsher and soul's needs are harder to fulfil here. A very young soul's idea of life is that God, its parents or the world should look after it and nurture it and make it feel safe, but it doesn't work that way here. The Devil could never accept this limitation on Earth and the Lower Realms. She refused to grow up and find this fulfilment within herself.

When a puppy is young it can be quite destructive. It may dig holes or gnaw on expensive table legs and shoes but it doesn't know any better. Its owner tries to set boundaries and limit access to certain things the puppy may ruin. Beings of Light do this for young souls. They don't stop the young soul exploring its new environment but try to limit the damage it can cause to itself and others.

A dog is most destructive when it is a young and rebellious juvenile. This is the best age to take it to dog-training school and give it boundaries and guidelines for coexisting with other dogs and with people. It can have a very fulfilling relationship with its owner and enjoy interacting with the other dogs. This is the same with some juvenile souls; they love their relationship with God, Beings of Light and other souls and the guidance they receive. It is very fulfilling.

Some juvenile dogs don't respond to training school. They just want to lie around at home being hugged, having their belly endlessly scratched and fed chocolate biscuits. They become very jealous and savage if asked to share this

A History of Angels

attention with a new pet and may even kill it when the owner isn't around. This dog expects the owner's life to revolve around fulfilling its every whim. It sulks if it doesn't get its own way. It may even become nasty and aggressive. The owner tries to discipline it but this dog refuses to give in.

The owner realises the dog has become dangerous around guests. The dog has also grown big and strong and is quite capable of really harming someone, even killing them. There is no love in this relationship. This dog has become unmanageable and destructive. It isn't even affectionate at home anymore but just sulks and snarls all the time and barks in the night at any noise. A sad but necessary decision has to be made. The dog has to be put down. The owner is very sad remembering what a beautiful puppy the dog was, how fun loving and affectionate and what a joy it was to have around. To live in this world the dog has to live by very similar rules as the owner and if it becomes a problem to society the owner will get in trouble also.

Some dogs run away and become feral. They run around in packs and relish killing needlessly. They don't even kill to feed themselves. Eventually some of these dogs are drawn to being with people and accept once more guidance and love. They are willing to leave the pack. But most love the killing and hunting too much, the thrill of the chase and sense of power it gives them. These dogs usually have to be hunted down and killed because they are so dangerous. You only have to look at the news or the history of the world to understand that just below the surface of a so-called civilised human lies a very savage and dangerous animal. That's why Gabriel used dogs as an example. They revert back to their original wild and savage state so easily.

Some dogs become working dogs. These are usually the happiest and most fulfilled dogs. They round up sheep and cattle and protect them and their owners at night. They have a close relationship with their owner, based on mutual respect and love. But unlike dogs and their owners, souls can become Beings of Light too one day.

A girlfriend and I had a sheepdog. Our dog had a brother that worked sheep in the country. The girl who owned him

Chapter Twenty-one

would visit us. This dog was so mature and responsible. It looked so fulfilled. Our dog seemed needy and naughty in comparison. The owner hardly ever had to tell the dog what to do, it read people so well. It surprised me how intelligent and wise this sheepdog was. The owner and her dog had a mutual understanding. The dog knew he needed the owner to get by in this world but he also knew she was very grateful for what a good job he did with the sheep and what a good friend he was to her.

I guess a lot of people would be insulted by me comparing the relationship of soul, the Beings of Light and God to that of an owner and their dog, but when soul is young it needs guidance and a strong hand to stop it becoming destructive to itself and others. Young souls can't really survive within the Lower Realms without some sort of help from God and the Beings of Light. It can be one of the most fulfilling adventures soul can have and also give them the most beautiful close relationship with God and the Beings of Light. It can also be a disaster. Compared to Beings of Light, which have existed for countless eons, we are like children or puppies. The savage animal in all of us is our ego. Beings of Light respect and love us but they also know that spoiling us will only lead to our downfall.

In the karmic circle everybody has an opportunity to be powerful. To soul this is all a game. Sadly though, it can become a very cruel and harrowing one and throw up a Hitler or a Stalin. When it's your time to have power, how will you use it?

If a soul, after many lifetimes, is adamant it wants to live in a destructive way, Beings of Light will place it with other destructive souls in a limited realm where they can play out this need until they have had enough. This is the Wild West Gabriel visited. They are the Lawless Realms. People often think these realms are Hell, but souls are there by choice. They can't leave until they let go of their attachment to their destructive ways. Eventually these realms will fade into nonexistence and the destructive souls with them. Earth used to be part of them, but Beings of Light have stepped in and, if you are observant, you may notice karma is working a lot faster on Earth now.

A History of Angels

Chapter Twenty-Two

SEX

In most religions the topic of sex is taboo. People fear the strong lusts, feelings and desires associated with sex. When a person's heart kicks in they are prepared to risk everything, and they are impossible to control. This explains why so many people fear their own desires and why those in authority try to suppress such feelings. People fear loss of control, if they give into these desires; that they may be easily manipulated or enslaved by the object of their desire. Some fear that if their repressed sexual desires are allowed to express themselves, they will take over their life possibly leading to sexual addiction, shame or degradation.

These are some of the reasons why sex is such a loaded subject and why people spend so much energy fantasising about it, and not fulfilling it and envying and judging others who are indulging their fantasies. Sex is a huge creative aspect of the soul. It is easily fulfilled without guilt, suffering and attachment in the God Realms but this is rarely possible on Earth. Why is it so hard to express our creative sexual side on Earth without becoming entangled in possessiveness, guilt and power games?

When soul first comes to the Lower Realms it is surprised how complicated relationships are here and how hard it is to be honest and open about one's desires without feeling harshly judged. Young souls will have the unhappy experience, in their early lifetimes on Earth, of being used and degraded through the sexual act, especially women. There is a bizarre and complicated game on Earth where men try to trick and coerce women to have sex with them in the most degrading way possible, then run off to tell their friends all about it. They want to prove how powerful they are.

When I worked with men out of prison I was told horrific tales of men raping other men or making them have oral sex with them. These men weren't homosexual. It was about having power over another, power to make them do the most degrading acts possible.

A woman, for example, may feel special with all the attention a male afforded her, before she agreed to sex. She would have hoped he was someone she could be herself with and feel free to express her love and desires with safely. Suddenly all that changes after the sexual act and she is treated like she is a slut.

This same man may even try to induce her to go to bed with him again and say many kind and consoling words to persuade her to trust him. But she is soon betrayed again and finds out that people are talking about her behind her back. Other men have decided she must be easy so they try to pick her up all the time, while girls despise and judge her. This same man who tricked her into bed may be having no luck bedding other women so he keeps coming back to her. He is very jealous of her talking to or seeing other men, even though he doesn't want to spend time with her after they've had sex.

This can happen to a young male soul too in a similar way. He might meet a woman who has been hurt many times by men, and uses them and then discards them because she doesn't want to be hurt any more. He might sleep with a girl who sees him as a potential provider so becomes pregnant to him, even though they haven't discussed children, then guilts him into marriage.

A young soul isn't equipped for these scenarios. In the God Realms souls are like glass. They can see each others' desires, there are no tricks or games. But Earth is all about people acting in a way that they believe will help them get what they want.

I knew a policeman once; women loved him. He was funny, charming and had the knack of saying the right

Chapter Twenty-two

thing at the right time. But when women weren't around he spoke of them in the most degrading way, and so did his friends. It was all a game to them. He married a really lovely woman who we all liked. She had no idea that he frequently had affairs and that he even joked to us about having contracted a sexually transmitted disease at the time, which his wife knew nothing about. I don't think his wife would have married him if she had known his true intent. It may take her many years to discover who she has really married.

There are also people looking for partners to take on the role of Mummy and Daddy. They use sex to attract them but after they move in together, all passion disappears. Soul is confused. What happened to all that love and desire? Sadly, the other isn't interested in mature intimacy and only wants someone who will meet their needs and make them feel loved and secure like a baby.

There are people who want another to help them play out their sexual fantasies. Soul may be excited and interested by this new experience at first but soon realises that the other person isn't interested in true intimacy.

Being used by others, or being just an object of another's desires causes confusion in young souls and makes them feel alienated and lonely. Young souls love to share another's desires and dreams but also love to be acknowledged and appreciated. They learn after bitter experience that most people just want a slave to meet their needs and will only express love if they give them what they want. If they deviate from this pattern, the controlling lover may become very angry and hateful and even try to destroy the other.

So soul pulls back and becomes wary and aloof. It can become quite lonely and disillusioned without the intimacy it knew in the God Realms. To overcome its fear of being misused and tricked, it may try to throw off its fears and inhibitions for a night, go out and get drunk and maybe even find someone it can love and be intimate with.

There are sexual predators who prey on people in this vulnerable state. They are usually the types that wait in bars and clubs hoping someone like this will walk in. They instantly latch on to this soul and try to trick it into fulfilling its needs. If the lonely soul ends up going home with this person, the sad old cycle starts all over again.

The soul will be angry with itself for being used again and feel more alienated and lonely than before. In its desperation it might go along with this person, or other predators like them, and allow itself to be used, in the hope that this will drive the lonely feelings away. Soul may even marry someone that it doesn't love or isn't really attracted to, just to have some company in its lonely existence on Earth.

Soul is naïve and vulnerable to what Beings of Light call 'sexual vampires,' the predators mentioned above who are as addicted to sex as others are addicted to drugs and gambling. They use sex to steal another's life-force. They are obsessed with looking desirable and are also incredibly competitive and ruthless about winning the object of their desire. They have a great hunger and emptiness in them that is impossible to fill. They are especially attracted to innocent young souls. A soul who has sex with them will feel unsatisfied. They may be fooled into believing they need to have a lot more sex with this person to feel fulfilled, but the need just intensifies. When the young soul walks away from this person, they will have a great sense of exhaustion, emptiness and despair.

People on Earth look for partners and have sex for very different reasons to those in the God Realms, where people feel secure and safe. They also feel loved and fulfilled and share this state of being with others. No one is starving or feels ugly, unwanted and powerless. All are free to express and create anything they want to. Love, sex and relationships are just an extension of this.

On Earth, sex and relationships are heavily linked to ego's idea of survival. This is where the games and the need for power over others begin. Soul is at first very confused that it can't just be loved for itself, that it has to offer people something they need or desire and be useful in some way. It has to be attractive or powerful or gifted or willing to serve another. Soul finds no love in this, but this is where ego usually takes over. The primal need for survival kicks in, as

Chapter Twenty-two

soul despairs and finds existence in the Lower Realms is a loveless process. Sadly soul may become very quiet at this time and observe its life from a distance and allow its ego to run the whole show.

Ego has strong needs and desires of its own, which are more base and animal-like. It misses the fulfilling feeling of soul and sharing in its experiences. It may look to satisfy this inner emptiness by becoming ambitious for success, power and fame. It may turn to things that give it a sense of momentary fulfilment like sex, drugs, gambling or living in fantasy. Ego is a sexual vampire. It only has an outer idea about fulfilment so is very attracted to good-looking people, flashy clothes and cars - any signs of outer power. It will obsess about marrying famous movie stars, models, musicians, royalty, the rich and powerful. Ego feels ill equipped to attract or control people like this so it has a sense of failure and loneliness. Even if it is capable of attracting such people, it finds the relationships very shallow and unfulfilling.

We have reached a time when soul and ego feel stuck. Both are incapable of finding lasting happiness. This is why Beings of Light have started to appear in this person's life, either in spirit-form or as incarnate humans. They only come when soul and ego have exhausted all possibilities of finding fulfilment. Soul is now willing to be guided and helped to take the next step and be reconnected with the infinite – with God. Ego feels threatened and is scared of stepping into such an unknown world.

Ego senses its time is short and fights desperately for its own survival. It tries to block all contact soul has with its higher self. But the higher self has all the time in the world; it is infinite. Long suppressed desires and longings spring up within the soul, longings it has been unable to fulfil on its own on Earth and in the Lower Realms.

Often when Gabriel visits women in either spirit form or incarnate at this time, great sexual longings are aroused in them that have long gone unfulfilled. This can be very confusing and make the women feel despair because Gabriel can't be their partner. But the reason the longing is aroused in the first place is because their soul feels that Gabriel and other Beings of Light are truly seeing, feeling and acknowledging them, which is true intimacy and what soul looks for in the sexual act.

Soul will be shocked by the strong sexual fantasies it has, which verge on the pornographic. Strong feelings of love and desire lie behind them, and its heart physically aches. Ego will try to make soul fear these feelings and remind it of the trouble it got into in the past trying to fulfil them. But soul will be offered an opportunity to fulfil them in soul-form in the Realms of God with people they have loved and trusted in the past or are in relationships with right now on other planes. These sexual experiences will be so real that while in bed they will even feel and maybe smell their lover next to them. They can fulfil all their sexual fantasies without having to meet someone in human form on Earth. Remember, these realms are only an illusion to soul. It is part of the infinite and can dwell in the Lower Realms and the Realms of God at the same time, especially if it isn't too attached to the Lower Realm's illusion.

This cuts ego out of the equation. Soul learns that it can fulfil itself in this way and accept the limitations of Earth where it is hard to find someone spiritually aware enough to share its dreams and desires. If this soul is willing to give up ego's outer ideas of security, it can feel loved and fulfilled with the most minimalistic lifestyle. All that the ego thinks is necessary for happiness in this world is unnecessary to soul. Soul recognises its connection to the infinite and also can be with anyone it loves at any time, even if they are dead, because death too is only an illusion.

Does this mean soul will withdraw from life? On the contrary, it will have a sense of flowing along with life, knowing its heart's desires will be fulfilled, either here or on some other realm. All the different parts to soul are now connected and a great sense of wholeness starts to radiate from within. When soul completely lets go of the need for outer fulfilment in this world, when it is no longer attached to its desires, it may find that the love it has longed to express and share with another can be freely expressed

Chapter Twenty-two

without all the suffering and feelings of alienation that used to occur. It doesn't matter if the partner isn't as capable of intimacy as this soul is, because this soul already feels whole and doesn't need the other for fulfilment, but will just enjoy expressing itself with this person. Both are enriched by the experience.

A History of Angels

Chapter Twenty-Three

BEINGS OF LIGHT

Beings of Light are direct extensions of God. They are like the fingers on God's hand. They are facets or different aspects of God, all distinctly different and individual.

I've met Gabriel and also one female Being of Light named Lara. Gabriel felt very male to me. Cool, collected and dangerous, he radiated vast strength. Lara felt like Spring to Gabriel's Autumn. She radiated a fresh, youthful, and very feminine energy. I felt she was far more complex and subtle than Gabriel, where he is more straightforward. Lara is great at fine detail and complex issues; Gabriel with simplifying an issue and pairing away the unnecessary. Where Gabriel feels like cool running water, Lara burns with an inner flame.

Imagine the two of them working in a garden together overgrown with weeds and thorn bushes. Lara feels daunted by the vast amount of work that needs to be done but Gabriel relishes the prospect. He takes to the garden with amazing strength and cool efficiency tearing out vast amounts of weeds and thorn bushes by their roots revealing small beautiful flowers, herbs and vegetables. Gabriel then helps Lara redesign the garden the way she wants.

Over the next few months Lara transforms the beds into a beautiful, fruitful garden. Gabriel takes note of diseases and pests affecting the plants and deals with them and removes plants that fail. He replaces them with plants that maybe Lara hasn't thought of that are hardier or more suited to the soil. He creates a watering system to water to the garden. When the major work is done Gabriel will move on to other projects leaving Lara to develop and care for the garden.

A History of Angels

He'll only return if Lara asks his help to extend the garden or deal with a problem she can't solve. Gabriel's work in the garden reflects his role in the Lower Realms. Most Beings of Light working in the Lower Realms, like Lara with her plants, foster and nurture souls interested in being part of the God Realms.

What all Beings of Light have in common is their immense compassion, wisdom, patience, humour and a great sense of their role in the infinite. They love, respect and are truly interested in the diversity of each other and creation in general. They love being part of the Creation Song. They interpret God's dream for the song in vastly different and original ways. But all these differences marry perfectly together and enhance each other to create the whole.

If your soul, like the garden, becomes clogged with weeds and thorn bushes and is unable express itself anymore, Gabriel can help clear away the unwanted and negative connections to dark beings and make room for your long lost dreams and desires. Gabriel will help connect you to God again and make sure that this connection stays open. He will help give you the strength and clarity to see what is truly important in your life and what isn't. He then helps you discard the rest through non-attachment.

Lara would follow Gabriel to help with your next phase of development. Your soul may feel barren and world-weary. She would remind you of your youthful and creative self and foster and nurture your soul's dreams and desires.

God offers all the opportunity to be part of the God Realms. Elders amongst the angels hope to become Beings of Light one day. Archangels start out as Christ realm angels. If they show the qualities needed by an Archangel they are offered an opportunity to join them. You have to be especially hardy, independent, and a natural warrior to be one. Amongst the angels these special individuals are known as eagles. Of the thirty Archangels, twenty are offspring of Gabriel. Many of his children are naturals for the role. Gabriel said he has two hundred children and most aren't interested in this violent and thankless task of policing the Lower Realms. Archangels are given extensive powers so they can handle Senior Fallen.

Chapter Twenty-three

You can be a very young soul and still be an Angel or Archangel but of course you are connected to God so you are guided. You are also full of a sense of your purpose for existing and have great compassion for all things that exist. When an Angel or Archangel falls they lose this divine connection and all the guidance and power that goes with it. Everyone has an opportunity to be an Angel, if they so desire, when they rise in the karmic cycle. It is an amazing experience and most young souls learn so much from it and also gain an insight into the workings of God.

Beings of Light are willing to have a living form on all planes of existence and be the direct link to God. They usually live humbly and try to support those interested in having a connection to God or need help in their suffering. A Being of Light won't interfere with your karma or that of your country. They have a sense of the big picture and understand that certain actions in the past have brought people to their moment of suffering. They can help turn a negative experience into something life-changing and beautiful. They won't take the problem away but help you face it and learn what you can from it.

Beings of Light create realms for God and all the beings that exist there. But, as explained earlier, they didn't create the Lower Realms, the Senior Fallen did. They are always developing and transforming their creations to keep pace with the ever-changing direction of the creation song. All have their own individual idea of how to express this and sometimes will come together with other Beings of Light to merge their distinctive energies so that something new comes from the union. This is the way Beings of Light make love. In their love-making they express the true divine dance.

There are male and female Beings of Light but all have both male and female forces within them in perfect balance. Although whole and complete they usually express one aspect more than another. When they make love huge energies mix and dance together through this intimacy. Their shared creation dreams merge and beautiful new young souls are born of the union and dwell for a time in the blissful God Realms created for them by the Beings of Light.

A History of Angels

These young souls have complete creative freedom and want for nothing. They explore their world and each other. When they feel they are ready, they will be drawn to the Lower Realms for a time of growth amongst the limitations and suffering found there. Then they will be guided back to the realm where they were born, to further their experience as soul and will find they have become far more powerful. They can create their own worlds and beings to exist there, but can also dwell and coexist with fellow souls in their place of origin. They become God Realm Angels.

They will be offered extensive guidance by the Beings of Light, who first created them. They will help them understand their original purpose for coming into being and guide them in fulfilling their own creative potential. Some of these souls will avoid this guidance and be drawn back to the Lower Realms again. Some will never return and may even go into nonexistence. The stories told earlier of Lucifer, The Devil, Satan and Isolte, were all about beings that were drawn back many times to the Lower Realms, at first as Christ Realm Angels, then as Fallen. Most of these beings aren't interested in their original purpose, they just want to exist on their own terms.

They are, of course, free to do this, but it usually leads to them into becoming very selfish and destructive. Their original creator tries to keep an eye on them and guide them away from this path. Gabriel was one of the original creators of some of those mentioned in the story. He tried to limit the damage and suffering these few rogues created amongst other beings [Satan and The Devil weren't created by him]. You can see how the dog analogy in Chapter Twenty-one illustrates the role and responsibilities that fall on the shoulders of original creators.

Archangels came from some of the souls created by Gabriel and another Being of Light. All the beings that Gabriel co-created have a distinctive maverick quality, quite different to other souls. This causes Gabriel great heartache and he spends a lot of time trying guide his headstrong and independent off-spring. He has asked many times why God encourages him to create such troublesome beings.

Chapter Twenty-three

God loves their originality of thought, their courage and their adventurous spirit. If they return, they are amongst the most adaptable and free-thinking of God's servants.

All Beings of Light are not like Gabriel. He is famous as a very adaptable all-rounder. That's why he leads the Archangels, specialising in combat and helping especially twisted souls. He thinks quite independently of the other Beings of Light and can anticipate unforeseen possibilities and outcomes that others haven't considered. All Beings of Light are masters of creation, but Gabriel is famous for cleaning up others' messes. If something is in the 'too hard basket' they usually ask Gabriel to fix the problem, especially if God wants something reworked and not 'unmade' [unmade means a creation or being is dissolved back into the infinite and never exists again] after it all goes wrong. Everything created is allowed to take its natural course of evolution with all existing beings affecting how that creation develops and if possible incorporating them into the Creation Song.

Sometimes these realms become a negative, tangled mess of suffering and ignorance. Gabriel can think laterally and be utterly ruthless to save what he can from a situation. God knows huge potential can be born from seemingly utter chaos. Gabriel is good at unravelling the mess and finding the potential within for something new and beautiful to be fostered and helped to grow – just as in the garden. Then other Beings of Light, like Lara, step in for the next stage. Our Lower Realms are one of these messes made by Senior Fallen separating themselves from God's Creation Dream and going it alone.

Most Beings of Light are known as 'The Silent Ones'. They sit and dream the creation song and help it change direction when the time comes. They can also change the mass consciousness of a country or whole world when the time is ripe, so that all are in tune with the coming changes. Because the Fallen had such a long free rein to create down here, the Silent Ones have had to move slowly to change and raise our vibrational levels or else they would unmake us.

A History of Angels

We live in an ego-based world. Ego is a very limited being with a low vibrational level. If this world's vibrational level were to be raised too quickly, ego would dissolve back into the infinite. Raising the vibration makes it easier for humans to hear and be guided by their soul, but it can cause great suffering to a person if they are not connected to their soul. We are all being helped to shift our focus back to our souls so that we can be part of the God Realms. Many won't make it. They will be shifted to realms that suit their low vibrational level. We are still free to choose but a separation is occurring between ego driven people and soul driven people.

We are seeing this polarisation of consciousness happening in the world today particularly in the way people view religion, politics and relationships. Some see serving God as blowing people up and having complete control of other's lives. This is the destructive and ultimately self-destructive path of ego. You only have to watch the news to see the suffering and war caused by fundamentalism and nationalism.

If you want to know God better ask to be connected through your higher self and these 'Silent Ones' will come to you. I used to dream of them when I first asked for help. They never spoke to me but were made up of the most beautiful kaleidoscope of coloured energies. Each specialised in helping me develop an aspect of my self that lay dormant and undeveloped. Each helped me open to a different aspect of my soul and to God. They are pure beauty and compassion and don't judge you at all.

They used my art as a way to help me get to know them better and feel the energy they were offering until I could find it within myself and express it. I was curious to paint the Silent Ones and Gabriel was kind enough to be an intermediary for me so I could ask them questions. Gabriel could feel their intent and what they were trying to express to me. He tried to put it into language I could understand. But if I hadn't been connected to my heart and feelings at the time, anything they tried to convey to me would have been meaningless.

Chapter Twenty-three

The Silent Ones [and Gabriel] express straight from their heart to your heart. Your ego won't understand what is going on. It took years before I understood the true beauty of the message they'd shared with me, much of which I had expressed with my art. But because of his job down here, Gabriel needs to be able to communicate on a level all can understand. It is one of his greatest challenges. People are terrified when their beliefs are challenged. Humanity views God through the mish-mash of myth, superstition, religion and self-serving politics, which has nothing to do with the truth of the Infinite being and why we exist.

Gabriel's female aspect is a Silent One. She pushes Gabriel not just to serve God but express himself creatively and enjoy intimacy when he can with like-minded souls. Such times I think are sadly rare for Gabriel. His eagle children incarnated here are especially attracted to him on Earth and try to find him and he enjoys catching up with them too, but is careful not to interfere in their journey down here. God wants Gabriel to have relationships with his children, especially his girls, because of how lost and lonely they are for like-minded souls, but Gabriel worries about the huge longings and needs he brings out in them and fears they may become dependant on him.

So Gabriel tries to help them in soul form and may even become their lover [in soul form] but won't see them in the flesh until they let go of their attachment to ego, otherwise they would feel torn asunder by their soul and ego pulling them in two different ways. This causes them great agony and makes Gabriel very sad. But he can't deny a true heart-felt desire if his children want to catch up with him, but often they have to wait many years even though they constantly feel his love and guidance. Gabriel will leave them alone if they wish and return again if they change their mind.

I asked Gabriel how many Beings of Light are incarnated on the Earth at this time. He said there were four including himself - two males and two females. Lara is one of them. These Beings of Light agreed to help Gabriel find those who want to become part of the God Realms. They are new to the Lower Realms and rely heavily on Gabriel for guidance in handling and helping people so cut off from their souls and their hearts. Ego only believes in something it can touch and feel, and even then may doubt it.

Lara explained that Gabriel's children are more suited to this kind of work and it is hoped more of them will make the crossover into becoming Beings of Light. They are better at the confrontational work of challenging preconceived ideas of ego and she and the two other Beings of Light are better at the subtle task of helping people find compassion for themselves and others. In the God Realms Lara and Gabriel are having a relationship. She hopes that they will be able to meet in the flesh soon but she understands that he is busy cleaning up some very dangerous situations in the world and he is trying to guide it away from another world war. Countries have collective egos, which are always looking for outer enemies, trying to destroy them and make the world into its own image.

Lara went on to say that Beings of Light don't want to be confined to just serving God and cleaning up other people's messes. They also like to live, love and create as God intended, no matter how bad things are. They live in the moment. That's why God is putting pressure on Gabriel to take time for personal relationships and to enjoy life when he can. If the world falls apart, so be it. The beings that live here created this mess. They should learn to clean it up or live with the consequences. Beings of Light could spend their whole existence patching things up and the same people would tear it apart again.

That's why they are separating people, so the ones interested in living a positive and constructive life can live in peace and freedom, and the other selfish, short-sighted beings can be clumped together to play out their destructive and pointless games until they fade into nonexistence. People's souls are already beginning to exist in the realms of their choice and when they die they will move there completely and not be torn between different realms of lower and higher. In other words, souls who have turned to the light will incarnate out of Earth and won't return here.

Chapter Twenty-three

That's what Lara meant when she said we will all eventually leave Earth in the next few hundred years, and all the souls who aren't interested in the light can end their existences here and do what they like to the planet and themselves. It won't be pretty. Gabriel is making sure, with the help of the three Beings of Light, that everything holds together until all are gone who want to go. But in a way it doesn't matter. If you are interested in the light, you've already got one foot in the God Realms and the death of your body, or this world, won't change that fact. And there are many alternate realities for Earth running at the same time that a soul can exist on too, that aren't as troubled as here.

A History of Angels

Chapter Twenty-Four

ATTACHMENT

Attachment is ego's idea of love. It is the one thing that Beings of Light talk to people about that causes them the most fear and denial, especially attachment to a person or people.

I had a friend who was having a terrible time. She was a single mother with a long line of abusive boyfriends and a family who treated her like dirt. When she was young she had been sexually abused by her father. She also found it very hard to keep a job. We were talking about attachment one day and she said, " As long as God doesn't ask me to give up my 'fake tan' I'll be alright. I couldn't bare to live without it."

At first I thought she was joking but when I saw this very petulant, pigheaded look on her face, I realised she was very serious indeed. This poor girl had so little to hold on to, her fake tan was her security blanket. She also clung to her family, to her own gradual self-destruction. My security blankets were art, hockey, beer and my car.

This was the dark period in my life when I started to question my relationship with my own family with whom I was having similar troubles. I used to travel a lot on my own and when I did I felt like a completely different person. All my insecurities seemed to fall away. I felt at peace with myself, safe and close to God and my soul. But when I returned home a dread would come over me.

Once we were sitting at the dinning room table having a late Christmas dinner. I had just returned from India and felt very clear and at peace. But my family were like strangers.

A History of Angels

They looked at me with such hungry eyes, it dawned on me that they had a great need for me. I remember sighing as darkness and despair slowly descended on me like sleep. I realised I had to accept this slumber of my soul if I wanted to stay with my family. I thought I loved and needed them, that I couldn't live without them, but I felt I was slowly suffocating. All my fears, self-hatred, and doubts returned. I felt confused, tired and world-weary.

A few things happened after that. First I had a dream. I was floating in the ocean far from the shore, my family was with me and they were scared. They all clung to me to save them so tightly that they pinned my arms and legs. We all started to go under. I said to them, "If you'd all let go of me I'll be able to help you, but if you cling to me so desperately we'll all drown." They refused to let go and we all drowned.

I started to feel an inner agony, an agony of my soul. I realised if I stuck around I'd go under. I felt suicidal. I started to drink heavily to dull the pain and stayed out more. I started to ask myself how much I was willing to sacrifice to be with my family. I realised my attachment was threatening my very survival.

I went and secretly did a 'cutting the ties that bind us' course. My soul found great peace because it knew I was listening to it. On the course we had to draw the first image that came into our minds. I drew a rainforest parasite vine, a ficus, which grows around a healthy tree and slowly covers it, completely taking it over. The poor tree rots from within and finally disappears and the parasite lives off the rot. By the end the vine looks just like a tree itself. My attachment to my family was rotting me from the inside out. They were living off my support.

While I did this course I felt the vine being cut away. My family must have felt something was up and started to put more pressure on me. They tried to treat to me like I was a silly child, but the old emotional buttons of self-doubt, so easily pushed before, didn't work anymore. I was shocked at how angry and desperate they got when it was obvious I was moving out.

Chapter Twenty-four

At this time the woman I was seeing for the cutting the ties course mentioned she had a vision for me. She saw me as a happy, independent man if I moved on from my family. If I stayed, I'd become a weak, sad, vague character who would slowly drifted away in defeat from reality and life and die young. Funnily enough I'd heard this a few times before from different sources. I knew it was true. It was time to move on. The inner agony left me as soon as I moved out but fears of abandonment and loneliness assailed me.

Something about these fears wasn't quite right. This was when I first realised our egos are psychically linked to our family and friends. I was feeling their fears but felt a sort of detachment when they assailed me. My soul would pull back and let me see they weren't my fears. I learnt to sit quietly when self-hatred, doubt and fears assailed me, and not act on them. Once I would have rung a friend or gone out for a drink to distract myself from these awful feelings. I noticed they would wash over me and not drown me in despair and suicidal thoughts anymore.

I became a bit of a hermit. This is when I realised I only drank when I felt lonely, so I drank very little. The lonely feelings disappeared as I listened more to my soul. I stopped painting for others, gave up being an animator and started using my art to understand myself better. Old friends hated the new direction my art was taking. They thought it was weird and spiritual. They also thought I'd gone weird and spiritual. We drifted apart. I went a long time without a girlfriend.

This was the first time in my life women weren't a factor. My mother, sister and grandmother were very strong characters in my life. I'd also had an eight year relationship with a girl who, in hindsight, was so like my mother it was scary. I lived in a share house with two other guys. They were so easy to be with. We all gave each other personal space and privacy and there was an amazing lack of drama, which was so refreshing and exactly what I needed at the time. All three of us were estranged from our families. Karma had brought us together as mirrors for each other.

A History of Angels

I decided it was time to catch up with a girl I was in love with who had moved north to a country town. She said I could come up and live with her for a while. When I got there all the old fears doubts and needs came back. We set off across Australia together in my old F100 pickup truck. We were so needy with each other. I felt empty and anxious for her love and she for mine. We started to emotionally unravel together. It was like we were in an emotional tornado or washing machine. I lost all sense of myself and became obsessed about her. She was the same about me. We were like needy demanding children.

When we were stuck in a tent in a dirt camp-site up in Northern Australia in the middle of the rainy season, it all came to a dramatic head. Mosquitoes attacked in clouds. Ants and bugs crawled all over and into everything. The last straw for my girlfriend was when all her clothes went mouldy. She completely lost the plot and started kicking the truck. She had the brains to realise we were killing each other and got the next bus out of town and went back down south. I was assailed by a terrible sense of abandonment. I didn't know what to do with myself.

I tried to drive south after her but luckily my truck broke down in the desert and I barely crawled back to town with no breaks or steering. I worked at a crocodile farm, a supermarket and a hardware store to try and raise enough money to fix the truck and pay for petrol. It was over 6,000 km back to Melbourne and I was broke. When my girlfriend first left I had the most irrational thought, 'At least I've got my truck, that's all I need'. Well that truck became an amazing stone around my neck by the end of the trip and I would gladly have walked away from it.

Before my girlfriend left she spoke to me a lot about feelings and wanted to understand what I felt about everything. Being a bloke I realised I had probably five or six basic feelings I recognised; the rest I ignored. I knew when I was angry, depressed, lonely, jealous, happy, or bored. I realised I hadn't ever really felt loved once in my life. I didn't even know how it felt. My frustrated girlfriend said people have thousands of different feelings.

Chapter Twenty-four

I'd started drawing mandala-like patterns in the dirt around the tent. I felt great peace when I did it. My girlfriend would point at them and say, "What do you feel when you look at that one or that one?" I realised they all made me feel different. Some were negative mandalas expressing some sort of emotional block or pain. Others were positive and left me with a sense of wholeness or clarity about myself.

While I looked at one negative mandala one day my girlfriend asked me, "How do you feel?" I said, "I don't feel anything, just sort of fuzzy and vague." "That's a feeling!" she said. I actually understood what she meant. All these vague uncomfortable negative feelings I had within me that I usually just ignored, stopped me recognising them and healing them. So the mandalas helped me listen to myself. I was able to see the negative emotions in my life that were shaping my decisions and actions in a sort of 'knee jerk reaction' without any conscious choice on my part.

When my girlfriend left I had months on my own to truly get to know myself better, and see how damaged I was. I also saw how my attachments to people, and need for them to fill my emptiness, was killing me. I stopped the blind panic rush back to Melbourne. I realised I'd find no peace or answers there. I was stuck up north because my soul wanted me away from all my old attachments.

Every night at about 3am I'd be woken up and I'd hear a soft but persistent voice in my head ask me, "Why are you friends with this person? What are their negative and positive traits?" I'd think about it for a bit and then I'd realised they were all mirrors to me and were helping me see things about myself I was unwilling to look at. I started to see the karma of all my friendships and an amazing lack of any real love in these relationships. All these friends and family members had a great array of attachments to things that ranged from the intellectual, the materialistic, to the emotional. All of them were unhappy needy people, just like me. I realised how complicated all these needs made me, and how unhappy. They were also unfulfillable needs too.

When I finally arrived back in Melbourne I realised I didn't need my family or friends any more because I was willing to look at myself. I no longer needed the mirror. I still saw some of them but I didn't need them anymore. I still had unfinished business with my girlfriend and we moved in together down the coast.

It was one of the most spiritual times in my life. We'd spend days talking about insights and dreams we'd had or helping each other understand a person or situation. It was the first time I realised I wanted to live and breathe a spiritual life. The old life was so empty and pointless and unfulfilling. I didn't care what people thought of me anymore. This is when Gabriel showed himself to us both, though I think he'd been working hard behind the scenes for many years. It was also when we learnt about angels and the Fallen and how people psychically influence you, especially your family.

My girlfriend is a spiritual healer. I remember one day she became frustrated trying to explain to a single mother why her attachment to finding a rich man to solve all her problems in life, was causing all her suffering and destroying her life. I was sitting in the lounge room and my girlfriend turned to me and said, "Rod, what can I say to her to make her understand?" I remembered another time this girl had visited us. She liked to talk to me to get a male's perspective. I'd listened to the list of all the things that were wrong about her boyfriend and asked her, "Do you have any idea what he wants, or what he feels about anything?" My question seemed to confuse her. I said, "It sounds like you don't know much about this guy at all, but you are willing to marry him as long as he gives you what you want." This comment, of course, killed the conversation.

When I sat there this time I was struck by how this woman was just a demanding little girl looking for a guy to come along and make everything alright. She'd feel loved and safe and he would be a cross between Santa Claus and Daddy meeting her material and emotional needs. I thought, is it really this poor guy's responsibility to try and fulfil such a huge need? Could anyone meet this need? This is something people look to God for, and he's the Supreme Being!

Chapter Twenty-four

I realised I was like this woman. I was like a scared little boy who wanted my girlfriend to make me feel loved and secure and she had the same need. So I said to my girlfriend to tell this woman that it was a childish idea of relationships. It was an attachment to an idea that was near impossible to fulfil and the reason most relationships fall apart.

When I realised how childish and needy I was and how this need had nearly destroyed me within my own family, a great peace came over me for the first time in my life. I walked out into the backyard with the dog and threw a tennis ball far into the air for her. She leapt so high to catch it, I laughed at her pure delight and exuberance. I felt like crystal clear water. I could sense and hear all life around me, around the world. The dog seemed to sense something and was so excited, she knew I could really see her with clarity and love and I could see she loved and trusted me. I felt one with everything.

I'm not saying I don't have attachments anymore, but after facing that big one, letting go of the others was a breeze. Another big issue I, my family and my girlfriend had was a need to control our environment. At the time I was the coach of a field hockey team. The year before I had the satisfaction of seeing my team win the premiership. The next year we had to go up another level and, being a small club, we were hit hard when half the team wasn't available due to work and family commitments. I watched everything we'd worked so hard to build fall apart. We only won one game for the season and I realised there was nothing I could do about it. I had to let go. I knew my players were trying their best and the players who helped us from the lower teams also.

So my speeches changed. Every week we just went out and had a crack at the opposition, with no expectations. We didn't ague or turn on each other in our frustration and we'd have a laugh after the game. I realised also I felt a great weariness about playing hockey and it was time to move on at the end of the season. I also didn't want to be in charge of anyone again. I was enjoying taking a back seat, where before I used to thrust myself forward. I had had a need for others to acknowledge me and I think I looked for that through coaching and excelling as a player. The need or attachment had gone.

Not long after this my girlfriend and I broke up amicably. I didn't have another relationship for two years. They were the two most peaceful years of my life. I also moved into an inner-city share house with four students. We only had a small kitchen and no lounge room or sitting area. Dinner time was chaos. My old needs for space and privacy went out the window. Renovations went on day and night on both sides of our house. People yelled and screamed as they fought in our street. Ambulances would roar past three times a day because we were near the commission flats where all the drug dealers, gangs and down-and-outs hung out. But I knew my soul was where it wanted me to be. I felt strangely safe and at peace. I realised I couldn't be bothered worrying about things I couldn't fix anymore. I learnt to flow with life.

Security is an inner thing. Without it, no matter how much control you have over your environment, you never find it. I saw that with the snobby millionaires who lived down the coast who were always complaining and taking legal action against each other over the silliest things. They were looking for complete control over their environment and the people around them and never achieving it. With all their money they were some of the unhappiest and most petty people I'd ever met. They keep looking for outer Utopia's, but outer Utopia's are impossible to achieve, especially when everyone around you is doing the same thing and exerting the same control over their environment and their neighbours as you are. So the struggle and conflict begins and the outer peace and harmony is lost.

People have this same attachment to outer ideas of happiness with spirituality and religion. They wrap themselves in the security of their faith and prayers, remove themselves from society and hope that chanting, solitude, burning incense and being around other like-minded people will bring peace, fulfilment, or nirvana. But people have their own ideas and will try and make others do it their way. They will become frustrated with those who don't tow the line. Rivalries and infighting begin. What you ran away from in the

Chapter Twenty-four

'big bad world' has followed you right into the sanctuary of your religious or spiritual retreat. Your dreams of a spiritual Utopia are crushed.

My story shows how different attachments bound me to people and ways of life that caused me great suffering and disillusionment. My life was so complicated back then, but now has a lot of breathing space, a lot of stillness and peace. It doesn't matter who I work with, where I live, whether I sculpt or paint or not, if I've got a girlfriend or not. This inner space and peace can't be taken away from me, because it doesn't rely on an attachment to anything, it just is.

I had a vision that I was an old and gnarled tree. I was covered with dead and rotting branches and also had many different types of trees grafted onto me. I saw myself pruned right back down to my trunk. At first I looked ugly, lifeless and bare. But new life sprouted from my old trunk. My new branches grew straight and strong. Lush foliage sprung forth, then the most beautiful white flowers like lotus blossoms. Golden fruit covered the branches and fell to the earth.

When I think of all those rotting and grafted-on branches, which were my attachments and other people's attachments to me, and how I had them pruned back, I realise now I am growing into the tree I was always meant to be. Not what someone else wants me to be, or what I think I have to be to be loved and accepted by others, but what my soul and God wants me to be.

A History of Angels

Chapter Twenty-Five

WHY I LEFT MY FAMILY

My mother, sister and grandmother became my whole family after the death of my father and grandfather in my late teens. The women in my family are remarkable, giving people who are very talented in their fields of expertise. Because of the suffocating relationship I had with them I lost all sense of myself and realised I had to walk away. I hope to illustrate how this came about by telling a bit of our family story.

My father and mother were very much in love in the early years of their marriage. They both came from great poverty and hardship. My Dad had an alcoholic abusive father who was a union man during the Depression. When thugs were sent by the bosses to beat up or murder union men, the union sent for my Grandpa to deal with them. He was a tough man and good with his fists. He even made money on the side as a street fighter and Dad said once Grandpa set up a tent in the back yard for fights and he and my two oldest uncles fought all comers for the purse put in by both fighters. Grandpa slugged it out once with one man, nonstop, for over two hours with bare knuckles till both were too tired to go on.

Grandpa had a dog. Three thugs, who were always after the union men, tortured and killed the dog. Grandpa tracked them down one night in the city. He beat them almost to death, punching one man through a plate-glass shop window. A broken shade of glass fell and sliced this man's nose off.

A History of Angels

Dad grew up the middle son in a family of two girls and six boys. Grandpa would come home late at night drunk. Grandma would yell at him so he would bash her. The children were naturally terrified of him. I don't think my Dad or uncles and aunties had any love shown to them in their whole childhood. To my grandfather, life was one big battle for survival. When he reached his sixties he'd had enough, climbed into bed and willed himself to die. My father said to him "You're just giving up, you silly old bugger." Two weeks later Grandpa was dead.

My mother, on the other hand, was an only child. Her father, who I called Pa, was a very jealous and possessive man. Pa and Nana came out as poor immigrants from England to Australia in the 1920s. They were treated very harshly and found it hard to get work. Pa became very sick with tuberculosis. He also lost one and a half lungs from working in refrigerators at an ice-cream factory in Melbourne. Ammonia gas was used for refrigeration in those days and the ammonia ate Pa's lungs away. He had to sleep sitting upright so he wouldn't suffocate in his sleep. In his powerlessness and unhappiness he was very hard on Nana. She was always a free spirit and would tire of it and run away for months on end, deserting my mother. From the age of eight my mother had to go work at Victoria market and feed and care for Pa on her own.

When my mother and father met they decided they wanted a better life for their children, so they moved away from inner city Melbourne where they'd both grown up into an undeveloped beachside area in the South Eastern suburbs that later on become a wealthy suburb. Both their families thought they were crazy living in the middle of nowhere.

These were very happy times for them both and it wasn't long before my sister was born and Mum had to stop working. This put a lot of pressure on them both while they were trying to pay off the mortgage as Dad only had a low paying job as a sales representative for a steel company. By the time I came along three years later, there was a lot of financial stress but they were still very much in love with each other.

Chapter Twenty-five

Mum's best friend was unhappily married and envied her romantic relationship with Dad. She determined to seduce my father. So it was about the time of my birth that my father started a secret affair that was to last eight years.

By the time I reached the age of four Mum started to suspect something was wrong, but she loved and trusted Dad so ignored her intuition and doubts. But my sister somehow sensed what was going on and would become distraught whenever Dad made an excuse to visit Mum's friend. My sister would have an asthma attack, which would nearly kill her, and Mum would sit up all night with her on her own. Dad started to be very aloof with Mum and our family life became one big struggle. It was at this time Mum had to go back to work again.

When Mum was out she would sometimes see my father from afar with her best friend. When she asked him about this he'd make out she was imagining things. It became so frequent and my Dad's denials so strong that Mum started to doubt her sanity. Dad even convinced Mum to see a doctor who advised Mum that she should have electric shock treatment, which my father encouraged. Mum was going to go ahead with this treatment when she saw him and his lover up close.

When Mum confronted Dad they went into the bathroom to argue and Dad punched Mum in the eye. I was four years old at the time and watching television when a terrible feeling of despair came upon me and suddenly I felt worried for Mum. I went looking for her and opened the bathroom door to a scene I'll never forget. Mum was sitting on the edge of the bath holding her head crying and my father was standing over her threatening her.

When my parent's realised I was standing staring at this horrific scene, Mum looked up, her eye already bruised and swollen. I asked her if she was all right. She was concerned for me and tried to rally herself. She put on a brave face and told me she was fine. I asked what had happened to her eye and will never forget the look on her face when Dad piped in and said she had fallen over and bumped her head. How can I describe her expression? It was like Mum, who had completely loved and trusted Dad, had just had her heart torn out. He had betrayed her and was even willing to let her think herself crazy and have shock treatment just to sustain a lie. Dad punching her in the eye was the last straw.

I didn't move. My Dad thought the discussion was over and I'd get the hint and leave. But I just stood there and looked at Mum, then at him. I was no fool. I knew he'd hit her. In that one moment, at four years old, I decided my Dad was a coward and I lost all respect for him and felt very protective of my embattled mother. I also started to notice and question my father's relationship with his brothers, who seemed angry with him. They had no respect for Dad because they knew about his affair and they all liked Mum.

After this assault Mum was a broken woman. She aged ten years and was depressed and despondent. One day she lay down on her bed and gave up the will to live. I was playing with my toys in another room and felt my mother separating from me, like she was drifting away. I jumped up and rushed into her room and was horrified to see her lying there as if she were dead. I grabbed her arm and started pulling it and calling her name desperately. Gradually Mum started to respond. I told her I needed her and she couldn't go. I asked her to make me dinner, and she dragged herself out of bed like a zombie and went into the kitchen and prepared a meal. I went everywhere with her for weeks after that always holding her hand and she slowly came back to her old self again. I've never felt so sorry for anyone as much as my Mum when she lay dying of a broken heart. No death could be crueller.

After this our family dynamics changed. Mum switched her love for Dad to me, which made my father very jealous, and he began to hate me. From that day on he hit me all the time, but I never cried, I didn't want to give him the satisfaction. I realised Dad had a bullying streak in him that made him worse if he saw weakness. I used to stare straight back at him when he hit me. I was waiting for the day when I was big enough to pay him back for all the beatings he'd given me. The worst thing Dad did to me was to constantly call me an idiot. Right up till I was thirty-five calling me an idiot was a very dangerous thing to say to me.

Chapter Twenty-five

I used to watch other boys with their Dads kicking a football or having fun and I envied them. My one memory of my Dad playing sport with me was when I was five. We were watching the cricket on television and Dad decided to take me out into the backyard to teach me the fundamentals of the game. It didn't last long. He started to hit me because I wasn't holding the cricket bat straight. In frustration he made me bowl the ball to him instead, but being so young, I had trouble bowling the ball over-arm, so he flew into a rage and hit me again and sent me inside. On another occasion he decided he wanted to teach me how to hammer a nail into wood and was furious that a five year old couldn't drive a nail in with a hammer that he could barely lift.

Two things came out of this almost daily treatment by my father. One was that it made me a very tough little boy. Not a week would go by that I didn't get in a fight at primary school. I wouldn't take crap from anyone, especially if they called me an idiot. And I frequently got into trouble standing up to teachers when they verbally put me down and was given many beatings. A gang of boys followed me everywhere I went and I liked to fight boys older than me. The second was that I considered myself stupid and had trouble learning at school until I was about ten years old.

Its funny but many boys' father's respected me and told my Dad how lucky he was to have such a tough kid for a son and Dad was proud of that. My sister, who is three years older than me, was very sickly and weak at this time. Children can be very cruel and would bully her. This made me angry, and I'd try to stand up for her. I always remember a huge redheaded boy and two of his friends, who were my sister's age, cornered us one day. They were twice my size but my sister was furious at them for their endless tormenting of her. She thought I'd sort them out for her. They began to pick on me and push me around as I tried to walk away, so my sister laid into them furiously with her school bag. I was so proud of her. They took off and left us alone. My sister turned on me angrily and asked why didn't I bash them? I pointed out that they were too big for me and there were three of them. She stood and thought about that for a moment and realised I might be tough but I wasn't stupid.

Dad still went off at night to visit this woman but Mum started to stand up for herself. She punished Dad in every way she could for the slightest mistake and made him feel like an incompetent fool. Dad began to hide in the garage all weekend until evening so he wouldn't feel the edge of Mum's sharp tongue. She asked my sister and I once if we wanted to leave Dad and go with her, but we burst into tears, so she stayed. It was the 1960s and women had few rights and little protection under the law if they left their husband and Mum would have had to support two young children on her own.

A lot of my early upbringing and happy memories are due to the times spent with my sister. We were on our own a lot because Mum had to work. My sister would take me everywhere with her and would even organise picnics and we'd go off with my billy-cart full of food, a blanket and drinks and find a nice park and have a little party.

Dad became aloof towards the family while he was having the affair, so my mother in particular, and even my sister, turned to me for the love and support they should have been receiving from him. Also because my Pa was so hard on my Nana, she too looked to me for support and we always got on well. I also respected the fact that she refused to let her bitter husband [Pa] ruin her love of life. I was the only one she'd listen to when she was being naughty.

Mum became very interested in spiritual things and also alternative medicine, because no cures could be found for my sister's chronic asthma. Mum also looked for something to fill the emptiness left by the failure of her marriage. By the time I was nine years old she had become a very well known and respected yoga and meditation teacher, which changed her life and ours because lovely people started to come to our house for classes. This took a lot of pressure off the family dynamics. My father was a broken man and hid more and more in the garage. He had no friends of his own and lived with his head in history books in his free time. My sister was a driven student, dux of our high school and later became a lawyer.

Chapter Twenty-five

When I was ten I was in a big fight at school with a kid who was into karate. A huge pack of kids surrounded us as we fought. I had this weird epiphany when I looked up at the crowd of kids surrounding me howling for my blood. It was so ugly.

I realised from this moment on I'd had enough of being a tough guy. I refused to be a gang leader anymore and my love of books and the library began. When I went to high school I fell in love with art and became a quiet and successful student. I had little trouble with bullies because most of them remembered how tough I was at primary school. I went on to study graphic design and animation at film school.

When I was fifteen I grew nearly one foot in a year. My father was scared of me then and didn't dare hit me anymore, but he changed tack and was always trying to insinuate, wrongly, that I was a homosexual. Also, no matter what I said, he'd contradict me. When I was sixteen Mum and Dad separated, and when I was eighteen my father died of a heart attack. At the funeral there was considerable anger aimed at my mother, sister and I by Dad's side of the family. I came home one night from college and my sister and Mum were in tears after my uncle had been very rude to them on the phone and it was obvious they didn't want us at the funeral. We were all completely confused by this attitude.

I rang up my uncle and told him I'd come around and punch his head in if he spoke to my Mum and sister like that again. My tough uncle laughed. He was the famous hard man of the Belchers after my Grandpa's death. It seems my Dad had been telling terrible lies about us to his family about how badly we treated him and also how I'd become some sort of 'arty poof' at high school. Well my uncle knew I meant business on the phone and knew I wasn't joking when I said I'd sort him out, so everything changed after that with him. He respected me for standing up for my mother and sister, and let us view Dad's body before it was cremated. Dad's new girlfriend had tried to make him change his will and cut my sister and I out of it. She too told terrible lies to Dad's brothers about us. Ironically, Dad died before he changed his will so my sister and I inherited everything.

The point of telling the family story was I wanted to show how my mother, sister and even Nana looked to me for support. I was happy to take on this role. But also how the battle between my father and mother also became very ugly. Both fought for control of the family and their environment in different ways. Dad would lose his temper and storm around threateningly, making us fear he'd commit some sort of violent act. He'd also turn anything said into an argument.

Mum, on the other hand, would undermine Dad and make him doubt himself and his manliness and, in later years, when she won supremacy and ruled the house and family, she'd storm around the house now instead and make sure we all knew who was boss. Mum became the one to fear. Because my mother had been treated so terribly by men, she understandably was never going to let men harm or have control over her ever again. Her very survival rested on her having complete control of her environment and everyone in it.

When people talk about the love we feel for our family we associate it with loyalty. Also within a family, love and tenderness can be in short supply from people who have been deeply emotionally scarred. They have a sense that they are struggling to survive in a very competitive environment. Families become a battleground where everyone is trying to wrest some sort of control and security over other members and maybe, if they win this control, someone will fulfil their needs. This is when love, compassion and acceptance are sacrificed and the family relationship becomes loveless.

I remember before I walked away from Mum, that we had begun to have ugly arguments. Terrible things were said. I realised there was no love for me anymore if I hung on to the family in this endless struggle. I'm not blaming Mum, it was just that our old relationship of mutual dependency forged out of this harsh family breakdown was suffocating us both.

Chapter Twenty-five

I realised something about myself and my family. We were scared of being alone and because of this we stayed in relationships long after all the love was gone. I knew that if I went back to my family I'd fall back into this old dependency and we'd all start playing the same roles again. I've had many years on my own now and I'm probably the happiest and most fulfilled I've ever been. When I was with my family, and even with my girlfriend, I felt lonely. Isn't it funny that the reason I stuck out these relationships well passed their used-by date was because I feared loneliness. I didn't realise the relationships themselves made me feel lonely.

I was looking to my family, especially my mother and my girlfriends, to fill the emptiness left by the loss of my connection to my soul. To lose your connection to your soul is like being damned. Its like we have abandoned our soul over many lifetimes to fulfil our ego's idea of happiness, and feel more lost and empty as time goes by, and I felt very lost indeed.

There is only one way to connect with your soul again; you have to start listening to your heart and feelings. This leads you deeper inside yourself to your soul. We can only do this great journey alone; no loved-one, priest, guru, mystic, or saint can do it for you. Ego always looks for someone or something outside itself for help, but no matter how religious or spiritual the person or people we turn to for help, or how wise the writings in some sacred text are, in the end we can only find our true self and God through intimacy with our soul. This is also why it would bother me if people judged my mother when I walked away, because to truly find myself I had to leave.

A History of Angels

Chapter Twenty-Six

CONDITIONING

What stops us being able to access our true feelings and our soul? Firstly, we bring in past-lifetime scars or memories and karmic connections. Secondly, from a very early age we are conditioned to act in a certain way, especially by our parents. In my own relationship with my father I learnt very quickly that any show of feelings was viewed as weakness. I learned to hide what I truly felt and by the time I was a teenager I was an aloof and cynical character with an unbending attitude towards others, very suspicious of anyone wanting to access me emotionally.

This is conditioning. My father moulded me into the character I became. I also was led to believe that to be a 'true man' I had to be aggressive and forceful. So I learned to view all relationships and communication with others in a combative way, which created a lot of unhappiness and loneliness for me. I felt competitive with men and aloof with women.

I remember learning about Pavlov's Dog. He conditioned his dog to associate the ringing of a bell with being fed. The dog would salivate every time the bell rang. A girl I knew always had relationships with alcoholic men. I asked her about it once. She said the only time her father was affectionate to her as a girl was when he'd had a few beers.

In life we are taught how to respond to nearly any situation. We should love and respect our parents, love our children unconditionally, respect people in authority, feel sad at a funeral and happy at a wedding. Further we should only desire our husband or wife, should feel proud of our country whenever we see the national flag, and that if we question our religious leaders we are evil. The list is

A History of Angels

endless. We even learn to say the appropriate thing in any given situation. It doesn't matter what we truly feel as long as we conform.

And so we become this sad puppet full of suppressed emotions, fears, desires, needs, and feelings. It takes a lot of energy, will power and denial to handle this. A psychologist friend once described this to me as being like holding hundreds of beach balls under water at the same time. They all keep trying to surface and it takes an amazing amount of energy to suppress them. No matter how hard you try to ignore them, suppressed feelings desperately try to surface and usually do at a time of great stress.

This tension causes us great fear. We continually worry that buried emotions will surface at the most inopportune times to shame us and make others spurn us, damn us, judge us, or avoid us. We also worry that we might unravel mentally and become insane, which will make us even more socially unacceptable. We innately know that other people are afraid of those who are unravelling or who's emotional beach balls are popping up at all the wrong times. People fear it could be contagious, so they drive the person away, or act like it isn't happening [denial], or its all a joke, or tell them 'to pull themselves together' and 'stop making a fool of themselves.'

At the time this was happening to me I had a reoccurring dream that I was naked, sitting on a toilet in the middle of a busy street and everyone was trying to act like they couldn't see me making a fool of myself.

To compensate for the fact that society won't accept us if we let all these suppressed thoughts, fears and desires surface, we look to others to do it for us. In Western society bad boy rock stars behave in a way we secretly envy, like sleeping around with lots of people, saying what they please to anyone, smashing up hotel rooms, taking drugs and getting drunk. We identify with comedians who get up on stage and act the fool [which we spend most of our life trying not to do], express their crazy unacceptable thoughts [that we secretly have], or with artists and writers who discuss or exhibit things that are thought taboo in normal society. We

Chapter Twenty-six

like to go along to shows and make believe we are the ones who are allowed to 'let it all hang out.' But then reality clicks in the next day when we return to work, or our families and friends. The illusion that we can finally feel free to be honest with ourselves and everyone about us and show how we truly feel about everything, no matter how ugly or shocking, is shattered.

Conditioning makes us believe that it is impossible for us to truly express ourselves without being completely unacceptable to loved-ones and society. We will end up ALONE. I think the fear of loneliness is one of humanity's biggest fears and explains why we see people put up with the most dysfunctional relationships, families, friendships and workplaces. We all make the most terrible compromises in life in the hope we won't feel lonely.

But what if you found out you'd never have to feel alone again, would you jump at the chance? I did. But I had to be willing to face some of my biggest fears. I had to risk letting those emotional beach balls surface and also be willing to risk being shunned when it happened. I guess when this was asked of me by Beings of Light, I was at the end of my tether. I was so tired of running around after people hoping to feel loved and accepted, and of all the compromises and sacrifices to my own desires, feelings and dreams I endlessly had to make. In the end I didn't even know who I truly was or what I felt about anything. I felt a great pointlessness to it all, because this sort of life didn't fulfil even the most basic of my needs.

So when I was asked to 'leap off the cliff and see where I landed,' I had nothing to loose. I didn't like the guy I was and was unhappy all the time, even though I was good at hiding it. The big move we first have to make is to look at all those suppressed desires, fears and dreams. Are they real? Are they truly yours or did you inherit them? When we detach ourselves enough to be able to view these suppressed feelings, we find that the huge energy behind them from years of denial is released. We find that they aren't such a big deal anymore, especially when they are viewed singularly and compassionately in the light of day.

A History of Angels

They don't fall upon us like an avalanche and drive us stark raving mad.

Also with the guidance of Beings of Light we are shown which suppressed emotions are doing the most damage and cutting us off from ourselves. The minor and more obscure ones will fix themselves as time goes by. Suddenly, without us realising it, we are looking at everything about ourselves in a way that once would have made us despise or fear ourselves. Also we become conscious of how these suppressed emotions were shaping our lives and making us unconsciously act in a way that didn't serve our soul.

Very subtly we are inviting our souls into our lives and soul helps and supports us through this difficult time. We often question our whole life and may be hit by despair over the waste of it. A natural curiosity about ourselves begins and the process can become very interesting and fulfilling, also enlightening. We start to understand ourselves better and the way people in our lives are affecting us. Wisdom comes from this.

We discover we are a very different person to the one we were made to believe we were. We become more peaceful, happy, less judgemental and very independent. We find our needs become less demanding and we are happy with very little. We find our feelings aren't tumultuous and a muddy mess, but clean and straight forward. We know if we truly desire to do something or not and all the old doubts and impetuousness is gone. We have more energy for everything, because we aren't wasting it trying to suppress all those forbidden feelings, or worrying about whether to act or not and what will people think if we do. What others think will seem less important because we aren't looking for acceptance now, or looking for guidance all the time. We know how we feel and what we truly desire.

Chapter Twenty-Seven

LIKE A MOTH TO A FLAME

I once saw a nature show on television that showed how moths find their way around by a sort of natural guidance system using the light of the sun in daytime and the moon at night. But since man came along there is so much artificial light the poor moths fly from one false light source to another and become completely confused and even die by flying too close to flames. Nothing is more tragic than watching a moth desperately trying to reach a lamp and its wings are burning.

Young souls are like this. When they were up in the God Realms 'the light', or God's love, was easy to find and it guided the young soul in every facet of its life. The young soul felt fulfilled, safe and secure.

But when this young soul comes to the Lower Realms and Earth, everything changes. Where once it felt loved and accepted, now it has to earn love by making many compromises. Even then the love and security it had unconditionally known once before may never be recaptured. This failure happens in many ways, the most common is the relationship between parents and children. This relationship is the closest on Earth to the relationship young souls have to God and the Beings of Light that guide them.

Naturally soul assumes it will find this close and fulfilling relationship again. But on an ego-based planet, where most people are cut off from their true feelings and souls, and are guided by their egos, this is very rarely possible. People try their best, but ego can only work with what it knows and how it was conditioned by its birth parents. Ego is all about survival and having control over its environment and those in it.

The second main way people try to find unconditional love and acceptance is in romance. This heady euphoric experience resonates with the sublime beauty and sense of love and passion young souls experienced in the God Realms. When a person is in love, fears of survival and conforming to society are swept away in the headlong pursuit of something akin to eternal happiness. But what happens if your lover leaves you for another, or dies, or you grow bored and disillusioned with them, or you think you may be happier with another? Suddenly this safe blissful bubble is burst and you are left feeling empty, disillusioned, confused and scared that you will always feel this desperate need for someone to fill this empty void within and they will always let you down.

This is one form of ' like a moth to a flame'. Another is where we turn to religion and spirituality in the hope it will fulfil our longing for love.

When I was growing up I watched my mother's endless search for fulfilment through religion, spirituality, gurus, psychics, astrologers, faith healers, numerologists, tarot readers, natural medicines, meditation, yoga, Eastern philosophies, psychology and dream analogy. She bravely travelled on her search, read countless books, stayed in many religious retreats and ashrams, and did endless courses.

By the time I was in my thirties my mother had an amazing body of hard won knowledge and spiritual wisdom, but one thing always bothered me; she still felt unloved. I, on the other hand, was a bit of a spiritual fence sitter. I went along when asked to spiritual and religious talks, gurus, chants and ceremonies, readings, and healings but something about it all left me feeling unconvinced. I saw how dependent people became on religious and spiritual teachers and mystics, even medical professionals like psychologists and psychiatrists, and how they stopped trusting in themselves and their own inner guidance.

Chapter Twenty-seven

Ego's idea of finding inner peace is to find someone who has it and get as close to them as possible in the hope they will share it or give it to them. Perhaps by being in their presence it will rub off on them, and after many years, will permeate them and transform them. To me it is like they are drenching or dipping themselves in spirituality or holiness in the hope they will come out covered in gold. A veneer of gold may impress those around you and fool them into believing you are somehow transformed into something divine, enlightened, and pure, but inside you are still the same unhappy, lonely, scared person you have always been.

But ego doesn't give up easily. It tries to copy everything that a 'holy person' or teacher does in the hope something they ate, wore, said, chanted, visited, or touched will give them this state of inner peace. So ego goes about studying and trying to duplicate this holy person's life, as if it were baking a cake, hoping to have the same success. Ego tries to obtain the most detailed recipe so it can't fail to reproduce the most perfect cake, identical in all facets to the enlightened one's cake. In theory it should have the same outcome. But why are there so few truly enlightened people on Earth even though there are so many instruction manuals and holy texts for devotees to follow?

Have you ever thought about how an ugly little crawling caterpillar transforms into the most beautiful winged creature, so different to its original form that it's impossible to see where it came from? It even changes from eating leaves to collecting nectar from flowers. This metamorphosis all happens from within itself. No outer agents make this transformation happen. Within us all is the potential and the tools for a similar amazing metamorphosis. All we need is the true desire and willingness. I find this concept far more comforting and empowering then thinking I have to wait for the next messiah or divine being to come along and touch me with their magic wand like the Fairy Godmother and make all my wishes come true.

The last time I went to a healer I picked up a spiritual magazine while I was sitting in the waiting room. It had the most interesting article about why certain Tibetan lamas

A History of Angels

who visited the West didn't believe Western people had any hope of truly understanding Buddhism and Eastern philosophy. At first I was a bit miffed at this condescending view of Westerners and our misguided ideas of spirituality, but then I read on. The article mentioned how in the U.S.A. all the major religions were under siege because of recent scandals. It spoke of how among Buddhists and other Eastern religious organizations senior devotees had been caught using and selling drugs and indulging in sexual excesses, fraud and other crimes like theft, rape, assault, blackmail, intimidation, and even murder.

What caused all these tragic incidents to occur, this lama said, was Westerners' outer or ego idea of spirituality. They used meditation and spiritual exercises to suppress unwanted unsavoury thoughts and desires rather than use the techniques to allow these suppressed desires to surface and be viewed without acting on them. So these Western spiritual adepts would try to act and feel the way they thought they should act [if they were enlightened spiritual beings] without ever really facing their 'Nasty Buddha' or dark-side, as we know it in the West. This suppressed or denied dark-side starts to rise unbidden and play out in these poor peoples lives and, before they know it, they are committing crimes, taking drugs, and becoming abusive to themselves and others.

Next the lama mentioned the problems faced by other religions like Catholicism where crimes of paedophilia, and other forms of abuse, were coming to light. This idea of following in Jesus's steps without any true inner searching or understanding of their inner demons and without the proper help needed to guide them through this time, was causing this self-same dark side in priests to raise its ugly head.

I knew exactly what this lama meant. I've known teenage girls who were molested by gurus and men and women sexually abused as children by clergymen. I've been in numerous ashrams and religious retreats and the one thing that always bothered me was the terrible in-fighting and manoeuvring for powerful positions that went on, just so

Chapter Twenty-seven

people could be closer to the guru, or spiritual teacher, or clergyman, and there were always people wanting to impose their will and ideas of the spiritual journey on others. These spiritual climbers actually strutted around thinking they were more enlightened than everyone else, just because they were in a position of power.

The few truly enlightened people I've met in my life couldn't care less if you were aware if they had achieved inner peace or not, or how close they were to God. That would be irrelevant to them. What amuses me most about these special people is how hard it is to corner them into taking on positions of power or getting them to sit around telling others how they should live and feel.

Dr. Carl Jung was once asked why he thought the horrors of World War One occurred in a civilised society like the West. He said the Western world suppressed its primal self or dark side and combined this denial with a sophisticated over-civilising of itself with a need for conformity of thought and actions. This caused the denied dark or primal side to express itself in the most savage way in mass warfare and murder. We deny our dark side at our own peril.

It isn't just a Western problem either. When I was about twenty-six years old I visited India. All facets of a Hindu Indian's life are governed by strict and detailed codes of religious practice, far more formal and strict than any Western rituals. A famous, much loved, local politician died, so a mob, in mourning for him, went on a mass riot where many men, women and children were murdered and homes and vehicles were torched. Things were out of control for two weeks. What amazed me most was that local Indians accepted this as a natural and regular occurrence. I asked a local Indian professor why the riot happened? He said that many Indians feel so trapped by their position in life, especially the Untouchables who have no hope of improving their lot because of the strict caste system in India, that every now and then they explode with suppressed frustration and rage. They usually vent this anger by attacking Muslims, who are in a minority in India.

A History of Angels

When my time to see the healer finally arrived, I felt quite distracted after reading this article. But an amazing thing happened. The young woman looked concerned and said to me that she had been told by her spiritual guides that I'd never need to come and see her again. I've never gone to a spiritual course, healer, talk, astrologer or mystic ever since. I realised no matter how clumsy or misguided my efforts may be, I wanted to find my answers for myself. I stopped meditating and using a mantra, because I understood I used it to calm and suppress my buried feelings. Now I sit quietly and explore them, and these self-same feelings I used to suppress and ignore have led me home to myself.

I remember being interested in the mythologist Joseph Campbell at the time I visited the healer. I was particularly struck by what he wrote about the legend of the Holy Grail. The quote said something along the lines of the knights on the quest for the Holy Grail arrived at the outskirts of the Dark Forest where legend held it the Grail was hidden. There was a clear well-trodden path that cut through the forest before them, but none of the knights chose to ride down it. They all rode off in different directions, because they knew no one had found the Holy Grail down another's path, and you only find the Holy Grail on your own.

To me the Holy Grail is your soul, and your higher self, which is your connection to God. I wish you luck with your personal quest, but you won't need it even if you stray off the path and find yourself lost in the dark forest of life because God will be with you every step of the way to guide you, and so will the Beings of Light.

Chapter Twenty-Eight

THE JOURNEY'S END

I would like to end with a story. You can make of it what you will.

There was a very wealthy and powerful family. Both parents had come from great poverty and with incredible drive, courage, personal sacrifices and perseverance each had become successful business people in their own right. When they met they realised that their union would enhance their already successful careers and their combined resources would offer them the opportunity to be very powerful indeed. The glittering possibilities in this union made them strongly attracted to each other sexually and soon were married.

As the years went by the couple had seven children. They were sent to the best schools and groomed to play important roles in their parents' business empire. The parents only showed affection to their children if they met their wishes in both thought and actions.

The parents were upstanding and highly respected members of the community. They supported many charities and went to church every Sunday where they had a private pew. The minister fawned over them after every service because they were the church's major benefactors. When church dignitaries visited the area they stayed at the couples' huge mansion.

The parents were known for their knowledge of the Holy Scriptures from which they quoted easily and regularly whenever they wanted to make a moral point or justify some action others may have thought questionable.

A History of Angels

The couple had two types of friends: those who wanted to be rich, powerful and respected, like themselves but weren't; and those who were their equals or rivals in business. The first type were people who were useful to the parents as pawns or tools to further the family's interests. But if one of these people fell on hard times or became a nuisance in some way, especially if they questioned what was asked of them, they were discarded without a moment's thought and the parents used their moral position in the community to have them shunned.

The second type, the successful type, were treated with respect and the parents were generous and kind to them and flattered them. But when they came home from a function with them, the children would hear the most scurrilous gossip about them and how much their parents secretly despised them and would love to ruin them. Nothing gave the parents greater joy than one of these friends falling on hard times or being caught in some unforgivable scandal. They would be giddy with elation over their fall from grace.

Their middle child was a boy who got on well with everyone in the family and did what he needed to fulfil his parents' designs for him. The one trait he had that the parents didn't like was that he was a bit of a dreamer. He also didn't seem to share their love of others' misfortune. His parents saw this as a weakness, in a world where only the most ruthless and toughest survived. There was also something that bothered the boy. He couldn't reconcile what he read in the Holy Book with how his parent's lived. It worried him that his parents weren't the least bit worried that their ruthless actions seemed to go against all the moral codes laid down in the holy texts that the parents were always preaching to their children. Also, that church dignitaries who stayed at their mansion weren't the least bit holy but were as ruthless and cynical as his parents.

When this young man had finished university he was expected to become an employee of one his parents' many companies, eventually to become a senior member of staff and run his own section. Already his older brothers and sisters were doing this. Most were married to partners that

Chapter Twenty-eight

their parents had chosen because they furthered their parents' business interests. All were resigned to their lives, but also seemed unhappy. They drank heavily and fought often with their spouses.

It dawned on this young man one day that he couldn't follow in his brothers' and sisters' footsteps. He felt pulled in two ways; one by the love and loyalty he felt towards his parents, who had given him everything [and reminded him of it regularly]. The other was a desire to walk away from this controlled, unhappy madness and find some sort of life for himself, no matter how humble or meagre. A great despair fell upon him and he took to hiding in his room for days on end. If he walked away, how could he honour his parent's wishes and the debt he felt he owed them? If he didn't, he knew his despair would only become worse and he would eventually kill himself.

He assumed that if his parents knew the truth about how he felt they would understand. Because they loved him and wouldn't want to see him unhappy, or suicidal, they would let him leave with their loving blessing. So at the dinner table one night he mustered enough courage to speak of his dilemma and he hoped that his parents would understand his desire to find his own way in life. A shocked silence fell on the family all sitting at the dining room table.

Never has the young man seen his parents so outraged. Hadn't they given him everything? Hadn't they educated him in the best schools? Hadn't they assured him of a great and secure future in their business empire? And this is how he repays them, this dreadful, ungrateful, wicked boy! They refused to hear any arguments from him and mocked him for being ignorant and ungrateful in front of his shocked and silent brothers and sisters who knew exactly how he felt.

So the son rose from the dinner table and silently went to his room where he felt a great sense of defeat. He had the most awful realisation. His parents would rather see him hang around and even die than have him thwart their plans for him. He realised they didn't love him at all. His happiness was not important to them. Some sort of tie of

A History of Angels

loyalty snapped within him and he quietly packed a few essential things, then waited till late in the evening when the household was asleep, and slipped out the front door.

One of the few things the middle son kept that was given to him by his parents was the car that he received for his twenty-first birthday. He travelled far and wide in it and lived on the small savings he had. Eventually he started taking on casual work always in towns where no one would know of him or his family. He shortened his name so it would sound more common and never spoke to anyone of his wealthy upbringing or education. One of the first things he did was throw his mobile phone into the sea. He also liked to take on 'cash only' jobs so he couldn't be traced through his credit card transactions. He also sold his flashy car and brought a knocked around old one that no one took any notice of and kept it registered in the last owner's name, an elderly man who didn't drive anymore.

He effectively disappeared. Sometimes he suffered great hardships, was robbed many times and even beaten badly when he hung out with the wrong crowd for a few weeks. But if things got too hard he only had to think of his life with his parents and what it would feel like to have to return home and he would feel peace about his decision to leave. He could always just move on to another town or city.

One legacy he had from his old life was an interest in God and a desire to know himself better. But even though he knew the Holy Book well, he found it unfulfilling and lacking any true insights and he was certainly sick of reading about these sheep-herders who went around destroying their enemies and thinking they were the 'chosen ones'. So he became very interested in all things religious and spiritual and spent many years travelling from one holy site to another, from one spiritual teacher to another, and he read endlessly. A great longing came on him. The searching seem to make the longing even worse, spurring him on to search even harder, but in the end he just felt more confused by what he saw, read and heard then when he first began.

One day he went to listen to a spiritual teacher who was quite famous, and had ashrams all around the world and

Chapter Twenty-eight

many devotees. He listened to this teacher speak and was struck by the great depth, strength and peace of the man. He realised he'd never met a truly peaceful person before. So he followed the teacher and became a loyal devotee. He worked hard and with his business training and knowledge of accounts, was given greater responsibilities within the organization. He was also given greater access to the Teacher and would sit and speak to him regularly, which always made him feel at peace. He'd long to be back with the Teacher again as soon as possible. The Teacher had a strange sort of bemused attitude towards him and talked to him differently than other people. He didn't quote holy texts to him or talk in parables to him as he did with everyone else. He just spoke to him directly and asked quite blunt questions right out of the blue.

After many years of loyal service to the Teacher he started to notice how dependant all the devotees were on him, how they hung on his every word, how they copied what he wore, ate, read, and even tried to mimic the way he spoke. People even stole pieces of the Teacher's clothing and secretly wore it. They took on fancy sounding Sanskrit names and took great pride in explaining their deeper meaning. Devotees within the organization had a habit of threatening people by saying 'the Teacher says you have to do this' or 'that's not allowed because the Teacher said so'. He knew the Teacher wouldn't talk to or order people around like that. He also noticed the senior devotees were always bitching about everyone else and seemed delighted when someone got in trouble with the Teacher.

Suddenly he realised that the ashram was amazingly familiar, and so were the people in it. It was just like being back with his family again. He felt he'd been hoodwinked. He was listening to a talk by the Teacher when this realisation struck him. It was like time stood still. The Teacher looked at him and gave him the most knowing smile. He also realised the Teacher was trapped by the devotion of his followers and there was a sort of sadness in him. Without a word the young man rose and left the talk, packed his things and moved on.

A History of Angels

For next few years he moved into a very different phase in his life. He lived in a small flat in an inner city suburb. He went a lot to bars and listened to live music, went to local theatres, and trawled through second hand bookshops. He got a job at a local café and waited at tables and made friends amongst the young staff there who worked and partied hard, drank alcohol heavily and took drugs frequently. They'd ask him along to see friends' bands play, to big warehouse parties and to art exhibitions. Every night of the week something was on if he wanted to go to some event, but he frequently went home and enjoyed the solitude of his flat and the peace he found in the quiet.

Ever since he left his parents he had had a reoccurring dream. To many it would seem an innocuous dream, but to him it was a nightmare. He'd wake to find himself back at his parent's mansion. He'd always wonder how he ended up back there again. He'd look around and see his brothers and sisters asleep in beds next to his, lined up in rows in a sort of dormitory. But it wasn't a dormitory, it was slave quarters. A terrible sense of powerlessness and despair would overtake him. He'd wake covered in sweat, relieved to see he wasn't back at the family mansion at all, but safely far, far away.

His taste in books changed and he started to read the old Beat writers, surrealists, and writers that came out of the sixties flower revolution. He loved their honesty, the way they spoke of the darkest facets of themselves and even how they revelled in what they discovered lurking there. He loved that they didn't seem to care how society judged them. All that mattered was a sort of honesty about themselves and a need to express it. It made him start to question his own dark thoughts and desires. He realised most people felt the same as these brave writers did but were too scared of showing this side of themselves to others. He found a lot of the young people he met and drank with were questioning themselves too. They loved to talk long into the night about their hidden fears and dark desires. Without realising it he became a hub for people interested in alternative ways of thinking. People dropped in on him at all hours and discussed books or films with him.

Chapter Twenty-eight

One night after seeing a friend's band, a group came back to his flat and brought all sorts of alcohol with them. They laughed and argued until morning. Amongst them was a pretty young university student who had a casual job as a waitress and worked with one of his friends. She kept staring at him all night and everyone noticed. They all knew he was a bit of a loner and they'd never seen him with a girl before. When everyone left, she stayed behind. They soon were kissing, then fell into bed and made feverish love at least three times, before falling into a sated deep sleep that lasted till late in the morning.

He woke to find the girl, nude, sitting on the floor in front of his small bookshelf. She was fascinated by all the unusual books she found there. She was studying literature at university but she'd never laid eyes on most of these books before. He was taken by how young and innocent she looked sitting there completely engrossed in his books, and how beautiful. He was surprised such a pretty girl would want to sleep with him. He asked if she'd like a cup of tea or coffee and she jumped in fright and turned around blushing and said she love one. He assumed she'd just run along as soon as possible, but she didn't, and they spent the rest of the day together and even made love once more. Eventually she had to go home to get changed for her job as a waitress. He assumed that would be the end of it.

But over the next few weeks whenever he met up with his friends, she'd be there, and would shyly hang around while he chatted to all sorts of weird and wonderful people. She loved to listen and was always surprised by his original and often off-beat view of life and how he always had a different take on books, films, music that she knew. She'd grown up in a very ordinary middle class family in the suburbs, had gone to a local high school and won her place in university from her high grades. But her family weren't interested in reading books, discussing films or plays or even questioning what they saw on the news on television. She found university a struggle, especially the way lecturers challenged students to interpret and understand what they read or saw on television. But after a while she realised

A History of Angels

there was a formula to it all. All the lecturers had a similar way of interpreting these things.

He even made the point to someone once that we are all trained to respond like robots to most situations, and people become very predictable and only say what they think will get them noticed, admired, or accepted. She thought about that and realised she was very careful indeed not to show her lack of political and social knowledge while people spoke of some outrage in a far flung third world country, or a terrible crime by a multinational company backed by some corrupt Western country. She felt like an alien, an outsider, like she came from a different planet and all this was so new to her.

She noticed that this older guy she liked seemed unimpressed by what these radicals ranted about so forcefully. He said it was just another religion with set doctrines and codes of conduct, thought and speech, and god help you if you don't follow the party line! You could just about predict every answer they'd give to any argument or situation, and when they reach their thirties they'll get bored of it all and become rich yuppies and work for the companies they used to loathe and have children and turn out amazingly like the parents they so despised before and said they'd never emulate.

At the end of every evening out she'd wait till it was time to go home or move on and hope he'd ask her back. He always noticed, with a sort of surprise, that she was still hanging around at closing time and would feel flattered and couldn't understand what she saw in a drab, uninteresting older guy like him. They'd go home and make the most amazing love and he always expected she'd soon tire of him. It took a mutual friend to point out what an idiot he was, couldn't he see she was crazy about him? After that he looked more closely and realised she only had eyes for him wherever they went. She started staying at his flat for days on end and they were very happy together. Her grades in literature rose because of the original take she now had on the old classics they studied. She found she wasn't scared of the radicals at university anymore and could hold her own in any discussion.

Chapter Twenty-eight

After many months she asked him if she could move in. This surprised him, and she felt insulted and hurt because he sat quietly thinking about it for so long that she stormed off to work. On her break she cried at the back of the restaurant where she worked, until a girlfriend comforted her and explained that it was a big step for a person who's lived alone so long to let another live with them. That didn't mean he didn't love her. Placated, she went sheepishly back to his flat where he still sat unmoved at the kitchen table. She'd never known a guy who could sit so still and peacefully and never get bored. He looked up and smiled at her and collected her into his lap and gave her a hug and said he'd love her to live with him but he didn't think her parent's would be too happy. She shrugged and said she didn't care what they thought, and for the first time in her life she meant it.

Their relationship went on harmoniously for over a year and he was truly happy. He loved her very much and she loved him. But he noticed things started to change. Whenever they went out she became jealous if he became engrossed in discussions with the usual 'weird and wonderfuls' he usually chatted to. He understood that and tried to include her in the discussion, or keep the chat short. She also needed to know where he was at all times and he grew tired of the continual cross-examinations. She would go out with her old school mates and friends from uni and he never asked her where she'd been, even though she might come home days later. All he cared about was that she was safe. This made her angry because she thought he should be jealous, especially of her many young male friends. She even contemplated sleeping with a few of them just to spite him, but the thought made her feel very sad and she'd burst into tears. He asked her why she sulked for days on end or stayed at friend's houses, but she always accused him of not loving her. It confused him because he knew he did love her and tried to show it in a million ways.

She even secretly followed him one night to see if he was seeing someone else but he just spoke to the usual crowd and sat happily on his own listening to the band.

A History of Angels

He didn't take any notice of the girls there. When he left the bar he walked over to a park and just sat for hours looking at the stars and the gardens around him, then he wandered home. She felt so ashamed of herself that she hid from him for days. But she couldn't help how she felt. She even stopped her friends visiting, though they liked her boyfriend, because she became jealous whenever he spoke to anyone, especially to the girls.

She tried to isolate him and even made his friends feel unwelcome when they visited. This is the only time he would look at her with a mixture of anger, pity, and sadness. She found herself yelling at him for the slightest thing, and turning every chat into an argument, but he always refused to be drawn into it. She started to cry for days on end and became incredibly depressed. He tried to help her, but she would refuse. He pointed out maybe it was time she spoke to a counsellor, that he'd help pay for it. It was like she couldn't bear to be without him and when she was with him she felt even more desperately needy.

In the end he couldn't see the love in the relationship anymore. He started to dread coming home to her. She was so desperate for something that no one can give another. It was like she wanted him to be her whole world, to fill her huge emptiness, but the emptiness was like a bottomless well and no matter how much love he poured into her, it didn't even touch the sides. He started to feel exhausted and depressed. She refused all offers of help even from friends and family. He started to feel like he was back at his parent's home again and he felt that same feeling of being torn in two. One part felt concerned and would do anything to save the girl he loved from her torment, although she made it impossible. The other part pulled him to walk away and find the sort of peace again he hadn't felt for a long time. He felt so confused and completely cut off from how he felt about anything anymore.

In the end, even though he loved her, he said to her that they were destroying each other by staying together. Though she sobbed, she knew in her heart he spoke the truth. She knew she couldn't go on like this much longer. When he

Chapter Twenty-eight

said it was time to end the relationship, she agreed. So he quietly helped her pack and rang her parents who kindly came around and without a word helped their daughter move out. Within a week he too was gone, never to be seen again by his friends.

He drifted for many years and spent much time alone, but an inner clarity came to him he'd never felt before. It was like he was watching himself and all around him with a renewed awareness. He started to pick up clearly how other's felt. He even felt people thinking about him. He especially felt his poor ex-girlfriend pining away for him and her desire to find him again and also her anger at him for leaving her. He also started to feel a dark intense hatred aimed towards him, which confused him. He felt two people wanted him to suffer and die horribly somewhere alone. At first he didn't recognise who these people were who felt such raw hatred towards him, until he realised it was his parents.

In a vision one night he saw a paper cut-out of his younger self being torn to pieces by his parents. It surprised him that they were still so angry with him after all these years, even though they had six other loyal children still by their side. He realised he needed some sort of clarity on this. He had another vision. He saw himself at the dinner table back at the family mansion. He was telling his parents again he was leaving. But this time he watched the whole scene from the sidelines. He observed himself rise and leave the table and the family finish the meal in stony silence. But he also noticed or felt something else. Some sort of hold or spell that the parents had over all the other children was broken by his rebellion.

He saw how over the next few weeks and months the parents said that he'd come crawling back to them on his hands and knees seeking forgiveness and that he couldn't survive without them. But to their horror and dismay, he never returned. They even hired private detectives to find him but they came up with nothing. This infuriated the parents even more. People started to talk about his leaving and the parents were incredibly embarrassed and felt he'd deliberately left them so they'd lose face in the community.

A History of Angels

The other children felt emboldened by their brother's courage and started to stand up for themselves with the parents. Three even left the family businesses and went out on their own successfully. Even the ones who stayed only came rarely to the mansion anymore and it was obvious to all the children that the parents needed them a lot more than they needed the parents. Also the spouses of the children generally despised the arrogant parents and would only visit on Christmas day if forced to. When alone with each other the parents blamed all their woes on their hateful son, who had deliberately left them to ruin their lives. How could this happen to good, honest, religious people like them? What had they ever done to deserve this? Didn't they give to all those charities generously?

He woke with a thoughtful look on his face. He realised his parents weren't the type of people to truly question that their actions may have created this situation. As far as they were concerned they were the victims and everyone else was against them, and jealous of their success. They couldn't understand why God didn't strike down their evil ungrateful son for all the woe he'd brought down on their heads. He knew he'd never return to the parents again.

His wandering finally ended one day when he took a casual job in a local family-owned hardware store in a small rural town. At first he just worked on the floor helping customers. But the owners soon realised he was handy with bookkeeping, computers and accounting and moved him to the badly run office. After a year he was offered a full time job as a junior manager. He made friends with some nice easy-going locals that he worked with and even visited an old hermit artist that lived on the outskirts of town with his ten cats. One of his friends offered his family's empty old house to him to rent at the back of their property. He gratefully accepted and moved in. Just over the fence was a Crown land Forest Reserve and he loved to wander for hours down the beautiful gullies and along the banks of the tree lined streams. He lived happily here for many years before anything unusual happened.

Chapter Twenty-eight

Now that he had a proper job his parents were able to have him tracked down by his taxation records and credit details. They had friends in the right places able to access this confidential material. The parents used the excuse of reconciliation, convinced their children and grand children to come along with them on their surprise visit to their long lost son.

One day he was sitting at home reading when a cavalcade of expensive cars drove up his dirt driveway in a cloud of dust. He could have easily slipped out the back and off into the forest unseen, but he didn't. Somehow he knew this day was coming. He was strangely unmoved and undisturbed by his family's arrival. He walked to the door to greet them and then let them come in. He spoke easily with his embarrassed siblings and enjoyed meeting all his little nieces and nephews and showed them where he climbed the fence to walk in the forest. They were so excited. They'd never walked in forests before. They spent their lives in endless weekend sports and school activities.

But he didn't have anything to say to his parents. They just looked shrunken and scared now and he noticed his siblings sort of ignored them too. And he could also feel the cogs whirling in their brains as they tried to find someway to manoeuvre him into returning. But one look at this grown man before them, a complete stranger, told them they were wasting their time. Black hatred and bile lay barely hidden behind their brittle smiles. The family noticed one thing, he never offered them tea or coffee, and waited patiently for them to leave. His siblings got the hint and started to round up the children and made their goodbyes. They were obviously glad to see him and were surprised at how peaceful he looked. Before the parents knew what was happening, they were bundled into their car by their children and were soon on their way home.

He sat for a while looking within himself to see if he was disturbed by this visit in anyway, but all he felt was a sense of calm. He realised he wasn't the same person who walked away from his family so many years before. Who was he then? He felt the calm deep within himself, like a huge lake of crystal clear water. But as he went deeper, rather than grow darker, the water became brighter and the lake was almost bottomless.

When he finally reached the bottom he found the lake led to another lake just as deep and beautiful as the first, but existing in a very different environment to his. He realised also that this lake was linked to many others all distinctly different. He felt, rather than saw, how all these lakes were different facets of himself existing simultaneously with all the others, but all leading to very different and more exciting lives than his. Something else struck him as odd. That he was aware of all the other selves but they were only aware of him and not of each other. Then he felt himself as the hub for all his different selves and how he was actually part of a vast ocean and that ocean knew him and loved him and was wise beyond reckoning and also immensely compassionate.

When he rose from his armchair near dusk, he climbed over his back fence and wandered down to a stream and sat there for a while. He felt older and wiser than time. He realised what an illusion his existence was here.

Back amongst his family the visit had caused a lot of excitement, especially amongst the nieces and nephews who wanted to know more about their mysterious uncle. Also his siblings, in quiet moments, especially when they were questioning their lives, would think of him and promise themselves they'd visit him on their own soon, but they never did.

He never had that reoccurring dream again. He was finally free.

Chapter Twenty-Nine

THE END and THE BEGINNING

I want to leave you with two images that have stayed with me all my life.

The first comes from a story about a spiritual Master who was head of a huge worldwide organization with tens of thousands of members and the author of many books. He wrote once how he believed he was God-Realised [enlightened] and that one night he had a vision in which he was taken into a study full of white light. A kind, wise Being of Light stood before him radiating power from every pore. He asked the Master with a quiet smile if he thought he was ready to take on the powers of a Being of Light now that he was God-Realised. The Master thought he was truly ready; he knew how special he was. The Being of Light pointed to an orb of clear glass on a pedestal. He explained that to have the powers of a god, as Beings of Light do, where their very thoughts create whole universes, they first have to truly know themselves or there will be dire consequences. The Being of Light pointed towards the orb and said, "Within this limited space I'd like you to imagine the world you'd truly like to create, inhabited by any beings and life forms you so desire".

The Master was excited. He had always felt he could have done a better job of Earth if he'd been the one to create it and how it would be a Utopia of peace and beauty. So he bent his will towards the orb and a world came into being, a world of vast oceans and continents, of beautiful complex flora and fauna inhabited by beautiful angelic-looking beings living in many large and impressive cities.

A History of Angels

The Master felt proud of what he'd created and looked up at the Being of Light and smiled confidently. But the Being of Light looked sad and pointed back at the orb and the world within. Terrible things were starting to happen. The angelic beings were murdering each other, warring against their neighbouring cities, burning, raping and pillaging. They were building vast temples to bloodthirsty gods and sacrificing their enemies to them. They were enslaving others so they didn't have to work anymore and they were laying waste to all the forests and polluting all the rivers and streams. Horrific diseases broke out amongst the populations and they died in droves and their bloated bodies clogged the streets. Rats and dogs fed on the corpses, and the angelic survivors fled into the wilderness and reverted to primal beasts. The land was forever scarred. Ugly weeds and scrub grew in desolation where once magnificent forests stood teaming with life.

The Master stood with his mouth agape in shocked horror. How could this have come about? That's not what he created. He turned to the Being of Light who explained, "The orb only expresses our thoughts and desires and manifests them. Do you think you truly know and understand yourself yet? All this [indicating the world in the orb] came from your own suppressed subconscious. If you were given the powers of a god to manifest all you desired, all the unresolved dark-side of yourself would manifest itself. How do you think the world you so harshly judge came about? The beings who created it all had just as good intentions as you, but look at the result."

The Master woke from his vision and was very quiet for many days. He realised if he was serious about becoming a Being of Light he'd have to explore very uncomfortable and ugly things about himself that he'd fooled himself and his devotees he was free from. If people realised the truth about him he risked losing all he'd taken so long to build. For all his gifts he was as base and dark as any gangster. But then all his devotees would lose his spiritual guidance and all his fine charitable works. So with these justifications for the good of all he went on with 'life as usual' and left the facing of his dark-side for a more opportune time.

Chapter Twenty-nine

THE SUNFLOWER

Many years ago, in my darkest hour, I had a dream. I saw my heart alone and surrounded by complete darkness. It felt lost and full of despair and hopelessness. A beautiful female Being of Light appeared next to my heart and planted a seed in its centre. A shoot sprung forth and grew quickly. On a long strong stalk, two green leaves unfurled, then from a bud at the apex blossomed forth the most beautiful yellow sunflower. Sunflowers always follow the light of the sun, so after that I felt that my heart would always know where the light is and follow it.

A History of Angels

www.ingramcontent.com/pod-product-compliance
Lightning Source LLC
Chambersburg PA
CBHW060944230426
43665CB00015B/2057